CAPTAIN STEELE

The Early Career of Richard Steele

CAPTAIN STEELE

The Early Career of Richard Steele

by Calhoun Winton

THE JOHNS HOPKINS PRESS

This book has been brought to publication with the
assistance of a grant from The Ford Foundation.

Preface and Acknowledgments

ADDISON AND STEELE had the good fortune of enjoying literary fame in their lifetime. Though this was not extraordinary in eighteenth-century England — so did Pope and Swift and Johnson — the even tenor of their critical reputation is perhaps unusual. Their major works, whether essays, drama, or verse, were on the whole favorably received when they appeared, without much dissent from the leading critics of the time, and the essays at any rate have continued to be esteemed for two centuries and a half. Addison and Steele were recognized in their own day as major writers of the second rank and that has been their niche since; "standard authors," if the term has any meaning at all. Most English-speaking readers of the past hundred and fifty years, it seems safe to say, have encountered some of the famous essays somewhere in school; by the *consensus gentium* Addison and Steele have retained a place in English literary history. This being so, it is striking how little critical attention Addison and Steele have received in this our own, allegedly Alexandrian age. Beyond a few conventional statements, reiterated over the decades, there has been scant discussion as to why or whether these authors deserve their place in literary history; indeed, even the biographical summaries prefaced to anthologies for students usually contain gross errors of fact.

Steele's memory, at any rate, has been well-served by his scholarly editors in recent years, especially Rae Blanchard and John Loftis. When Donald Bond completes his editions of *The Tatler* and *The Spectator* and John C. Stephens, his of *The Guardian,* almost everything Steele is known to have written which survives will be easily at hand in print, soundly edited. The historical studies of Richmond Bond and his research students have opened much new ground, and John Loftis in his

v

Steele at Drury Lane has set forth with meticulous care Steele's later career in the theater. The materials for discussion in Steele's case are becoming available. The present volume is intended to further that discussion by presenting in convenient compass the details of Richard Steele's early life and career, that is, the years before the death of Queen Anne in 1714, when Steele was undergoing his apprenticeship as a writer and acquiring renown as a dramatic author, as a pamphleteer, and as an essayist. The subtitle implies that the focus is on the career, on the facts of biography and literary history; extended analyses of Steele's works are not attempted, though surely no literary biographer is entitled to suspend entirely his critical judgment. The book is intended to serve as an introduction to the career of one of English literature's most engaging individuals, and the starting point for further investigations. Interpretations of Steele's character and actions are limited as far as possible to the evidence of the years treated; he is presented as he was in those years, according to contemporary sources. The final summing-up may await a later volume. Under these conditions, some of the early years remain tantalizingly obscure, especially those during which Steele served as a trooper in the Life Guards, and I have resorted to conjecture here and there, labeling it as such.

Much of this account will be familiar to those who have maintained an interest in modern scholarship about the eighteenth century; some is new. If more is made here of Steele's career as a political journalist and politician than is perhaps usual in treating a man of letters, it is because such activities occupied a large proportion of his time and energies in those years; one recognizes, of course, that Richard Steele's reputation stems from his essays and, to a lesser extent in our time, though not so in his own, from his plays. In his view, however, his political activities were the most important aspect of his public career, the "common cause," as he was to put it, in which "I am engaged to the end of my life." As will be seen, his interest in politics appeared early and was a condition of his subsequent literary achievement. One may state the matter flatly: Steele's successful political career enabled him to escape Grub Street sooner than would otherwise have been possible. When he settled in London his artistic gifts and material resources were scarcely greater than those of Samuel Johnson three decades later, and Johnson was forced to endure many years of literary hackwork before he was, to use Pope's significant word, *déterré*. It is a commonplace to observe that literature and politics were interwoven in eighteenth-century England; the interweaving was supremely true of Richard Steele's early career.

In the context of the book, then, the term career does not apply solely to Steele's literary undertakings. Actually, Steele ordinarily pursued more than one métier, and for a time during his young manhood was attempting to maintain simultaneously careers in politics, literature, and the army. He had to. Steele was a young Irishman, with almost no resources of family and little or no money. Activity, above all, was essential. This book tells of that activity, often misdirected, often misrepresented by malicious contemporaries, but finally successful; it is, if one will, the success story of an energetic and appealing man who left few areas of experience untried. It ends before the final Whig triumph of 1714, before he became Sir Richard; this is the account of Captain Steele, as he was known to his London friends and acquaintances.

A word on documentation. I have attempted to document every matter of fact *not* included in *The Correspondence of Richard Steele,* ed. Rae Blanchard (Oxford, 1941). Since this edition is reliable, arranged chronologically, and readily available, I have followed the practice of Joseph Addison's biographer, Mr. Peter Smithers, and employed it as a primary source without, ordinarily, making specific reference thereto.

This book was begun in 1957, and over the years since I have benefited from the advice and help of many individuals as well as the support of a number of institutions. It was a source of personal satisfaction that my research trip to England and Ireland in 1960 was made possible by the generosity of the American Philosophical Society, whose founder, Benjamin Franklin, acknowledged in the *Autobiography* his literary debt to the authors of *The Spectator*. The grant was made from the Penrose Fund. I should also like to acknowledge with thanks the generosity of the Research Council of the University Center in Virginia in making a grant for summer travel and research as recommended by the Committee on Research of the University of Virginia, Professor C. J. Bishko, Chairman. My present institution, the University of Delaware, granted me a leave of absence for the first semester of the academic year, 1960–1961, and opportunity for research during the academic sessions since by way of a reduced teaching schedule, for which I am most grateful.

Libraries and librarians everywhere have been generous of holdings and time, but I must cite especially the Baker (Dartmouth College) Library, the Library of the University of Virginia, the Bodleian, and the British Museum. Dr. Richard J. Hayes, Director of the National Library of Ireland, opened with Irish grace many doors for me in Dublin, at considerable expense of time and effort to himself. Mr. William O'Sullivan, assistant in charge of manuscripts at the Library, Trinity College, Dublin, gave me expert guidance on several important points. My thanks also are offered to the Fellows of Merton College, and especially to the Librarian, Mr. J. R. L. Highfield, for permitting access to the college records and to their extensive collection of Steele's printed works.

Others who have provided guidance are Mrs. A. Henderson-Howat, Archivist, the Society for Promoting Christian Knowledge; Mr. D. W. King, Librarian, The War Office, London; Professor Kathleen Lynch of Mount Holyoke College; Mr.

F. G. Emmison, Director, County Public Record Office, Chelmsford, Essex; the Rev. G. H. P. Karney, Embleton Vicarage, Northumberland; the Very Reverend Cuthbert Simpson, Dean of Christ Church, Oxford; Professor Harlow Shapley, Harvard University; Mr. G. Webb, Librarian, All Souls, Oxford; Dean Thaddeus Seymour, Dartmouth College; Professor Shirley Strum Kenny, Gallaudet College; Mr. Peter E. Thornton, Seale, Surrey.

Many scholars living and dead have been laid under contribution by way of their published works, and these men and women must be thanked, unfortunately, by citation only. To many others I have not been able to extend even these minimal thanks. On the works of two, however, I have relied extensively and have profited also by personal conversations with both: Miss Rae Blanchard, Steele's editor, and Dr. J. H. Plumb, author of the fine Walpole biography. Professor and Mrs. Louis Landa of Princeton, he my former teacher, have provided encouragement at critical times and much good advice. June Banker Noll was good enough to undertake the arduous task of transcribing all of Katherine Mildmay's letters from microfilm and to read the entire manuscript in early draft. Professor Ricardo Quintana of the University of Wisconsin read the manuscript and made many helpful suggestions. Finally, my wife, Elizabeth J. M. Winton, supported the project from its earliest stages and, with extraordinary fortitude and patience, saw the book to completion, typing several drafts of the manuscript herself.

CALHOUN WINTON

Newark, Delaware 1963

A NOTE ON REFERENCES

References to Steele's life and quotations from letters to and by him, unless otherwise noted, are derived from *The Correspondence of Richard Steele,* ed. Rae Blanchard (Oxford, 1941). Since this work is chronologically arranged, I have not ordinarily given page references. When cited this work is abbreviated *Corr.* References to other volumes in Miss Blanchard's edition are as follows:

Engl.: The Englishman (Oxford, 1955).
Per. Jour.: Richard Steele's Periodical Journalism, 1714–16 (Oxford, 1959).
Tracts: Tracts and Pamphlets by Richard Steele (Baltimore, 1944).
Verse: The Occasional Verse of Richard Steele (Oxford, 1952).

Titles of scholarly journals, after the first reference, are abbreviated in accordance with the *Style Sheet* of the Modern Language Association of America. Other abbreviations used frequently:

Add. MSS.	Additional Manuscripts
Aitken	George A. Aitken, *The Life of Richard Steele* (London, 1889)
BM	British Museum
CSPD	*Calendar of State Papers, Domestic*
CSPEI	*Calendar of State Papers, Colonial Series, East Indies*
HMC	Historical Manuscripts Commission
Journal	Jonathan Swift, *Journal to Stella,* ed. Harold Williams (Oxford, 1948)
DNB	*Dictionary of National Biography*
London Stage	*The London Stage, 1660–1800,* Part Two: 1700–1729, ed. Emmett L. Avery (Carbondale, Ill., 1960).
PRO	Public Record Office [of Great Britain]
Plays	*Richard Steele,* ed. G. A. Aitken, The Mermaid Series (London, 1903).
Smithers	Peter Smithers, *The Life of Joseph Addison* (Oxford, 1954).

Reliable editions of the major periodicals are much to be desired; none of those mentioned in the preface to this volume had appeared in time for use herein. Editions used were *The Tatler,* ed. G. A. Aitken (London, 1898–99); *The Spectator,* Everyman Edition, ed. G. Gregory Smith (London, 1907); *The Guardian,* Tonson 12mo. ed. (London, 1745).

I have modernized spelling and, to the extent necessary for coherence, punctuation, except in a few cases (as in the correspondence of Lady Mildmay) where orthography and pointing have an interest of their own. Quotations from the poetry of Pope and Swift are not modernized.

Contents

CAPTAIN STEELE

The Early Career of Richard Steele

CHAPTER I

Irish Roots

RICHARD STEELE was born in Ireland. Such roots as he had were in that land. Though he departed for the other island in his boyhood and though he left no mark on the sod like that of his friend and contemporary Jonathan Swift, he was bound to his birthplace by his Irish kin, Irish friends, and not least important, Irish habits of mind. A Hibernian nativity was, of course, something less than a recommendation in the London society to which he in later life aspired (as in a similar case the young Scot James Boswell was to find of his own heritage), but Steele, like Boswell, never denied his native land. In either case any such attempt would have been useless. An estranged friend, the critic John Dennis, averred of Steele that "God has marked him more abundantly than he did Cain, and stamped his native country upon his face, his understanding, his writings, his actions, his passions, and above all his vanity. The Hibernian brogue is still upon all these, though long habitude and length of days have worn it from off his tongue." [1] This in the heat of controversy it is true, but the statement was based on an association of over twenty years' duration and the better portraits seem to confirm Dennis' description: there is a rough-hewn cast to Steele's features. One is persuaded, too, to find in his temperament characteristics often associated with the Irish: Steele's affection and concern for children in a thoroughly adult century,

---

[1] *The Critical Works of John Dennis,* ed. E. N. Hooker (Baltimore, 1939–1943), II, 213.

for example, and his unquenchable cheerfulness; or on the darker side, his pugnacity and a certain notorious fondness for the product of grape and grain. But this may all be supposititious; more important than real or fancied Hibernian temperament or physiognomy is the fact that he was born in Ireland, the third generation of a family permanently settled there.

As Steele put it many years later (*The Englishman*, No. 46, 19 Jan. 1714), "I am an Englishman born in the City of Dublin." The phrasing is interesting. Steele, speaking to Englishmen, wished them to think of him as an Englishman, a member of the Anglo-Irish Ascendancy, a compatriot of Spenser and Raleigh, born as if by accident in Dublin but really a native of St. James's and the Strand. In seventeenth-century Ireland, however, the term "English," as used by, say, the census taker, had no honorific connotations as such but simply denoted a Protestant, "Irish," a Catholic.[2] Many candid observers in the twentieth century, some of them Irish, will admit that the role of the Protestant Ascendancy, the relationship of its members to Ireland, was always to a considerable extent mysterious. Proclaiming their Englishness, yet bound to Ireland by years or even centuries of struggle and suffering (much but not all of their own making), these people finally yielded a Yeats as their bard. In the seventeenth century the Ascendancy may have been less self-conscious than in the twentieth, but its position, that of a dominant Protestant minority in a Catholic country, was fully as precarious. In the seventeenth century religious differences were ordinarily settled by gunfire, Samuel Butler's "infallible artillery."

Despite its position (or perhaps because of it), this was a society remarkably productive of effective men. The career of an intelligent male child not of the peerage, born into the Ascendancy, was more or less foreordained in the seventeenth

---

[2] See, e.g., 1660 census of Monkstown quoted in F. E. Ball, *A History of the County Dublin*, Part I (Dublin, 1902), p. 9.

and eighteenth centuries: he would if possible go to Trinity
College (or better still Oxford or Cambridge); then, unless he
were the heir of an estate or a trade, he would enter the army,
the Church, or become a lawyer or a writer. Ireland's bloody
soil has always nurtured fine soldiers in the image of the Irish
troops who fought it out for Protestant England and Catholic
France toe to toe across western Europe. Less celebrated are
the Anglo-Irish churchmen of this period, at their best men
like William King, ecclesiastical statesman and Archbishop of
Dublin, or George Berkeley, philosopher and Bishop of Cloyne.
More remarkable than churchmen or soldiers, though, was the
splendid succession of writers crossing the Irish Sea in the
eighteenth century. Consider a random list: Congreve, Swift,
Steele, Farquhar, Goldsmith, Burke, Sheridan, to name only
the best. Surely this was in at least one respect an extraordinary
society.

Into this society Richard Steele, son of Richard Steele and
Elinor Sheyles Symes Steele, was born in 1672, and baptized at
St. Bride's parish church on 12 March of that year.[3] The *soi-
disant* Englishness of this Dubliner is suspect. His father's
family, though of course ultimately sprung from the numerous
English Steeles, had been settled on the land in Ballinakill,
Queen's County (Leix) before the Civil War. Old Richard
Steele of Ballinakill, the essayist's grandfather, was an empire
builder of heroic mold, charged with those qualities of energy,
courage, and practical sense which during three centuries made
England the most effective colonial power since Rome. Known
to and mentioned by both Coryat (whom he befriended in Persia) and Purchas, the grandfather deserves his own chronicler.
As a young man he had gone out from Bristol to Aleppo to
learn the cloth trade at its source. After two years there he
struck out alone overland to Persia in pursuit of one John

[3] Trinity College, Dublin, MS. 1478. Early copy of St. Bride's baptismal
register.

Mildenhall, who had absconded with some goods, arriving finally at the English settlement in Surat, without Mildenhall (who had died during his flight) but with some of his booty and with a sense of the possibilities of Persian trade. In 1615 he was commissioned by the East India Company factors in Surat to return with one companion to Persia and open that area to trade. This he did, sending back also a report on Persian prices, weights, and measures for his successor's use and proceeding overland once more himself to the Mediterranean and England, which he reached in 1616. Steele's later voyages, his life in Persia and India, his friendship with the Great Mogul, his shipwreck in the East Indies, his marriage in the East to a Kentish servant girl, Frances Webbe, and the beginning of their family with the birth of a son in India — all these are beyond the scope of the present narrative.[4] The career of merchant adventurer which Richard Steele quit in the late sixteentwenties had, however, importance in the life of his grandson the writer in at least three ways. First, it provided the basis for much of whatever position of influence his grandson was to enjoy before he made his own fortune and reputation as a writer. Richard Steele, in his role of explorer, was known personally to both Charles I and James I and enjoyed the favor of both. Steele's necessary self-confidence, or as his enemies saw it, sense of self-importance, is a trait noticeable enough in the character of his grandson; in both cases the quality attracted much contemporary comment. Finally, the excitement of a merchant-adventurer's career, the vision of national greatness through trade was communicated by some means to the grandson who was to write, eighty years later in *The Spectator,* "It is a stupid and barbarous way to extend dominion by arms; for true power is to be got by arts and industry."

---

[4] For Steele's voyages, see *The Embassy of Sir Thomas Roe to India 1615–1619,* ed. William Foster, Hakluyt Soc., 2nd Ser., Nos. 1 and 2 (London, 1899) and CSPEI, *passim.* See also Michael Strachan, *The Life and Adventures of Thomas Coryate* (London, 1962), pp. 213–14.

On his return to England from his final voyage to the East, Richard Steele set out on another career, a more traditional road to wealth and station, that of being a courtier. He was at a disadvantage in certain respects; he had no family influence (a most potent disability) and, apparently, not a great deal of money. Furthermore, tugging and pulling behind the scenes in the Royal Court was increasing year by year as the British Isles drifted toward civil war; a courtier's life was no assured employment. Nevertheless, Steele seems to have had the enduring confidence of Charles. He was straightway appointed a Gentleman of the Privy Chamber, about 1631 was awarded a pension of £200, and sometime in this period acquired land in Ireland, around Ballinakill in Queen's County and near New Ross in County Wexford. Several of his associates at the Court were holders of Irish land: among others, Lord Edward Conway, the sponsor of his tour to the Far East; Sir George Rawdon, Conway's private secretary; and Sir Thomas Ridgeway, Treasurer of Ireland and later Earl of Londonderry. Ridgeway had "planted" the settlement at Ballinakill during the reign of King James with more than the usual landlord's care, and by the time of his death in 1631, the town had a castle and park, several hundred Protestant settlers, and the beginnings of a flourishing ironworks. Richard Steele settled his family at Ballinakill and began paying off the mortgage on the castle park, held by the daughter of the Earl of Castlehaven. Included in the Steele's household were nine children and the family's Eastern servant, Fortune, whose native religious persuasion was said to be "Indian-Pythagorean." [5] The entourage must have added an interesting tone to the Irish countryside. Richard Steele became a leading citizen in those parts, though he kept his position at court as Gentleman of the Privy Chamber. (See Appendix A.) All things considered, his rewards appear dis-

[5] Fortune, see Trinity College, Dublin, MS. F. 2. 8, fol. 85.

proportionately high for a minor courtier. One guesses that he was employed in the Stuarts' intelligence service; in a petition of 1635 for pension arrears due him, he refers to his nine children and asks payment "In consideration whereof and for other causes well known to you." [6] By 1641 he was still Gentleman of the Privy Chamber and had acquired a military title, Captain Steele. Seven decades later his grandson Captain Steele was also a member of the Royal Household, Gentleman-Waiter to the Prince Consort.

At King Charles's court in the sixteen-twenties was a young Irishman of deeper roots and more significance than these other new-planted Irish: James Butler, a Protestant of an ancient Catholic family, twelfth Earl and later first Duke of Ormonde. Ballinakill was near that part of Ireland which the Anglo-Norman Butlers controlled, in fact if not in theory, from their seat of Kilkenny, and which they had ruled off and on for centuries, settling their differences with the Irish peasants and another ruling Anglo-Norman clan, the Geraldines, in the Irish manner, by force of arms. It may be that Butler had a part in Steele's selecting that region of Ireland as his home; on many other occasions, as will be seen, he aided the various descendants of Richard Steele of Ballinakill.

James Butler and Richard Steele had one common bond: unswerving loyalty to the Stuarts, whom Butler regarded as the means for solving the great Irish problem, the religious issue which divided the country and his own family. As events proved, Charles I was a weak reed on which to rely. Butler was by nature a compromiser and a friend of religious toleration in a century which placed little value on these qualities. Though roundly damned on all sides for his efforts, in history's perspective James Butler appears rather more enlightened than some

---

[6] PRO, Domestic Series, 16/306/81. See also CSPD, 1631–1633, p. 110; and Trinity College, Dublin, MS. F. 2. 7, fol. 358–59, Steele's deposition on the 1641 uprising.

of his celebrated contemporaries. In 1641 his and Ireland's and the Steeles' troubles began in earnest.

In that year, while Richard Steele was in England with the King, a group of Irish leaders, predominantly Catholic, gathered in Kilkenny and announced Ireland's independence and return to the ancient faith. The Irish Protestants fled in panic to centers of resistance before the armies of these Confederates. Some nine hundred persons, including Frances and her children, gathered for safety in the castle at Ballinakill. The castle was invested by the Confederates and a long siege began; Steele's pleas to the English Parliament were in vain. King Charles had more important matters before him than the fate of a few hundred Protestants in rural Ireland. A force sent out from Dublin was turned back after a half-hearted effort at raising the siege. As is usual in religious wars, siege and defense were conducted with great ferocity; in the last months both sides adopted the classic technique of decapitating prisoners and throwing their heads back across the lines. It was said that women could be heard moaning within the castle during the lulls of battle.[7] In the spring of 1643, the Confederate General Preston brought up heavy guns from Wexford and the garrison, now hopeless and reduced by almost half, accepted the besiegers' terms: safe-conduct to Dublin. The Steeles, all of whom seem to have survived, left their home for a time. Within a few years, in the way of Irish history, General Preston and the Earl of Ormonde were allied in support of Charles II. Ballinakill then became the scene of determined resistance to Cromwell's forces, who besieged the Castle once more, took it, and razed it with Cromwellian thoroughness.

Of the Steele family during the terrible years following the siege, little is known. Perhaps they drifted back to Ballinakill

[7] Steele's MS (note 6) ; R. Bellings, *History of the Irish Confederation and the War in Ireland, 1641–1643,* ed. John T. Gilbert (Dublin, 1882), I, 150; *A Contemporary History of Affairs in Ireland,* ed. John T. Gilbert (Dublin, 1879), I, 64–65.

and were involved in the second siege or perhaps, reunited, they followed the Stuarts into exile. Some of the Ballinakill estates were sequestrated by Cromwell, but as Protestants the Steeles escaped deportation with their Catholic compatriots to "hell or Connaught." When old Captain Steele died in 1658, he still possessed property in Ballinakill and Wexford.[8] The knowledge that he had been able to do something for his family must have consoled the aging veteran of Ispahan and the Java Sea, but he could not know what would have pleased him most: that in less than two years the Stuarts, in the person of Charles II, would regain the throne.

What of his children, all of whom must have reached majority by Captain Steele's death? A family which has undergone stresses of the order and variety which this one had suffered may disintegrate altogether, or it may generate a strong internal cohesive force to resist those stresses. The Steeles had much earlier chosen the latter course. In the face of the worst the world could send, they would cling to their identity and watch over their own. As a first step, Frances gave up all her rights in the estate to the eldest son, John. John, however, possessed of some of his father's fiber, had chosen the sea as his vocation; within a few years he would become a skillful privateer captain for King Charles in the undeclared cross-channel warfare against the Dutch and the French. John gave up or sold his interest in the Irish lands to those who wanted to stay; evidently this remained an option in the family for some time because Richard Steele the essayist, a member of the next generation, later wrote that "he lost the succession to a very good estate in the county of Wexford" when he joined the army.[9] There could not have been land enough to go around and possession of Irish land has

[8] Irish Genealogical Office, MS. Reg. Ped., Vol. 248, p. 18.
[9] *The Theatre*, No. 11. John Steele, CSPD, for 1667, 1669, 1671, 1672; will, Probate Registry, Somerset House, London, July, 1673, fol. 95. Dr. R. J. Hayes, Director of the National Library of Ireland, has indicated that such stipulations were not unusual in seventeenth- and eighteenth-century Ireland.

been for many a mixed blessing anyway. While some of Captain
Steele's children could stay in Ireland, others like John would
have to seek their fortune elsewhere. In the early sixteen-sixties
two of them important to the present account, Richard, the
essayist's father, and Katherine, his aunt, were acceptably occupied in London, the one studying law at Clifford's Inn and the
other seeking a husband.

Beside old Captain Richard Steele, the explorer, and his colorful offspring, Katherine and John, Richard Steele (II) is a pathetic figure, almost a cipher. No single person, on the evidence
of the few records that survive, ever expressed an opinion favorable or unfavorable of him except his son, and that only once
in fictionalized form; and the Steeles were for three generations
a family that evoked comment. His health was bad; perhaps his
constitution had been weakened during the siege at Ballinakill
when he was a child, for his life appears to have been a struggle
against blows of fate too heavy for him to bear. With the help
of friends and family, however, Richard Steele and his sister
were able to observe the forms proper to Irish gentry. As we
have seen, the law was a correct activity for the younger son of
an Irish Protestant family, and a daughter was expected to
marry as well as she could.

In 1662 Katherine succeeded, in spectacular fashion. Sir
Humphrey Mildmay, a widower of seventy, a distinguished
Royalist partisan in the Civil Wars and hereditary head of the
renowned Mildmay family of Essex took, in the twilight of a
busy life, the young Irishwoman as his second wife. This romantic coup created a distinct and unpleasant sensation among
the Mildmays; the family took steps to protect their interest and
especially that of the eldest son, John. In July, 1663, there was
a preliminary agreement; in October, formal documents were
signed by which Katherine Steele's rights to the Mildmay estate
were purchased in a cash settlement of £80 a year.[10]

[10] Essex County (England) Record Office, MS. D/DPL 39.

The articles of the settlement appear to suggest in their dry, legal English an ominous foreshadowing of troubles for the Steele family. Associated with Katherine's brother Richard as party to the indenture is one Thomas Deane, goldsmith of London. Since goldsmiths were moneylenders in those days, one may conjecture that Richard Steele was in debt, a situation in which his son was often to find himself.

Katherine Steele Mildmay, from the surviving fragments of her letters, does not strike one as an adventuress, though that is doubtless the role in which she was cast by the Mildmays. A woman who knew the value of money — assuming that there have been women who did not — but no adventuress. Though limited in her financial expectations to £80 a year, she was not to be deprived of her title. Lady Mildmay Katherine Steele was, and Lady Mildmay she remained to her life's end, even after her second marriage, to Henry Gascoigne. An interesting person, Katherine Steele; warm-hearted, extravagant, vain, a trifle petulant; in some respects much like her nephew, the subject of this work, whose foster mother she became and for whose education and upbringing she was largely responsible.[11]

Richard Steele, senior, returned to Ireland to seek employment, leaving his sister to nurse Sir Humphrey in his declining years. The English institution of which Steele had been a member, Clifford's Inn, was an Inn of Chancery, at that time a preparatory institution for the Inns of Court, especially the Inner Temple, with which it long had been associated. Steele was, that is, not yet a practicing attorney, but he secured minor preferment in Ireland of a legal sort: as clerk of the Registry of the Court of Claims, a judicial authority attempting to straighten out the property claims of Catholic and Protestant, which had been grievously tangled by the Civil Wars and especially by Cromwellian ministrations. The advantages for the Steele fam-

[11] National Library of Ireland, MS. Ormonde 183, fol. 323–403: letters and fragments of letters by Katherine, mostly addressed to Henry Gascoigne.

ily as a whole were obvious; no doubt the appointment came through influence of old friends, perhaps the Conways or the Duke of Ormonde himself. On 11 June 1667 "Richard Steele, Gentleman," (having paid his fee of two pounds, thirteen shillings, fourpence) was duly admitted to the membership of the King's Inns of Dublin as an attorney.[12] The King's Inns, like its English equivalent the Inns of Court, was and is the training institution and certifying authority for Irish lawyers; Steele had thus become a duly accredited attorney. The previous year Jonathan Swift, father of the future Dean of St. Patrick's, had been admitted into the same society. Relative prosperity seems to have come to the young lawyer about this time; perhaps he was able to advance a property claim of his own through the Court, perhaps fees for the private practice of law came his way from friends of the family. At any rate, in June, 1670, he was living in Monkstown, a pleasant country village south of Dublin, now a suburb, overlooking the sea. And he was, in Lemuel Gulliver's phrase, thinking of altering his status.

On 1 June 1670 the Archbishop of Dublin issued a marriage license for Richard Steele of Monkstown and Elinor Symes of St. Bride's parish, the marriage to take place in Monkstown.[13] Richard Steele's status was indeed altered by this ceremony, for his wife's first husband, Thomas Symes of Dublin, to whom she was married in 1663 had died in 1667, leaving her three hundred pounds and three children, one of them unborn at the time he made his will. Elinor Symes' maiden name was Sheyles. She was, that is, of Celtic extraction, for the name Sheyles or Sheills or Shiells is derived from the clan O'Sheill of County Antrim (though also known in Scotland). Perhaps Elinor

[12] Library of King's Inns, MS. Black Book, under date (pagination unsatisfactory). For a fuller summary of Richard Steele, senior's life, from which some of the details herein are drawn, see my "New Documents Concerning Richard Steele's Father," *Journal of English and Germanic Philology,* LVIII (1959), 264–69.

[13] Aitken, I, 11. Original apparently destroyed in fire at Irish Public Record Office, 1922. Symes' will, also destroyed, Aitken, I, 11n.

Steele herself came from Antrim; years later an anonymous Tory opponent intimated that Richard Steele was born in Carrickfergus.[14]

This, then, was the couple joined together that June morning in the Monkstown parish church long since demolished, whose ancient cemetery, now choked with weeds and the debris of centuries, still overlooks the Irish Sea from the hillside: a newly-fledged lawyer of the Ascendancy, whose political influence, and hence whose practice, must have been extremely modest; and an Irish widow, mother of two or perhaps three children and heiress of three hundred pounds. No very promising union for these children or for those to come.

As a sensible first step the new family of Steeles and Symeses moved to St. Bride's parish, Dublin, where Elinor lived, probably in a house left her by Thomas Symes. This had been a fashionable address, better than Monkstown, and Elinor's son Richard may have learned from his mother that a good address is important. Though fine houses were being built to the eastward of the Castle in the sixteen-seventies, this western parish was still near the center of Dublin life, between St. Patrick's Cathedral and the Castle; crowded into the tiny parishes of St. Werburgh's and St. Bride's were hundreds, thousands of more or less prominent and prosperous Dubliners.[15] Within a few hundred yards (for such were the dimensions of these parishes) dwelt Counsellor Godwin Swift in St. Werburgh's parish, uncle and foster parent of Jonathan, who was to receive the orphaned child into his home a year or two later. And yet, crowded as St. Bride's parish was, it would have been pleasant enough for parents and children: abutting the grounds of St.

[14] O'Sheill: Edward MacLysaght, *Irish Families* (Dublin, 1957); Carrickfergus: *A Second Letter From a Country Whig, to His Friend in London.* . . . (London, 1715), pp. 17–18. I am indebted to Professor Shirley Strum Kenny for the latter reference. The possibility that Elinor Steele was of Scottish lineage must not be overlooked.

[15] Cf. Maurice Craig, *Dublin, 1660–1860* (London, 1952), pp. 12, 44.

Patrick's on one side, the river Liffey an easy walk to the north, St. Stephen's Green just to the southeast. In a few decades a slum, but now, in thriving post-Restoration Dublin, a good place to live, and near the Castle, the center of influence and power, absolute necessities if gentlefolk without money were to continue gentlefolk.

In March, 1671, the couple's first child, a daughter, was born and baptized Katherine in honor no doubt of Lady Mildmay, now a widow herself. A year later the son, Richard, had joined them, a male heir for the Steeles. Now indeed was the time for redoubled efforts on the part of the head of the household; Richard Steele manipulating, we may imagine, every source of influence obtained preferment. James Butler, his father's acquaintance in the Stuart court, now Duke of Ormonde and Viceroy of Ireland, appointed Richard Steele subsheriff of County Tipperary.

One imagines the jubilation that the Steeles must have felt at this appointment. Here was preferment; no grubbing clerk's job but a position in the hierarchy of the House of Ormonde, and, best of all to anyone who knew politics, a position involving the collection of public revenues. Revenue, King and Parliament had discovered, was the key to public power; revenue was one road to private wealth. To be sure, the post of subsheriff was a modest one, involving as it did the collection of certain forfeited fines and bonds from the impoverished inhabitants of County Tipperary. Still, Richard Steele could tell himself, it was preferment and the possible source of wealth and position for his family. Then too, Tipperary was not far from Ballinakill; he could keep an eye on the family holdings and see that rent due was collected a little more promptly and honestly.

Though that was the region of Richard Steele's boyhood, he had been living in London and Dublin for at least ten years. He was, in short, a city dweller assigned to collect fines from country people hostile to the Ascendancy, and as well disposed toward revenue agents as rural folk generally are, that is, not at all. Many miles from Dublin and the family, among an unfriendly people, Richard Steele learned that there was preferment and preferment. Through 1672 and 1673 he toiled, attempting to reduce the sums which were charged against him for collection. Whether his health had broken before he came to the post or whether the chills of Tipperary beset him during his time there, he was in any case afflicted, as he later put it, with "much sickness." He gave the post up and returned to Dublin and family. But the worst blow was yet to come; the hapless ailing man was ordered to indemnify the High Sheriff for all sums charged against him but uncollected. Richard Steele summoned up his strength and dispatched a "Humble Petition" to the Duke of Ormonde begging relief, pleading that "The persons from whom [the fines] became due being at that time insolvent, & having since so withdrawn, or absconded themselves that your petitioner could never meet with their persons nor find out any substance to answer the charges. . . ." [16]

The Duke, though somewhat pressed for money himself because of many responsibilities in England and Ireland, ordered the court having jurisdiction of these matters to "take such course for the petitioner's relief as is used in his Majesty's Courts at Dublin to such sheriffs. . . ." Apparently nothing was done, however, for the former subsheriff was forced to submit another petition sometime in February or March, 1675, once more setting forth his pathetic circumstances: ill health, "divers losses," and "a great charge of children." Again the Duke endorsed the petition favorably. Though the infant Richard Steele could not realize it, the House of Ormonde had twice in his short lifetime provided help at critical junctures.

Nothing later than the second petition is certainly known of Richard Steele, senior, but Steele's *Tatler* No. 181 contains an

[16] Petitions: Bodleian Library, Oxford, MS. Carte 160, fol. 95^v, 99^v, 100^r.

account of the death of Bickerstaff's father which is so striking
that it has always been taken as at least in part descriptive of the
death of the writer's own father:

> The first sense of sorrow I ever knew was upon the death of my
> father, at which time I was not quite five years of age; but was
> rather amazed at what all the house meant, than possessed with a
> real understanding why nobody was willing to play with me. I
> remember I went into the room where his body lay, and my
> mother sat weeping alone by it. I had my battledore in my hand,
> and fell a-beating the coffin, and calling "Papa"; for I know not
> how I had some slight idea that he was locked up there. My
> mother catched me in her arms, and transported beyond all pa-
> tience of the silent grief she was before in, she almost smothered
> me in her embrace and told me in a flood of tears, papa could
> not hear me, and would play with me no more, for they were
> going to put him under ground, whence he could never come to
> us again. She was a very beautiful woman, of a noble spirit, and
> there was a dignity in her grief amidst all the wildness of her
> transport. . . .

His grave is unknown. The houses and streets of St. Bride's
parish have long ago disappeared, the church and cemetery
razed in the last century to make way for a slum clearance
project. A few headstones still are preserved in the neighboring
church of St. Werburgh's, but Richard Steele's name cannot be
made out on any of them. Perhaps, it is pleasanter to imagine,
his body was taken back to Monkstown and buried there in the
hills beside the sea, or to Ballinakill. The stones there too are
mute.

In 1676 or early 1677, it may be supposed, Elinor Steele was
left, for the second time, a widow with two small children, and
this time presumably two or three larger ones as well. It was
indeed a test for her noble spirit. Help was at hand, however,
and once again its ultimate source was the House of Ormonde.

In 1675 Katherine Steele Mildmay had married Henry Gascoigne, private secretary to the Duke of Ormonde.[17] It was undoubtedly an advantageous match for both, because Lady Mildmay — as she insisted on being known — brought to the marriage an unflagging sense of her own worth and some important friends, and Gascoigne brought a greater than average amount of sagacity and determination, and, of primary importance in a relationship with this family of Steeles, a highly developed acquisitive sense. In short, she had position and he money, or at least the means of getting money.

Gascoigne is an early and interesting example of what today would be called a civil servant. That is, under the patronage of an influential man he and others like him performed the day-to-day routine tasks involved in governing, carried out the policies of the lawgivers and formulated *de facto* policies of their own when none existed, drafted letters, transmitted commands, sought favors for friends. They were paid largely through preferment, by appointment to sinecures or to posts where duties could be performed by subordinates, themselves on the servant's payroll. There was, of course, no hint of disgrace in such a position; indeed, the machinery of government depended on men like Henry Gascoigne and a later patron of Steele's, John Ellis. Moreover, it was a way of acquiring wealth acceptable to gentry like Gascoigne and his new wife who perhaps did not want to venture down that other and widening road to riches, trade. This career, for such it was, of being associated with powerful men was, it should be understood, essentially the career Richard Steele later chose for himself. Literature and politics were, had to be, subordinate to patronage in this society.

To be accounted successful, a man in Gascoigne's position needed the ear and confidence of his patron and a continuing supply of substantial preferment. In both respects Henry Gas-

---

[17] Between June and December. National Library of Ireland, MS. Ormonde 62, fol. 211–14, and 63, fol. 163. Aitken (I, 21) is mistaken.

coigne was pre-eminently successful. A letter from a friend written in 1665 signalizes Gascoigne's first recorded service for the House of Ormonde; the exact nature of the deed is unknown and unimportant. Gascoigne's manner of doing business is everything. I have, the writer informs Gascoigne, "delivered the inclosed you sent to my Lady Duchess [which] was prudently done on you by sending, considering from whom it came, and the welcome news it brought. . . . I have been always very confident of your honour and must thank you for this last." [18] Prudence, trustworthiness: these are the key qualities. A few months later Gascoigne was in the full employ of the House of Ormonde; by 1674 he had become private secretary to the first Duke as well as keeper of the records in the Birmingham Tower and Chief Chamberlain of the Exchequer in Ireland. Preferment followed preferment as year followed year. The enormous collection of correspondence among the Ormonde Manuscripts in the National Library of Ireland reveals the source of Gascoigne's success. In the early years, the sixteen-sixties and early sixteen-seventies, there are many letters in the Duke's own scrawl. These become fewer, and more and more in Gascoigne's neat hand appear over Ormonde's signature or, increasingly, over his own. He was, that is, complying with the first requirement of a successful civil servant: making himself indispensable. Soon important men were writing him directly, seeking access to the man who had the Duke's ear. Thus in his quiet way Henry Gascoigne acquired a respectable income and exercised, prudently, considerable power. He was obviously a valuable kinsman, or husband of kin, for an impoverished widow's family.

Fortunately, he was also a kind and thoroughly decent human being. The family of Steeles had, after all, no real claim on his generosity. He was, in his position, the constant target of appeals of every sort. Why should he bother, he might have asked himself, with his wife's poor relations? But Katherine was a

[18] Aitken, I, 19.

strong woman and a loyal Steele. "My uncle Gascoigne to whose bounty I owe a liberal education," as the essayist referred to him years later, took the responsibility for the children's rearing.[19] Katherine and Henry's marriage was a curious one by modern standards. She became a member of the Countess of Arran's household and consequently spent much of her time at the residence of the Earl (Ormonde's son) at Chapelizod, a few miles outside of Dublin. Gascoigne had secured a house in the city near the Steeles (on St. Nicholas Street, just across the River Poddle from St. Bride's parish),[20] but was forced by his employment to follow the Duke on his travels to Kilkenny, to Dublin Castle during the years the Duke was Viceroy, and to London. Lady Mildmay must have seen to the education of the two children, making sure that young Richard Steele received the necessary tutoring in Latin. Though a school had recently been established in Dublin, the Bluecoat School (the King's Hospital), it was still regarded as a charity institution and would have been beneath young Steele's station. No such odium attended the Kilkenny Grammar School where William Congreve and Jonathan Swift were preparing for Trinity College, but for whatever reason Richard's primary education was private.

Ireland was enjoying the relatively tranquil and prosperous years between the Restoration and the Williamite Wars beginning in 1688. Despite the attitude of the English Parliament which wavered between indifference and outright oppression, the Irish economy was flourishing. Dublin was bursting through the limits of the old walled city in every direction; Sir William Petty's estimate put the population in 1682 at 58,000 in a total of perhaps 1,000,000 for all Ireland. The parish of St. Bride's may have been rapidly becoming a slum, but for children having foster parents in the Gascoignes' positions of influence the fu-

[19] *Corr.*, p. 44.
[20] HMC, *Ormonde MSS.*, New Series, IV, 27, 31.

ture did not appear dark. Indeed, Elinor Sheyles, if she was still alive in 1680, could have reflected that Richard Steele's children now had greater prospects than when their ineffectual father was living.

A quiet and relatively prosperous period for Ireland, these years (1677–1685) of Ormonde's second viceroyalty, but a busy time for the Duke and his staff, shuttling across the Irish Sea to London, then back to Kilkenny and Dublin. Gascoigne's friends occasionally reported to him that Lady Katherine was comfortably situated in the Countess of Arran's household but Gascoigne must have wished sometimes for a more sedentary occupation.[21] In April, 1682, Ormonde went to England to stay for more than two years, naming his son, the Earl of Arran, as his Deputy in Ireland. It was probably during this period that Gascoigne determined to bring his wife and the young Steele children to London.

There were several good reasons for this step. Besides desiring, presumably, to end the exile from his wife, Gascoigne realized by virtue of his employment that the calm in Ireland was a prelude to further trouble. The position of the moderate Ormonde in King Charles II's court, long secure because of his faithful and effective service to the House of Stuart, was weakening under pressure from Protestant extremists and from Catholic followers of the Duke of York, soon to be James II. In the fall of 1684 Charles informed Ormonde of his intention to replace him as Lord Lieutenant. Though disappointed by the King's diminishing confidence in him, Ormonde expressed to a friend the relief of a man grown old and weary: "From this difficulty, I thank God and the King, I am delivered. . . ."[22] Before Ormonde's appointed successor, the Earl of Rochester, arrived in Ireland, King Charles died. In February, 1685, Or-

---

[21] HMC, *Ormonde MSS.*, New Series, VI, 372, and VII, 336.
[22] T. Carte, *An History of the Life of James Duke of Ormonde* (London, 1736), II, Appendix, p. 118.

monde gave a farewell official dinner in Dublin, toasted the
new king and left the land of his ancestors, never to return.
With the appointment of the Earl of Tyrconnel as Lord Deputy
a few months later, the battle lines between Catholic and Protestant began to form once again. Prudent men like Gascoigne
commenced liquidating their Irish holdings. Assured by an old
friend that Dublin's future was bright, Gascoigne endorsed the
friend's letter for the Duke's eyes before he filed it away.
"These are fine promises if they hold, but if you are of my mind
you will put very little confidence in them." [23]

Like the Duke of Ormonde, young Richard Steele had also
left Ireland forever. On 17 November 1684 he was registered
in the Charterhouse as follows: "Richard Steele admitted for
the Duke of Ormond, in the room of Phillip Burrell — aged
13 years 12th March next." [24]

The Charterhouse, then at Charterhouse Square near the
heart of London, was like the Bluecoat School in Dublin, a
curious mixed institution, geriatric home and boys' school. As
were most of the other great public schools of England, Charterhouse was by origin a charitable foundation built, a contemporary of Steele's wrote, "on the maintenance of decayed gentlemen's children" and "for the relief of poor men." Admission was
as usual dependent on influence: the same author put the matter
quite explicitly: "The way to obtain a place for a young lad or
an old gentleman, is much the same: *viz.* to make an address to
any single governor the person has most interest in, by way of
friends, petition, or any other method of application." [25] In
addition to being the child of a decayed gentleman, Steele had
another advantage, for the Duke of Ormonde was a very strong-
minded governor of the foundation.

During Richard's years at Charterhouse he and his sister
were full members of the Gascoigne ménage at Fulham which

---

[23] National Library of Ireland, MS. Ormonde 152, fol. 87.
[24] Aitken, I, 24.
[25] Samuel Herne, *Domus Carthusiana* (London, 1677), p. 189.

included Katherine's widowed sister, Bellindia Steele Lynn, and Bellindia's spinster daughter, Penelope. Lady Mildmay and Henry Gascoigne were the actual, if not the legal, foster parents of the two children. Nothing further is known of Elinor Steele except that she was not living with the Gascoigne family. Perhaps one of her older children by Symes took her in; it may be that she followed her husband to an early grave, but a reference to her by Richard Steele much later makes it appear that she lived many years — somewhere.[26]

From the time of his registration at Charterhouse, Richard became in most respects an English schoolboy. Though we can imagine the hoots of his schoolmates upon hearing his Dublin accent, Steele was, unlike Jonathan Swift, not taking the usual course of a young man of the Ascendancy. He had come to England, but Ireland was still around him; for many years yet his education and employment were to depend on Irish influence and patronage. His foster mother, Katherine, thought of herself as transplanted to England from her native land and was none too happy at having traded Chapelizod for London, where memories of her notorious marriage to Sir Humphrey Mildmay were still green, and for Fulham, the country suburb in which the Gascoignes crowded into a small house. In Fulham she nursed her many ailments with complaints, white wine, and the waters of Tunbridge Wells.

The children, it is true, could scarcely have been much of a burden to her. Katherine soon found employment away from home, and Richard lived at Charterhouse during term time, where the school day commenced at six in the summer, seven in winter, and lasted until six in the evening. The Master of the Charterhouse was the redoubtable Low Churchman Thomas Burnet (not to be confused with Bishop Gilbert Burnet's son, Thomas, later Steele's friend and ally in the pamphlet wars). Burnet's religio-scientific work, *Sacred Theory of the Earth,* touched off a controversy upon its publication in the sixteen-

[26] *Corr.,* p. 287.

eighties that continued for decades. The influence Burnet had upon Steele is, of course, only conjectural; it is a fact that the writer throughout his life maintained an intense amateur interest in scientific matters and discussed the *Theory* in *The Spectator* (No. 146).[27] Burnet was also a protégé of the Duke of Ormonde, and had been the companion of his grandson. Thus the web of preferment in those days.

The curriculum was like that of the other public (i.e., private) schools of the time: heavily classical, with emphasis on translation from and into Greek and Latin. Here Steele was immersed in Cicero, the primary literary influence of his life; here also he learned Horace, the English Augustan's Augustan. Discipline was strict and simple; the masters' meditations, like those of Fielding's Thwackum, were full of birch. To this method of discipline Steele reacted violently; years later in *The Spectator* No. 157 he voiced a memorable plea, almost the first of its kind, against education by stripes, then and for a century and more afterward the accepted pedagogical method.

I am confident that no boy who will not be allured to letters without blows, will ever be brought to any thing with them. A great or good mind must necessarily be the worse for such indignities; and it is a sad change, to lose of its virtue for the improvement of its knowledge. No one who has gone through what they call a great school, but must remember to have seen children of excellent and ingenuous natures, as has afterwards appeared in their manhood; I say no man has passed through this way of education, but must have seen an ingenuous creature expiring with shame, with pale looks beseeching sorrow, and silent tears, throw up its honest eyes, and kneel on its tender knees to an inexorable blockhead, to be forgiven the false quantity of a word in making a Latin verse. The child is punished, and the next day he commits a like crime, and so a third with the same consequence. I would fain ask any reasonable man, whether this lad, in the simplicity of his native innocence, full of shame, and capable of any im-

---

[27] For a full discussion of the Burnet controversy, see Michael Macklem, *The Anatomy of the World* (Minneapolis, 1958), *passim*.

pression from that grace of soul, was not fitter for any purpose in this life, than after that spark of virtue is extinguished in him, though he is able to write twenty verses in an evening?

For this Irish orphan had remained through a turbulent childhood a sensitive boy. In his earliest letter still preserved, written to Lady Katherine Mildmay from school, some of that sensitivity is manifested, and some of the grace and warmth which were to become distinguishing characteristics of Richard Steele's prose style at its best. Evidently Henry Gascoigne thought the letter unusual, for he placed it in the Ormonde Correspondence, where it remains. The schoolboy had neglected to write home; Katherine was a generous person but conscious always of what was owed her. Perhaps she had chided him in one of her misspelled notes.

HONOURED MADAM,
Out of a deep sense of your ladyship's goodness towards me, I could not forbear accusing myself of ingratitude in omitting my duty, by not acknowledging your Ladyship's favours by frequent letters; but how to excuse myself as to that point I know not, but must humbly hope [that] as you have been always so bountiful to me as to encourage my endeavours, so you will be so merciful to me as to pardon my faults and neglects. But, Madam, should I express my gratitude for every benefit [that] I receive at your ladyship's and my good Uncle, I should never sit down to meat but I must write a letter when I rise from table; for to his goodness I humbly acknowledge my being. But, Madam, not to be too tedious, I shall only subscribe myself, Madam, your ladyship's humble servant and obedient though unworthy nephew,
R. STEELE [28]

In 1686, after Steele had been at the school for two years, Joseph Addison enrolled at Charterhouse as a private (that is, non-scholarship) student. English literature's most famous friendship was, one can imagine, natural enough. On the one hand, Addison must have found Steele's ebullient spirits and

[28] *Corr.*, p. 3.

Irish vigor attractive; while on the other hand, Steele could admire his young friend's obvious intellectual gifts and his famous self-control. Above all, though, Addison's settled, harmonious family circle, presided over by his distinguished father, Lancelot Addison, Dean of Lichfield, appealed to Steele, representing as it did an existence of which he could scarcely have been aware. More than three decades later, after Addison's death, Steele was to recall nostalgically his admission to that family circle: "[Nor] had [the father] a child who did not prefer me in the first place of kindness and esteem, as their father loved me like one of them. . . ." [29]

Outside the Charterhouse the English political situation grew worse. Faithful to his convictions, King James II attempted to remake England as a Catholic country, appointing those sympathetic to the faith to various positions of trust and influence. England was agitated as political factions rose; Ireland was in a turmoil, on the very brink of war. During this hectic period the Charterhouse itself was the scene of a historic act of resistance to the King's activities, an act commemorated yet by Carthusians in their triennial pageant. King James directed the admission to the Charterhouse (that is, to the hospital) as a pensioner one Andrew Popham, who was to be exempt from taking the required oath of allegiance. The governors, led by Ormonde, forced to choose between the law of the land and the king's prerogative chose the former, twice flatly refusing to admit Popham. A contemporary pamphleteer recognized the event's significance, calling it "the first stand that was made against the dispensing power, by any society in England." [30] Thus young Richard Steele was a student at the Charterhouse during one of the most celebrated constitutional tests of the time, in which his patron Ormonde, despite a lifetime's devotion

[29] Dedication to Addison's *The Drummer* in *Corr.,* p. 514.
[30] *A Relation of the Proceedings at Charter-House.* . . . (London, 1689), p. 4.

to the Stuarts, led a determined and successful struggle for limitation of the royal prerogative. Years later Steele was involved in a number of partisan controversies having to do with the prerogative; whereas Ormonde had once, regretfully, pressed for the limitation of royal power, Steele made the quest for such a limitation part of his mature political philosophy.

The next year, 1688, was that of the so-called Bloodless Revolution. The old Duke was mercifully spared a final choice between Stuart King and Protestant religion; he died in July before the November Revolution. His grandson and successor, the second Duke, only twenty-three years old, decided for William of Orange and aided his entry. Of more direct importance to young Steele was the retention of Henry Gascoigne as private secretary to the new duke and the second duke's election on the death of his grandfather as Chancellor of the University of Oxford.

The "Bloodless" Revolution, meanwhile, was proceeding in a decidedly sanguinary manner in Ireland. Protestant was set against Catholic by the landing of James II with French support in March, 1689. Gascoigne's forebodings had been correct. The Protestant minority in Ireland was in great danger; an overwhelmingly Catholic Parliament assembled in Dublin at James's call and passed an Act of Attainder by which about two thousand persons, including the Duke of Ormonde, were to stand convicted of high treason unless they voluntarily surrendered by August, 1689. Among the names on the list were those of many of Gascoigne's friends and acquaintances. Ireland was doomed to choose between James and William; months of bloodshed lay ahead.

In his maturity, Steele's high regard for Protestantism was accompanied by an excessive distrust of Roman Catholicism. The attitude is surprising in a person so naturally tolerant, a man by no means bound to conventions of the age, one of which conventions was violent religious partisanship. The explanation

lies partly in his Irish background. The siege of Ballinakill was
recalled in family legend. The Williamist wars confirmed once
and for all the mistrust of Irish Catholic for Irish Protestant
and the reverse; erased almost all of the *modus vivendi* which
Ormonde and others of similar vision had attempted to work
out in the post-Restoration years; fixed the determination of
the English to dominate Ireland and discourage all signs of
Irish independence. Intervention by the French seemed to support the opinion many Irish Protestants held: that Catholicism
and political subversion were synonymous. Richard Steele, then,
could like many other Irishmen be tolerance itself on every
matter but the most important, religion. From his earliest writings to the latest, his distrust of Catholicism in civil affairs did
not waver; Catholicism represented in his mind civil discord
and subversion.

In 1689 it was time for Richard Steele, then seventeen, to
make some decision concerning his future. He might have decided to enter the army; war flamed in Ireland where young
Ormonde led a troop of horse. But several important considerations worked in favor of Steele's continuing his education. For
one, Charterhouse was a wealthy foundation and supported
some twenty-nine scholars at the universities. For another, the
Duke of Ormonde had become Chancellor of Oxford in succession to his father. For a third, Henry Gascoigne continued to
be a minor but powerful political figure, one whom men liked
to please. He had even been given academic distinction: a doc-
torate of laws from Trinity College, Dublin, in 1681. Furthermore, in the new reign as in the old, Gascoigne demonstrated
his marked capability for securing preferment: James had appointed him Tail-Cart Taker to the Board of Green Cloth in
1687; William was scarcely crowned before making Gascoigne
Clerk of the Bakehouse in Ordinary with "the wages, board-
wages, fees, profits, perquisites, and advantages thereunto be-
longing. . . ." [31] He was, in short, fully able to get a promising

[31] Aitken, I, 21–23.

young student into a respectable Oxford college, if the student was so disposed.

Richard Steele was so disposed. Joseph Addison had left Charterhouse for Queen's College, Oxford, two years earlier. But Gascoigne had other, closer sources of influence: the second Duke of Ormonde had been a student at Christ Church and his tutor, Henry Aldrich, became Dean of the college in June, 1689, largely as a reward for his opposition to King James's Catholic Dean. The way was open. As Lady Mildmay knew, Christ Church was a fashionable college; young Richard Steele must be decently fitted out for his entry into university life. "[P]ray give him a pare of gloves and Send him a Sord," she wrote Gascoigne, "and Show him how to put it one, That he may be like The young Lads nex doer. . . ." [32]

With gloves and sword, Richard Steele left Charterhouse, London, the Gascoigne household which had been his home, and went up to Oxford, where he signed Dean Aldrich's Entry Book at Christ Church on 21 December 1689.

APPENDIX TO CHAPTER I

The Steeles of Ballinakill

THE GENEALOGY of the Steele family must, at this date, be patched together by many guesses, less or more informed. The origins of Richard Steele (I) are uncertain. Though referred to by contemporaries as a young Bristol merchant (cf. CSPEI, 1513–1616, p. 360), no reference to him has been found in Bristol or Somerset printed records of the seventeenth century. The undated note mentioned by

[32] MS. Ormonde 183, fol. 355.

Aitken (II, 354) as being in the Harleian MSS. has the virtue of identifying his wife correctly as Frances Webb[e], of Ingham, Kent. The note traces the elder Steele's descent to Sandbach, Cheshire. If this is correct, he was probably related in some way both to William Steele, later Cromwell's Lord Chancellor of Ireland and to the Reverend Richard Steele (1629–1692), Dissenting minister and author of *The Tradesman's Calling*. He would have been unsympathetic, of course, with their religious and political views and there is no record of Richard Steele's having been in touch with any relatives in Cheshire. Lacking evidence to the contrary, however, one guesses that he was, in fact, one of the numerous Steeles of Cheshire and that he sought his fortune in trade at Bristol. If he was a young man in 1614 (CSPEI, 1513–1616, p. 316), he may have been born around 1590. He died about 1658 (Probate Registry, Somerset House, *Book of Administrations,* 1658, fol. 159).

Richard (I) and Frances had nine children living by about 1635 (PRO, Domestic Series, 16/306/81), the eldest of whom (presumably John, the eventual heir) was a son born in India in 1617 (CSPEI, 1617–1621, pp. 94, 131). Of these nine, four daughters signed Steele's deposition on the uprising of 1641 (Trinity College, Dublin, MS. F. 2. 7, fol. 358–359) : Frances, Bellindia, Mary, and Ellenor. Since Katherine and Richard (II) were married and studying law, respectively, in the decade of the sixteen-sixties, they were probably minor children during the siege of Ballinakill, too young to sign the deposition. The nine children, in approximate reverse order of their ages, then, would be:

John. Will at Probate Registry, Somerset House, *Book of Wills,* July, 1673, fol. 95.

Bellindia. According to John's will, Mrs. Lynn, a widow of Westminster with two daughters, Mrs. Bellindia Sumpner and Mrs. [i.e. Miss] Penelope Lynn ("Cousin Pen" of the *Correspondence*). By the sixteen-eighties Mrs. Lynn and Penelope were living with Henry and Katherine Steele Mildmay Gascoigne, as were Richard Steele (III) and his sister. (National Library of Ireland, MS. Ormonde 183, fol. 393; *Correspondence,* pp. 1, 208, 209.)

Ellenor or Elinor. According to John's will, a spinster, living in London.

Frances. Mary. Nothing known beyond their signatures on the 1641 deposition. Perhaps one of the two was the Mrs. Steele who was a companion or governess in the Conway family at Lisburn, County Antrim, between 1679 and 1682. Richard Steele (I) had known Sir Edward Conway, later Viscount Conway, in the court of Charles I, and Katherine Steele Mildmay Gascoigne was a friend of the daughters of Sir George Rawdon, who was private secretary to the third Viscount Conway in 1683 and also a member of the Lisburn household. (CSPEI, 1625–1629, p. 48; CSPD, 1683; and *The Rawdon Papers,* ed. Edward Berwick [London, 1819], p. 411.)

Daughter or son. Nothing known.

Richard (II). See text. Children: Richard (III) and Katherine.

Katherine. Katherine Steele Mildmay Gascoigne, foster mother of Richard Steele (III). There is no evidence that she had children. The Henry Gascoigne mentioned by Aitken (I, 157) is certainly not her husband Henry and probably not her husband's son.

Son? Perhaps the George Steele mentioned in John O'Hart's *Irish Pedigrees* (New York, 1923), II, 530, as a resident of Balloughmore Castle, possessor of "a large tract of land" in Leix and father of a large family. Presumably it was his descendants who came into possession of the estate in Wexford, of which Richard Steele (III) gave up the succession when he entered the army (see text).

CHAPTER II

Oxford and the Guards

UNIVERSITIES ARE generally no more disposed to change than rivers; like rivers they are inclined to cut their course deep and then flow somnolently on or stagnate within their selected bounds. But rivers from time to time do change course; impelled by some catastrophe — a rising flood, an earthquake — the river will shift its path, become almost a different river, irrigating new land with its flow. Soon though it will settle into its newly-cut banks and continue seaward. And so it is, metaphorically, with universities. The University of Oxford had undergone, in the years before the Revolution of 1688, an unsettling series of events which were regarded there as catastrophes and which indeed would have been thought in ordinary civil life mischievous or serious. Nowhere did James Stuart, James II, flaunt his political ineptitude more egregiously than in his continued efforts, at last successful, to alienate one of his main sources of strength, strongholds of bedrock royalist conservatism, the universities.

Not, of course, that he set out to do so. James's intention at Oxford was to foster what he believed with all his heart to be the true religion; this was his intention in Ireland in 1689. His method, however, was to assault the very Ark of the Covenant, academic prerogative, by appointing his coreligionists to fellowships and administrative positions in the place of Protestant members of an overwhelmingly Protestant faculty. Those appointed were exempted by royal decree from receiving the Anglican sacrament and, as in the Popham case at Charterhouse, from taking oaths of allegiance to the reformed religion. In December, 1686, the King appointed a Roman Catholic, John Massey, Dean of Christ Church, a post which combined the headship of the college and the decanal direction of the Anglican cathedral. Henry Aldrich, subdean and friend of Henry Gascoigne, grudgingly went through the installation ceremony while undergraduates and townspeople in the congregation hooted throughout the proceedings, and refused to assist in the customary bellringing afterward. Anthony Wood, historian and crusty fellow of Merton, took a long, gloomy view of the matter:

> Whereas, before Xmas or about a week or fortnight, there were in Ch[rist] Ch[urch] 26 gentlemen commoners, there were not in the latter end of Jan. following above 6, and two noblemen. This winter the proctors walk not because of the troopers for fear of being affronted by them; whore houses increase, surgeons have work, and great salivation used. O tempora! o mores![1]

An even more serious case of James's interference took place the following year (1687), involving another one of Henry Gascoigne's close friends, John Hough. Hough had served in Ireland as domestic chaplain to the Duke of Ormonde and was a fellow of Magdalen College in 1687 when, upon the death of the college president, he was elected president by the other fellows, contrary to a mandate of King James ordering them to elect one Anthony Farmer. Despite the mandate, Hough was formally admitted by the Bishop of Winchester and sworn into office. The case quickly became a *cause célèbre,* with both sides not only refusing to move, but actively maintaining the propriety

---

[1] *The Life and Times of Anthony Wood, antiquary, of Oxford, 1632–1695, described by himself,* ed. Andrew Clark (Oxford, 1891–1900), III, 202. Details of Oxford life following from this source and from *Corr.,* unless otherwise noted. For a good account of the installation see BM Loan MS. 29/135, letter from Paul Foley to Robert Harley.

of their actions. After several months of threats, protests, and rejoinders, James sent a special commission to Oxford, escorted by three troops of cavalry, to discharge Hough from the presidency. At a hearing in the great hall of College, Hough refused to surrender, saying that he submitted to the commission "so far as it is consistent with the laws of the land, and the statutes of the College, and no further." [2] Though removed along with all the college fellows from ecclesiastical preferment by the commission, Hough, as a final token of resistance, declined to hand over the keys of his rooms, which had to be broken open.

The statement that the Revolution of 1688 was a conservative revolution is now a cliché, but not the less true for being one. Men like Aldrich and Hough were fundamentally conservative scholars, Church of England men who distrusted both Dissent and Catholicism, but who in the late sixteen-eighties had found the latter more threatening. "The laws of the land," they discovered, provided a buttress for their personal position and a refuge from the King's prerogative. When William displaced James, the lessons they had learned were reinforced; they were rewarded for their stubbornness, Aldrich becoming, as we have seen, Dean of Christ Church in 1689 and Hough, Bishop of Oxford in 1690.

Into the hands of men like these, then, Gascoigne delivered the young Steele. He was forthwith accepted for what he was, the protégé of an influential man who had the ear of the University's Chancellor. "I have been with Dr. Hough," the matriculant wrote in his first letter home, "who received your letter and enquired very civilly after your and my Lady's health. When I took my leave of him he desired me to inform him, if at any time he could be serviceable or assistant to me for he could very readily do it. Dr. Aldridge gives his service to you, and told me he should write to you himself by this post." Hough would be

---

[2] *Magdalen College and King James II, 1686–88,* ed. J. R. Bloxam (Oxford, 1886), p. 120.

"serviceable" to this seventeen-year-old Irish orphan because Gascoigne might be helpful to him. Such was the accepted way of seeking one's fortune in seventeenth-century England.

Richard Steele was not long in learning. In his next letter to Gascoigne he acknowledges the receipt of money from home, then turns to business, the business of securing a scholarship:

> Our Dean, whom you expected, is, I suppose now at London, the election of students is not very far off now; if you would be pleased to speak with him or purchase from my lord [the Duke of Ormonde] a word or two, it would perhaps get me the most creditable preferment for young men in the whole university: there are many here that think of it, but none speak their mind; the places are wholly in the Dean and Canons' dispose without respect to scholarship; but if you will vouchsafe to use your interest in my behalf there shall be nothing wanting in the endeavours of
>
> S^r, Your most obedient nephew,
and most humble servant,
R. STEELE

In the meantime studies proceeded. A tutor had been appointed and once more family interest was present. The tutor was Welbore Ellis, sometime "customer, comptroller and searcher for the provinces of Leinster and Munster" in Ireland, now a student preparing to take orders. His brother John, of whom more later, had recently become a secretary of the Duke of Ormonde, having served the first Duke in the same capacity. Like Hough and Aldrich, and for the same reason, Welbore Ellis was glad to welcome Richard Steele to Oxford. "I shall endeavour to take such care of him," he wrote his brother John, "that I may gain Mr Gascoigne's favourable opinion of me and continue yours to me." [3] Fortunately for all concerned, Steele was progressing in his work. Despite some time spent drinking claret in an Oxford tavern with fellows of other colleges, he was able to report

[3] BM, Add. MSS. 28931, fol. 36, and DNB.

to Gascoigne in May that Dean Aldrich had seen his work and said that "if I went on in my study he did not question but I should make something more than ordinary. I had this from my Tutour. I have I think a good character through the whole College. I speak not this, Sir, out of any vanity or affectation but to let you know that I have not been altogether negligent on my part. . . ." A renewed request for Gascoigne's help in the forthcoming selection of scholars follows.

Two characteristics of the mature Richard Steele are noticeable even in this college boy's letter. One is, despite the denial, a high opinion of his own worth, a tendency perhaps to inflate his abilities and performances beyond life-size. The second is the virtual craving for preferment. Both no doubt have something to do with his position: that of a penniless Irish orphan who existed solely by preferment and by his brains. Stories of his father's and grandfather's struggles, memories of his widowed mother's plight must have served to sharpen the hunger for place and preferment which was so noticeable throughout his life and which caused him at times to posture in a ridiculous manner, to expose himself to charges of sycophancy. It was not as a sycophant, however, that Richard Steele sought favors from persons like Gascoigne well able to bestow them. It was as a young man beginning to realize his abilities, perhaps beginning to magnify them somewhat out of proportion, who knew that he was condemned to obscurity and poverty unless he exerted himself. Like his grandfather before him, Richard would exploit his opportunities.

Gascoigne was happy to oblige in this case. A studentship (that is, a scholarship) would make up Steele's expenses over the amount provided him by his Charterhouse scholarship and relieve Gascoigne of tavern bills and money spent for white gloves and swords. The Duke of Ormonde was accordingly invited to "be pleased to befriend Dick Steele, who is now entered in Ch. Ch., by getting him a student's place there, or something else. . . ." Apparently nothing came of his request : Gascoigne's influence with young Ormonde was not equal to his power with the first Duke.[4] But Steele all his life worried with only half his mind; life was not unpleasant for the young undergraduate in 1690 and 1691. Joseph Addison was studying at Magdalen and already well known in the University for his ability. Christopher Codrington, a native of Barbados and later an associate of Steele's in London pamphlet warfare (still later donor of the magnificent All Souls' Library), was a student at Christ Church. Dean Aldrich was revered on all sides for his wit and kind nature. There were intellectual currents stirring too. John Locke, though no longer in residence, had been for many years a fellow of Christ Church. When his *Two Treatises of Government* appeared in early 1690, the college must have sounded with discussion of its merits and defects. The work became for Richard Steele the foundation of his political philosophy; time and again in later years he was to refer to Locke as to a final authority, and Steele's effect as a popularizer of Locke was considerable.

Oxford, in short, was a friendly and interesting place for Richard Steele: he delighted in later life, like alumni of other universities, in recalling his days there. Acknowledging his debt in 1706 by way of a "Prologue to the University of Oxford" written to be read before a theater audience there, Steele began :

> As wandering streams by secret force return
> To that capacious ocean whence they're born,
> So for their doom their toils our poets bring
> To the famed Oxford where they learnt to sing:
> These happy seats would rudest minds inspire,
> And all that see must feel poetic fire ; [5]

[4] He was succeeded as secretary in 1693 (HMC, *Ormonde MSS.*, N.S., VIII, xxxiii). Katherine Mildmay's letters (see note 11, chap. 1 above) reflect her uneasiness about the second Duke's generosity, though, as she put it, "bagers can't be choosers." Gascoigne's note as quoted in Aitken, I, 36; original not located in the Ormonde MSS.

[5] *Verse*, p. 45.

In July, 1690, word reached Oxford of King William's decisive victory over James at the Battle of the Boyne in Ireland. The stubborn Stuart king who had alienated his conservative support at the universities had now lost for the time being his last foothold in the British Isles. Richard Steele must have rejoiced more than his English schoolmates; no doubt he had a hand in kindling one of the innumerable bonfires which lit up Oxford and in pealing the bells of celebration. Tempers continued high. One Sunday night in July three hapless Dutchmen, inquiring at the Crown Tavern for lodging, were seized by a mob who took them from their accent to be Frenchmen come, of course, to set fire to the city. Hailed before the mayor that night, the strangers were finally identified as Hollanders, fellow countrymen of King William, and released shaken but unharmed. It was a time, many felt, for action.

If town had its excitement, so in its own manner did gown. In August, 1690, Convocation voted that a book by Dr. Arthur Bury, Rector of Exeter College, called *Naked Gospell* "containing a great deal of Socinianism should be burnt. Whereupon a fire being made in the school quadrangle, it was accordingly burnt." But not forgotten; theological disputes inclined toward heat in those days. Defenders of Bury and his doctrines arose; opponents replied in sermons and pamphlets like that written by Dr. John Wallis and, Wood records, "printed at London to shew to the world that some of Oxon did stand up against Dr. . . . Bury." Richard Steele maintained all his life a lively interest in matters theological; his religious beliefs were by no means unexamined. There is no evidence, however, that his years at the university were the immediate occasion of such an examination; though what he heard and read and saw at Oxford doubtless provided part of the basis for his later writings on religious subjects, those writings were still many years away. The picture of Addison at Oxford, his biographer judges, "is one of overmuch gravity for a very young man." [6] Steele's

[6] Smithers, p. 18.

undergraduate character, one feels sure, never provided material for such a judgment; his interest in the Bury controversy probably extended to its pyrotechnic rather than its theological aspects.

Steele continued his studies at Christ Church but without preferment, for the Duke of Ormonde had other concerns. The second Duke found his calling in the army; unlike his grandfather, he displayed little aptitude for the life of a courtier. There was a campaign to fight every summer, and as Chancellor of Oxford he was forced to perform almost from the saddle whatever duties devolved upon that office. He was first a cavalryman and a good one, and had less time and inclination for politics and preferment than had the first Duke. In any case, Gascoigne had friends elsewhere in Oxford than Christ Church, and Richard Steele was learning to make his own way. In 1690 he had acted as an intermediary for some transaction between Gascoigne and William Sherwin, Fellow of Merton, and had shared oysters and wine with fellows of that college including old Anthony Wood, who knew anecdotes concerning grandfather Richard Steele of Ballinakill.[7] Perhaps the Mertonians were impressed with young Richard's intelligence and good humor, a combination of qualities usually in demand among academic groves. Or did the smallpox, sweeping through Oxford in 1691, provide a place for Steele in the way sudden death was to do throughout the eighteenth century, opening opportunities for some and graves for others? At any rate, and for whatever reason, Steele entered Merton in August, 1691, as a *portionista* or postmaster, the name Merton has used over the centuries for its endowed scholars.

Though Steele's sojourn in Merton was comparatively brief, he regarded the college with special favor and is thought of there as a Mertonian. He had at Merton, of course, improved status; important to academic happiness generally and doubly

---

[7] Wood's anecdote (about Steele and Coryat): *Athenae Oxonienses*, ed. Philip Bliss (Oxford, 1813–1820), II, col. 211.

important to Richard Steele. The appointment signified approval; it is doubtful that any amount of pressure from Ormonde would have induced the college to grant it if the fellows had not been convinced of Steele's intellectual promise. Years afterward Steele recalled his feelings about the college and revealed some of the studies he had pursued there (*The Englishman,* No. 34, 22 Dec. 1713):

> Some business lately called me to Oxford, and it was with infinite pleasure that I beheld an university of which I had once the honour to be a member. The sight of that college I am more particularly obliged to, filled my heart with unspeakable joy. Methought I grew younger the moment I stepped within the gate, and upon my entering the hall in which I had so often disputed, I found my logic come afresh into my head, and that I could have formed syllogisms in figures whose very names I had not once thought of for several years before. The libraries, quadrangles, and grove, all renewed in my mind, an hundred little pleasant stories and innocent amusements, though in the last place I could not help observing with some regret the loss of a tree, under whose shade I had often improved my acquaintance with Horace.

At Merton, Steele, according to an early account, attempted a comedy, but destroyed it on the advice of a fellow postmaster and lifelong friend, Richard Parker.[8]

Excitement over King William's and Marlborough's conquest of Ireland culminated on 26 November with a formal Thanksgiving Day for the taking of Limerick. Fireworks and bonfires blazed everywhere. By midwinter, however, some of the excitement had been rubbed away by the presence in Oxford of troops returning from Ireland who conducted themselves as troops returning from a difficult campaign will, committing "many rudenesses and rogueries." Now that Ireland had surrendered, King William could pursue his war on the continent against France and an even larger army would be needed. Press

---

[8] *Biographia Britannica,* under "Richard Steele."

gangs passed through Oxford early in the year, as well as more
orthodox recruiting parties. Invasion by the French was rumored; who could stand idle? Certainly not Richard Steele. In
December he left college for almost a month, presumably going
to London to stay with the Gascoignes over the holidays; in
mid-January he returned for a few weeks and left again at the
end of February, with his friend Richard Parker. He spent
eleven days in college in May and went down this time for
good, though his name was kept on the kitchen rolls for another
year and a half.[9] Of Steele's decision to leave Oxford without a
degree we know nothing for certain beyond his own statement,
somewhat dramatized as usual, of a quarter-century later:

> [When] he mounted a war-horse, with a great sword in his hand,
> and planted himself behind King William the Third, against
> Lewis the Fourteenth, he lost the succession to a very good
> estate in the county of Wexford in Ireland, from the same humour
> which he has pursued ever since, of preferring the state of his
> mind to that of his fortune. When he cocked his hat, and put on
> a broad sword, jackboots, and shoulder-belt, under the command
> of the unfortunate Duke of Ormonde, he was not acquainted
> with his own parts. . . .[10]

It is a conjecture but one that accords with what we know that
Richard enlisted in early March, spent the next two months
learning to sit his horse and use the broad sword, and returned
to Merton in May to cock his hat for the benefit of his fellow-
students before going overseas. Fighting was a warm-weather
occupation in those days; Steele may well have told the fellows
of Merton that he intended to return and take up his scholarship
when he had helped the English finish Louis that summer.

The regiment he had chosen has always been a good one, good
in the opinion of the *haut monde,* and, as Napoleon was to find

---

[9] Merton College Buttery Books. These are quite clear; Steele was not in
residence after May, 1692.
[10] *The Theatre,* No. 11, pp. 87–88.

to his sorrow at Waterloo, composed of good fighting men. The Second Troop of Life Guards had been formed by Charles II in 1660 with two others as the royal bodyguard. Commanded in 1692 by the Duke of Ormonde, the Second Troop was officially composed of officers and "private gentlemen," and the rankers were addressed as "Mister"; Lady Mildmay need have no fears of society's disapproval. Each private gentleman provided his sword, two pistols, a carbine, and his own horse, and, as befitted a horseman in an equestrian society, was paid more than a private of foot: four shillings per day against eightpence. The gentlemen of the ranks, furthermore, looked toward a commission by appointment or purchase in another regiment within a few years.[11] It was, in short, an appropriately cavalier unit for this grandson of a cavalier. The jack boots and gauntlets and sword worn even yet in full dress by the mounted Guards were, of course, then utilitarian protection against weather and foe, but young Richard Steele put them on, one feels certain, with plenty of dash and swagger.

The troop's commander was the Steeles' family patron, and life around London in such a regiment would have been pleasant enough for Richard, but there was, in the modern expression, a war on. Men were scarce; some commanding officers, the chronicler Luttrell reported in April, had asked the Queen's leave to resort to the desperate measure of filling their ranks with convicted criminals. Recruits were being shipped to Flanders every month that spring and it seems entirely probable, though no documentary evidence exists to prove it, that Richard Steele joined the Life Guards in Flanders shortly after his final weeks in Oxford, that is, in June, 1692.

A bitter summer was ahead for the British army. King Wil-

[11] Captain Sir George Arthur, *The Story of the Household Cavalry* (London, 1909–1926), I, 24, 37; Clifford Walton, *History of the British Standing Army. A.D. 1660 to 1700* (London, 1894), pp. 6, 647.

liam was a determined fighter but no very skillful general. "He was no more," judges Sir Winston Churchill, "than a resolute man of good common sense whom the accident of birth had carried to the conduct of war." [12] Casualties under the King's generalship were high, campaigns long and exhausting. His main object in life was to defeat by any means the political and military aspirations of France, toward which country he bore a distrust amounting to an article of faith. A young soldier in the Life Guards, naturally suspicious like all other Irish Protestants of France, which for two centuries supported invasion of their home island, imbibed some of William's Francophobia and carried it to his grave.

Personal loyalty to friends and leaders was a strong element in Richard Steele's character; at a time when such loyalties were likely to be transitory and determined by interest, Steele clung to friendships as treasured possessions. His defense, years later, of the Duke of Ormonde, turned Jacobite, is a case in point. Unlike Addison, he would not allow friendship to cool; it must continue or break in a quarrel. To William's memory and to many of his principles, insofar as he understood them, Steele remained devoted with the dogged fidelity of which he was capable, and which, at its best, was a mark of genuine moral courage.

With the perspective of history, scholars have judged that much of William's activity was self-serving and that his Dutch followers were rewarded far beyond their deserts. The early enthusiasm of many Englishmen for William, kindled by his victories in Ireland, waned as they grew to know the dour Dutchman better and as the campaigns in Europe stretched on from year to year, bleeding the armies white. But in 1692 public support of the new king was high and was raised further by the prospects of a French invasion. In May, 1692, the British fleet under Admiral Edward Russell defeated the French off Cape La

[12] *Marlborough: His Life and Times* (London, 1933–1938), I, 342.

Hogue in one of those decisive sea battles which the British, century after century, have managed to win when victory is essential. William was free to pursue his mismanaged campaigns on the continent.

In August, 1692, the King prepared for battle without his most skillful general, Marlborough, who had been suspected of intriguing with the Jacobites. All detachments of the Life Guards were under Ormonde's command. Battle was joined at Steenkirk in Flanders, with the Allies (largely British and Dutch) attacking the French in strong positions among woods and ravines. During a long day's fighting the British infantry was frittered away, while the cavalry was held off from attack until it was too late for them to win the battle but not too late to suffer heavily in charges across the ravines. The Dutch general, Solmes, was accused in the British ranks of sacrificing them to save his fellow countrymen, and British casualties were in fact extremely heavy, perhaps half of the troops engaged. All in all it was a bloody, discouraging campaign with which to begin a military career.

Perhaps it was a memory of the charge at Steenkirk that furnished Steele the image he used in the 1716 preface to his second *Englishman,* in which he had rashly defended the personal qualities of the same Duke of Ormonde, then recently attainted for treason and exiled to the Jacobite court in France. The metaphor is that of a man who knows what he is talking about:

> It ordinarily happens that the same men who make an attack very bravely upon troops in good order, do least execution upon them when they are put to flight or ask quarter. But I never heard it said that they were the less zealous for the cause, or that they were held deserters from the service, because they have been overrun in pursuing a defeat, by their friends, who were in the rear at the onset.

Better days were ahead for the Second Troop after Steenkirk. In September the survivors embarked for England, where they re-equipped in Northamptonshire and were mounted on black horses throughout. During the winter the Second Troop relieved the Blues on duty at Whitehall, and by 1693 Richard Steele's life must have settled into a mild garrison routine. The Gascoignes were in London, of course, to provide a roof and a mailing address for the young soldier. In April Steele's Oxford tutor, Welbore Ellis, was commissioned Chaplain of Ormonde's troop.[13] One imagines that Steenkirk would have slaked a trooper's thirst for battle and made standing guard at St. James's palace and Whitehall seem positively restful. During the summer of 1693 Ormonde left his troop in London and joined the army in Flanders for a bloodbath even greater than Steenkirk, at Landen, where the Duke himself was wounded and captured leading a charge. According to the custom of those times, the Duke was quickly exchanged, and in the spring of 1694 he prepared to lead the Second Troop into Flanders once more for the summer's campaign. This was soldiering under King William.

Before the Troop shipped out for Flanders, in April, 1694, Steele had apparently written a conventional Valentine poem entitled, "Upon having Mrs. Selwyn, by Lot, my Valentine." If Mrs. Selwyn was Mrs. William Selwyn, her husband was Colonel of the Second Regiment of Foot; Steele seems to have been pursuing military promotion — as Marlborough himself had — by indirect means. The careful qualification "by Lot" suggests a gentleman-ranker's caution.[14]

The campaign of 1694 provided much marching, some skirmishing, and not much bloodshed for the Second Troop; Richard Steele got a general view of the Low Countries if nothing else. The Life Guards went into winter quarters at Breda, but Steele did not stay there; he returned to London, probably with

[13] *English Army Lists and Commission Registers, 1661–1714*, ed. Charles Dalton (London, 1892–1902), V, 21. Movements of Ormonde's troop based on Narcissus Luttrell, *A Brief Historical Relation of State Affairs from September 1678 to April 1714* (Oxford, 1857), *passim*.
[14] *Verse*, pp. 32, 88.

one of the detachments of Life Guards escorting King William. In 1695 Richard Steele proceeded to seek promotion more directly and made his formal debut in English letters doing so.

Queen Mary's death from smallpox in December, 1694, was followed three months later by an elaborate funeral. There were sound political reasons for this pomp: Mary was the English member of the reigning couple and hence the better liked; the Jacobites, moreover, were becoming bolder. A show of royal pomp and power was in order, and the dead Queen provided the occasion for a state funeral. On the literary side there was the normal outpouring of poetical tributes, addresses of loyalty from towns favorably disposed to King William, and an elaborate book of verses bound in purple from the University of Oxford, presented to the tearful King by the Chancellor, the Duke of Ormonde.[15] In early April, 1695, a small folio pamphlet appeared in London, modestly priced fourpence, entitled *The Procession. A Poem on Her Majesties Funeral*. The author was revealed only as "a Gentleman of the Army" and the poem was dedicated to John Baron Cutts, at thirty-four one of the army's boldest soldiers and commanding officer of the Coldstream Regiment, the Second Regiment of Foot Guards. The poem recalls in florid hyperbole the funeral procession, the mourners, objects of Mary's charity ("There mothers walk, who oft despairing stood,/ Pierced with their infants' deafening sobs for food"), and the mourning nobility including the Countess of Derby, the Duke of Ormonde's sister, who is singled out:

> But Darby hides in vain her gushing tears,
> In her affliction takes an abject state,
> Something so very low, yet very great;
> No single cause so different grief could send,
> She weeps as subject, servant, and a friend:[16]

[15] Wood (see note 1), III, 477–78.
[16] *Verse*, p. 6.

Though no critic's work of art, the poem displays sound Williamite politics and a lively interest in the important people of the day. It is an ambitious young soldier's poem, a set piece of the sort it was well for budding men of promise to write. Thus young Jonathan Swift addressed King William in inflated verse (though he was later to change his mind about the Dutch king), and Addison's poem on Marlborough's victory at Blenheim was to attract great attention and provide in part the foundation for Addison's political career. The early poetic efforts of all three contemporaries were at least quasi-political.

The Procession had no such public success but its unsigned, conventionally florid dedication to Lord Cutts apparently served. In 1695 Richard Steele left the Life Guards and joined the Coldstreamers: the Second Foot Guards, but as their motto proclaims, *Nulli Secundus,* second to none. In April, 1697, he was commissioned ensign in Lord Cutts's own company.[17] There was more to the assignment than the window dressing of rank. Steele, who at first was probably a "gentleman of the company" pending his promotion to ensign, became Cutts's private secretary, but his duties did not end with seeing to the numerous details, private, military, and political, of that office. As ensign of the colonel's company, he was, in fact, second in command of a company of guards, the colonel being the titular and the lieutenant the actual company commander. The Coldstream second battalion, of which Steele's company was part, was assigned before 1697 to guard duty in London while the first battalion fought with King William in Flanders, and guard duty at Kensington, Whitehall, Hampton Court, and elsewhere was more than ceremonial; attempts on the sovereign's life still occurred, a notorious one in 1696. For this responsibility guards' officers were given extra pay and brevet ranks

[17] Dalton (see note 13), IV, 173. See also Mrs. Manley, *The New Atalantis* (2nd ed.; London, 1709), I, 188.

higher than their actual commissions; no later than 1697 Steele
thus acquired the title by which he was known in London for
many years, Captain Steele.[18]

This transfer was an important step forward in several respects. Cutts was an outstanding soldier and also a successful
minor poet and a rising politician, as full of ambition as is a
ripe grape of juice. For his services in the Irish wars he had
been created Baron Cutts; in 1693 he had received a rich political reward, the governorship of the Isle of Wight, which sent
six members to Parliament, all subject to pressure from the
Governor, and Cutts delighted in pressure. Though only eleven
years Steele's senior, he was no easy superior; a contemporary
described him as "pretty tall, lusty and well-shaped, an agreeable companion, with abundance of wit, affable and familiar, but
too much seized with vanity and self-conceit." [19]

Some conceit was perhaps justified; wounded three times,
Cutts, whose very name signifies bloodshed, distinguished himself in one campaign after another by his favorite tactic: leading
the point of the assault on foot with sword drawn; thus he
earned his nickname, "the Salamander." This aggressiveness naturally endearing him to general officers, he was frequently to
be seen with nobility at Court, accompanied from time to time,
no doubt, by his private secretary.

The Baron's lieutenant governor and deputy on the Isle of
Wight was Joseph Dudley, the first of two Americans with
whom Steele was to be closely associated, both of whom probably served as sources for much of the writer's persistent interest
in the new lands. Dudley was a native of Roxbury, Massachusetts, a Harvard graduate, and a veteran of the ever-rugged

---

[18] Walton (see note 11), pp. 410, 415–16, 443, 446. This brevetting, Mr.
D. W. King, Librarian, the War Office, has informed me, was universal in
the guards, mounted and foot. For Coldstream duties and service, see Daniel
MacKinnon, *Origin and Services of the Coldstream Guards* (London, 1833),
II, 308, 417.
[19] DNB.

school of Massachusetts politics. Caught in one of the twists of that colony's political course, he had come to England to repair his fortunes; though many years older than Steele, the two became good friends in Cutts's service, where they smarted under the pressure the Baron habitually exerted on his subordinates. In 1702 Dudley had his reward, returning to Massachusetts as Governor.

In 1696, though, he and Steele were subordinates, emphatically so. Cutts's method of dealing with Dudley as with Steele was to combine exhortation with promises. "I dare venture telling a discreet man," he wrote Dudley at the end of a letter of most explicit instructions "[that] I don't much doubt of succeeding in my pretentions, which will put me in a fair way. Be assured I don't forget you, but will effectually take care of you. . . ." Between them, the two were manipulating the six seats in the House of Commons held by the Isle of Wight; Cutts spelled out for Dudley exactly what candidates should be presented, how the electors should be treated ("I wonder how Captain Phillips comes to be cowed by Sr R. Worsely. I beg of you to talk with him; and if good words, promises, or money will do, secure him; & pray don't omit this a moment. And let all things be done with calmness & gravity.").[20] Such were Richard Steele's lessons in politics and such the schoolmasters and sound the precepts they taught. Politics was a personal business in the eighteenth century; a typical seat in Parliament was controlled by a few electors or a few score, and the best way to secure an elector to one's interest, as now, was to do that elector a favor — good words, promises, or money. Men not measures, to reverse Chesterfield's slogan, dominated English politics. With respect to measures, Lord Cutts was a sound Williamite, like Welbore Ellis of the Whiggish persuasion, but his major concern was self- rather than party-serving.

[20] "Letters of Lord Cutts to Joseph Dudley," *Proceedings of the Massachusetts Historical Society, 1886*, pp. 177, 184.

No doubt Cutts's political machinations interested Steele and occupied much of his time, but there were other things to do. London society was as attractive as ever to the young guardsman; after 1698 Lady Mildmay and Henry Gascoigne had a house in Bond Street which Steele used as a mailing address, always referring to the house as "my aunt's" or "Lady Mildmay's" lodgings. The Isle of Wight where his duties apparently took him was remote, but amours could be pursued there as well as in London and Richard Steele before his marriage was Cupid's faithful follower. "There is no poem extant," he wrote a friend in London, "so perfect a description of a true wood-nymph, as my mistress. I must dispatch two or three clumsy rivals, besides a large attendant mastiff that always follows her, before my access is easy. She has an excellent wild beauty and wit; and everything that nature only can bestow." Steele pursued his nameless wood-nymph at a funeral and assured his London correspondent that he and the nymph would lie in the same bed.[21] Perhaps the verses he sent to London about this time (first printed many years later) were written in pursuit of the nymph. They are of the seventeenth rather than the eighteenth century in manner, not without minor poetic merit and reminiscent of the songs from Restoration plays:

Love's Relief
A wretch long tortured with disdain,
That hourly pined but pined in vain,
At length the God of Wine addressed,
The refuge of a wounded breast.

Vouchsafe, oh Power, thy healing aid,
Teach me to gain the cruel maid;
Thy juices take the lover's part,
Flush his wan looks, and cheer his heart.

[21] *Corr.*, pp. 430–31. I follow Professor Blanchard in accepting these letters to Mrs. Manley as substantially genuine.

Thus to the jolly god he cried;
And thus the jolly god replied,
Give whining o'er, be brisk and gay,
And quaff this sneaking form away.

With dauntless mien approach the fair;
The way to conquer is to dare.
The swain pursued the god's advice;
The nymph was now no longer nice.

She smiled, and spoke the sex's mind;
When you grow daring, we grow kind;
Men to themselves are most severe,
And make us tyrants by their fear.[22]

Whatever one may think of Bacchus' strategy, the poem reflects an impetuous disposition on the part of the poet, and, indeed, Steele was soon to be confronted with the results of his endeavors in the form of an illegitimate child. A memorandum in Steele's handwriting exists, telling a story in brief which the imagination can fill in: of debt, threatened blackmail, remorse. "Mrs. Phips a midwife in Watling-street at the sign of the Coffin and Cradle. Her bond she obtained by threatening to expose the occasion of the debt it is 22£: 5£ of it is paid."[23]

Steele's eighteenth-century world was a small one; the mother of a daughter born to him was Elizabeth Tonson, a girl of nineteen or twenty when the event took place and sister of the man later to be Steele's publisher, Jacob Tonson the younger. To Steele's credit, he accepted the consequences of his adventures and assumed the responsibility of rearing and educating his

[22] *Corr.,* p. 433 and *Verse,* p. 64. See also p. 102 where evidence for attribution is summarized.

[23] Blenheim MSS., reprinted in *Corr.,* p. 437n. Mrs. Manley, turned hostile, refers to two of Steele's illegitimate children. One girl ("Mrs. Temperance") seems to have died (*Corr.,* p. 427). Elizabeth Ousley survived; see *Corr.,* p. 399n, and note 24 below. There is no reason to believe Steele fathered other illegitimate children.

natural daughter, who bore the name Elizabeth Ousley and was the only one of Steele's children to produce surviving offspring. According to the statement of Elizabeth's grandson, Steele's second wife, Mary Scurlock ("Prue"), upon learning of the existence of the illegitimate daughter insisted that she be brought into the household and reared as their own. Elizabeth Ousley is, of course, known to readers of Dr. Johnson's *Life of Savage* where her intended betrothal to that other celebrated bastard is described.[24]

By 1700 or thereabouts, Steele's amorous impetuosity had been tempered by experience. It is well to see his peccadilloes in proportion, because his political foes made so much of them later. They were those of a young man without responsibilities in a great city. Macaulay's treatment of Addison and Steele as poles of virtue and vice must be regarded as a literary device. Samuel Johnson remarked most justly to Boswell, "Steele I believe practiced the lighter vices." In his young manhood at least, Steele drank heavily; so did almost every one of his friends. It was a hard-drinking society and a hard-drinking century. When his contemporaries spoke of "Poor Dick Steele," they chose the adjective because of his rashness, his occasional obtuseness, not, as Thackeray was to do, because of Steele's fondness for alcohol. And so with his sexual adventures. They were the mistakes of a night, and the young guardsman addressed himself to his responsibilities when it would have been entirely acceptable, in fact the usual course, to ignore them. After his first marriage, all evidence argues, he was completely faithful to his vows, an exemplary husband, for Richard Steele, except in one area of his character, could and did learn from experience. Not a scholarly or even a deeply-read man, Steele made experience his principal

[24] Prue's action: *The Epistolary Correspondence of Sir Richard Steele,* ed. John Nichols (London, 1809), II, 672n–73n. Mr. Benjamin Boyce (in *Johnsonian News Letter,* December, 1961, p. 9) conjectures that because the girl's surname, Ousley, is the same as that of Savage's supposed godparent, she and Savage may have been reared as infants in the same establishment.

teacher, searched always in his own biography for life's directions. It is a Spartan school, experience, and ultimately an incomplete one; Richard Steele's writings tend to be in large part skin deep, but they have the corresponding advantage of being, though skin deep, of his flesh. Fortunately for his art, his life was rich and full.

In one area, though, Steele never learned: for one so interested in making money he was curiously unable to hold on to it. All his life he labored to amass a fortune, spoke hopefully, as he had of the Oxford scholarships, of good times ahead, lived on hypothetical future earnings. And all his life he was pursued by bailiffs, besieged by creditors, harried in the courts by moneylenders and merchants. The truth is that Richard Steele's attitude toward money was that of the gambler rather than the businessman. Though he admired businessmen extravagantly and chanted their praises in *Tatler* and *Spectator,* he did not bother to emulate their methods of thrifty care, of living on interest rather than capital. Steele always hoped for the scheme that would speed him to riches. As if symbolic of his entire financial career, his earliest major commercial venture was with alchemy.

The scientific revolution of the seventeenth century brought about, among other more important developments, a renewed interest in the search for the philosopher's stone. Milton locates it on the sun ("That stone, or like to that, which here below/ Philosophers in vain so long have sought") and not only poets were grappling with the problem; Leibniz himself busied his creative mind with alchemy. Historians of modern chemistry see alchemy as a kinsman of chemistry. No doubt Richard Steele felt some of the intellectual curiosity in the late seventeenth-century air; perhaps Thomas Burnet's influence from Charterhouse days was still on him. Certainly mixed with his scientific questing, however, was a pronounced interest in finding a quick solution to his financial difficulties.

Sometime in the late sixteen-nineties, Steele undertook an alchemical project. His associates apparently included John Tilly, Warden of the Fleet prison; Tilly's mistress, Mrs. Mary Delarivière Manley, a colorful lady who was to be associated with or working against Steele for many years; and William Burnaby, a Mertonian of Steele's time at Oxford, now writing plays for bread in Grub Street.[25] These furnished the capital; the actual experimenter was later identified as Sir Thomas Tyrrel, presumably the last survivor of the well-known Buckinghamshire family. Mrs. Manley's account of the enterprise in the *New Atalantis* is partly confirmed by other sources and, though perhaps exaggerated, probably summarizes the affair adequately. Steele, according to her, met the "operator" (Tyrrel?) and agreed to back his trials. "Well, a house is taken, and furnished, furnaces built, and to work they go; the young soldier's little ready money immediately flies off, his credit is next staked, which soon likewise vanishes into smoke." Tilly then became a partner and presumably Burnaby, also, who had inherited a few hundred pounds. "Still the furnace burnt on, his credit was stretched to the utmost; demands came quick upon him, and grew clamorous; he had neglected his lord's business and even left his house, to give himself up to the vain pursuits of chemistry." Finally he lost everything but his commission. In view of the character of his "lord," Cutts, it is surprising that he was able to keep that; Cutts must have eyed his subordinate's scheme with contempt.

Steele's letters written during these experiments reflect the man: buoyant optimism followed by black despair. "I give you this trouble," he wrote Tilly, who was evidently involved in the actual work, "to desire you'd do me the favour of a line or two, that I may not look upon myself quite out of your thoughts when

[25] Sources summarized in *Corr.*, pp. 429–30n. See also Gwendolyn B. Needham, "Mrs. Manley: An Eighteenth-Century Wife of Bath," *H.L.Q.*, XIV (1950), 259–84.

you come to an *eureka*. My implicit faith deserves some consideration; and when the philosophick world is to be disposed of,
I hope there will some corner or other in it fall to my share."
Later, disillusionment: " 'Tis to me," he wrote Mrs. Manley,
"since my late reflections and selfdiscourses, a plain illusion of
some evil spirit, that anybody of sense believes in chemistry.
. . . I am heartily glad I am cured of all those hopes, and prefer jealousy of my mistress to the torment of a philosophick
doubt. . . ."

Despite the alchemical fiasco, Richard Steele's circle of acquaintances was growing if his fortunes were not. As Cutts's
secretary he had become well acquainted with that London society always beckoning to him and to other Anglo-Irishmen.
The Peace of Ryswick negotiated in September, 1697, had put
a temporary halt to King William's endless wars with France;
Steele's army duties consisted largely of garrison and guard,
with time enough for talk in the London coffeehouses. In 1700
he became involved in a complicated pamphlet war, more interesting for its participants than for the literary productions
themselves. The lines of warfare were drawn between the
ponderous physician-poet, Sir Richard Blackmore, and his old
foe, John Dryden. When in early 1700 Blackmore produced a
Satyr against Wit, directed against Dryden and his followers
who gathered at Will's Coffee House, those followers published
in reply a volume called *Commendatory Verses, On the Author
of the Two Arthurs, and The Satyr against Wit; By some of his
particular Friends.* Among the contributors were names well-
known in London literary circles, such as Sir Charles Sedley,
John Dennis, Vanbrugh, and Samuel Garth; Steele's Oxford
friend, Christopher Codrington, was a contributor and so was
Steele himself. His "Commendatory Verse" is a defense of Addison who had been mentioned, though gently, by Blackmore.
The poem's quality is not high ("Must I then passive stand! and
can I hear/ The man I love, abused, and yet forbear?") But

neither are the contributions of the others very distinguished. Blackmore or one of his cohort replied in *Discommendatory Verses* with "To the Noble *Captain* who was in a Damn'd Confounded Pet, because the Author of the *Satyr against Wit,* was pleased to Pray for his Friend." The controversy soon wilted, Dryden was dead by late spring, and Steele, years later when Blackmore's Whiggism shone more brightly, came to call (*Englishman,* No. 52, 2 Feb. 1714) the author of *Prince Arthur* "not only . . . a good poet, but a good Englishman." In 1700, however, Steele was for the first time in his life one of the lesser cynosures of the London *beau monde.* Readers wrote "Captain Steele" on their copies of *Discommendatory Verses,* thus identifying Blackmore's "Noble Captain." [26] This was the sort of tempest that erupted sporadically in the literary world, providing revenue to the booksellers and notoriety to authors with a taste for controversy. The Irish soldier was in the eyes of the world he valued a certified wit of Will's Coffee House.

Though he had received some publicity as an author of sorts, Captain Steele's constellation was still dim in the London sky. His personal friends were army acquaintances like Colonel Dudley, or Irishmen come to London to seek their fortune; the days of his pledging toasts with Whig politicians in the Kit-Cat Club were still several years off.[27] Despite his part in the *Commendatory Verses* controversy, Richard Steele in 1700 was a very minor figure. In June of that year he acquired some additional notoriety by fighting a duel with another Irishman in Hyde Park and almost killing his opponent. The antagonist was probably one Henry or Harry Kelly, an officer of the Queen's Regiment of Dragoons and an acquaintance (perhaps a kinsman) of Steele's and Congreve's Irish friend, Joseph

[26] *Verse,* p. 76. Controversy summarized in R. C. Boys, *Sir Richard Blackmore and the Wits* (Ann Arbor, 1949), from which, with *Verse,* this account is drawn.
[27] Fritz Rau, "Steeles Eintritt in den Kit-Cat Club," *Germanisch-Romanische Monatsschrift,* Neue Folge, VI (1956), 396–98.

Keally of Kilkenny.[28] The eighteenth-century legend, and it is only a legend, ran that Steele fought the duel with the greatest reluctance in defense of a lady's honor and wounded Kelly while attempting to disarm him. Certainly Steele regretted the episode, but he felt that he could not have avoided the duel. Writing to Colonel Dudley nine days after the affair, he said "the circumstances of that matter are such that you yourself, as wise as you really are, would have done the same thing. . . ." Nevertheless, the memory remained on his conscience and became transmuted directly, as was the way with Steele, into a call for action; his writings henceforth are full of denunciations of dueling. In an era when dueling was regarded as a fully acceptable, even desirable masculine activity, Steele waged a sort of crusade all his life against the practice.

The beginning of a century is an arbitrary act of man, of course, but somehow it provides fit time for reflective pause: 1700 was an important year to Richard Steele, a year in which he seems to have begun to meditate creatively on his experience, to take stock of himself and his future as if aware of time's passing. Stationed in and around London on guard duty at various public buildings, he was in his off hours becoming a member of the London literary world, as his participation in the Blackmore controversy attested. He had, or would soon have, a natural daughter; he had almost killed a man in a duel. What money he possessed was gone in the smoke of the alchemist's furnace; he was twenty-eight, an Irish ensign in the Guards, without prospects. A less thoughtful man than Steele might have paused for a backward look; a less ambitious man might have taken some action to enhance the future. Steele did both. The results of his meditations and the instrument of future success appeared in the form of a small volume of instruction and his first successful play.

[28] *Corr.*, pp. 8–9, 25–26; Kathleen M. Lynch, *A Congreve Gallery* (Cambridge, Mass., 1951), pp. 23–36.

The Christian Hero, published in April, 1701, is an extraordinary performance in several respects.[29] The subtitle gives some idea of its burden: *An Argument Proving that no Principles but those of Religion are Sufficient to make a Great Man.* The publisher, as if to demonstrate that his family did not bear grudges, was Jacob Tonson, uncle of the aggrieved Elizabeth. The book is dedicated to the man who could help Steele most, his commanding officer, Lord Cutts. And yet the book is an entirely serious manual of piety, written by Steele in all sincerity for the improvement of his and his fellows' moral lives. This was the sort of ambiguous action which Steele's enemies were later to use against him, employing such epithets as "hypocrite" and "dissembler." Thus Mrs. Manley, his old associate in the philosopher's stone project, wrote after the two had quarreled, "[H]e affected to be extreme religious, at the same time when he had two different creatures lying-in of base children by him." Steele himself mournfully recalled the reception of the work by his friends: "This had no other good effect, but that from being thought no undelightful companion, he was soon reckoned a disagreeable fellow. . . . [E]verybody he knew measured the least levity in his words and actions, with the character of a Christian hero." [30] Yet it is fair to say that Richard Steele never understood what his enemies were aiming at. Steele's capacity for rationalizing his own motives was considerable. Always ready to admit the errors of his actions, he was at the same time entirely convinced of his own worth and promise, of the moral rightness of his intentions. He could, he felt, speak with greater authority on the subject of right action because he had himself

[29] Reprinted in *Tracts,* pp. 1ff. For an analysis, generally accurate, of Steele's formal philosophic position as expressed in *The Christian Hero* and elsewhere, see Bertrand A. Goldgar, *The Curse of Party* (Lincoln, Neb., 1961), pp. 10–27. Dr. Goldgar concludes (p. 16) that his "moral theories would appear more as assumptions and general tendencies than as clearly formulated ethical systems." The subject might, however, bear further study.

[30] Mrs. Manley, *The New Atalantis* (2nd ed.; London, 1709), I, 188. Steele: *Tracts,* p. 339 (*Apology* of 1714).

been guilty of wrong ones. Thus he could denounce dueling more effectively because, not in spite of the fact that, he had dueled. Steele's attitude in these matters was, then, almost never a pose, though his enemies were quick to assume that it was. He genuinely intended to reform. At the same time he did not hesitate to play his strong cards. The slight tincture of self-serving in his moral pronouncements is not, however, so far from ordinary human experience as to be unrecognizable. Many people even today are willing to show their best face to the world. Steele's dedicatory epistle to Lord Cutts was no doubt sincerely felt; if it helped his military advancement, so much the better.

Considering its subject matter, the book is surprisingly lively, full of illustrative anecdotes of the sort later made familiar by *The Tatler* and *Spectator,* and charged with a certain excitement of purpose. It was, he tells Cutts in the Dedication, "Writ upon duty, when the mind was perfectly disengaged and at leisure in the silent watch of the night, to run over the busy dream of the day; and the vigilance which obliges us to suppose an enemy always near us, has awakened a sense that there is a restless and subtle one which constantly attends our steps, and meditates our ruin." Steele analyzes the lives of Cato, Caesar, and Brutus, showing how their philosophy was deficient whereas that of the early Christians, especially St. Paul, was effective because of the Christians' trust and confidence in God. In the last chapter mutual benevolence is enjoined ("Thus are we framed for mutual kindness, good will and service, and therefore our Blessed Saviour has been pleased to give us . . . the command of loving one another. . . ."), and King William is presented as the type of modern Christian hero "whose every day is productive of some great action. . . ."

Whatever his fellow officers of the Guards may have felt, Steele's reading public seized upon the book and bought up ten editions within his lifetime, endearing Steele to Tonson. As he so often was to do, Steele provided at the proper moment what the public wanted to read. This sort of courtesy book, combining religious instruction with hints for a gentleman's conduct, was finding an expanding audience in the late seventeenth and early eighteenth centuries as the middle class gained strength and numbers.[31] The reading public wanted moral instruction and entertainment, and they were especially curious about how gentlefolk lived. *The Christian Hero* appealed to all three interests: its success was not lost on Richard Steele.

Steele's meditations and ambitions in 1700 were not exclusively devotional. He needed the consolation of religion; he also needed reputation and money. In that same year his good friend and fellow Irishman, William Congreve, though only two years Steele's senior, saw produced his last, and in some respects his greatest, play, *The Way of the World*. Congreve was the victim of unfortunate timing. In 1698 and 1699 the stage had been under attack by one of the most resourceful detractors in dramatic history, the Reverend Jeremy Collier, whose *A Short View of the Immorality and Profaneness of the English Stage* had taken Congreve's works as a special target. There was much uncrystallized resentment against the stage in the air; whatever the merit of Collier's strictures, they proved capable of calling forth the criticism of others hostile to the London theater. In 1700 the Middlesex county grand jury proclaimed that many plays were "full of profane, irreverent, indecent, and immoral expressions," tending to the "debauching and ruining of youth. . . ." [32] In the midst of the controversy, *The Way of the World* appeared, to all appearances unmistakably a play in the tradition of which Collier was critical, the tradition of the Restoration comedy. Audiences and critics were not amused; the play had only limited success. Steele was thus thrown into a quandary. On the one hand, an intimate friend was under attack, had seen his work

[31] See George C. Brauer, Jr., *The Education of a Gentleman* (New York, 1959), pp. 13–33.
[32] Aitken, I, 71.

apparently come to nothing. On the other hand, Steele was inclined to agree silently with Collier, especially with regard to
the stage's treatment of clergymen and its apparent applause of
vice rather than virtue. His own tangled personal life, Steele
may have felt, demonstrated that the debauching of young
women, that staple of Restoration comedy, was in reality no
longer a matter for laughter. ". . . Virtuous principles," he
wrote in *The Christian Hero,* "must infallibly be not only better
than any other we can embrace, to warm us to great attempts,
but also to make our days in their ordinary passage slide away
agreeably. . . ."

Steele's reaction was characteristically personal. He defended
his friend's play (and stood almost alone in doing so) in a
poem, to which he added his name: "To Mr. Congreve, Occasioned by his Comedy, called, The Way of the World." The
defense is adroit. The play's failure he implies is due to the declining taste of the "well-dressed barbarians" fascinated by
spectacle and farce. Congreve's comedy, Steele asserts, is teaching morality by a sort of dramatic therapy, though the audience
which sees itself reflected on the stage is not willing to acknowledge that reflection:

> You check unjust esteem and fond desire,
> And teach to scorn, what else we should admire;
> The just impression taught by you we bear,
> The player acts the world, the world the player,
> Whom still that world unjustly disesteems,
> Tho' he, alone, professes what he seems;

Perhaps overingenious, but his praise of Congreve's "tragic
part" is unalloyed: the muse "conquers and she reigns in every
heart. . . ." Steele pleads with Congreve not to leave dramatic
writing (as he was in fact to do; no doubt Steele had personal
knowledge of his intentions): "Then still, great Sir, your moving power employ,/ To lull our sorrow, and correct our joy."

On the whole it was a generous and courageous defense.[33]

But Steele was not through with the stage, even if Congreve was. The appearance of *The Christian Hero* had chilled his London acquaintanceship, to Steele's annoyance. His defense of Congreve perhaps was of small help to that dramatist, but it fired Steele's critical meditations on the stage and on dramatic theory. "[I]t was now incumbent," he later wrote of himself, "upon him to enliven his character, for which reason he writ the comedy called *The Funeral,* in which (tho' full of incidents that move laughter) virtue and vice appear just as they ought to do." [34]

Captain Steele now knew his way around London and even the Court; he was always good company and he acquired friends easily. *The Christian Hero* had been successful from Tonson's point of view, but it was not the sort of work that secured preferment in the Guards. Captain Steele was still Captain Steele.

[33] *Verse,* pp. 12–13. See also E. L. Avery, *Congreve's Plays on the Eighteenth-Century Stage* (New York, 1951), pp. 32–33.
[34] *Tracts,* p. 339.

CHAPTER III

Landguard and London

DURING THE SUMMER OF 1701 Captain Steele retired to lodgings at Wandsworth in Surrey, across the Thames from Chelsea, to work on the play. Army life in peacetime was not arduous; there was time for writing and for sharing a pot of ale with the town miller and, of course, for bowing to the young ladies of Wandsworth. Financial troubles provided discipline enough; he was still in debt, probably as a result of his alchemical ventures, though Steele never lacked occasion for multiplying his obligations. His old friend and associate, Mary Delarivière Manley, may have chosen this inopportune time to approach Steele for a loan and receive his refusal; years later, a bitter political foe of Steele's, she was to make much of his ingratitude. But Steele had not the wherewithal for gratitude. "I shall I [hope] pay my debts with my play," he wrote an army friend, "and then in spite of [D]elia, be very easy, for whatever I may tell her, nothing can really make my heart ache but a dun, from which Lord deliver you and your most obedient servant." [1]

The Deity seldom chose this method of easing Steele's heart, but other solace was at hand. Christopher Rich of the Theatre Royal, Drury Lane, read the play and liked it well enough to contract in October for its production. Soon afterward, probably early in December, Richard Steele's first dramatic effort (if we except the legendary Merton comedy) opened: *The Funeral* or

[1] Delia, one guesses, refers to Mrs. (Delarivière) Manley. See her account in *The New Atalantis* (2nd ed.; London, 1709), I, 193.

Grief à la Mode. His literary talents, Steele discovered, were stronger in the dramatic than the lyric mode. With a first-rate cast including Colley Cibber and Anne Oldfield, *The Funeral* scored an unexpected success.[2]

Those of Steele's friends who saw the play would have noticed that the author had drawn heavily on personal experience. Lord Hardy, the protagonist, is a young army officer and a Christ Church man. Some of the action involves recruiting, an activity with which Steele was thoroughly familiar. The heroines are orphans, and almost everyone is in debt. Though remembered by those who have not read it as a satire on undertaking, *The Funeral* is hardly a satire on anything. There are satirical touches on marital duplicity, on gossips, on hypocritical mourning, but the play is a thoroughly good-humored comedy. Toward the end, as if reminded of his purpose, Steele introduced some blank-verse dialogue (much like that in Vanbrugh's *The Relapse*) for the reunion of the lovers, and there is more blank verse in the high style for Lord Brumpton's patriotic resolve to follow his son onto the field of battle. ("My rough plebeian Britons, not yet slaves/ To France, shall mount thy father's son/ Upon their shoulders.")[3] Despite the blank verse, the play was successful because it deserved to be; it is a competent piece of dramaturgy, with some excellent sight-comedy scenes and generally good theatrical construction. Steele, in fact, had learned a great deal about the theater; if he learned from Congreve, Congreve taught well.

In a little more than six months Richard Steele had made his literary debut (his earlier efforts in verse represented only the more or less required writing of an Augustan gallant) with considerable successes in two different genres. His problem was

---

[2] Colley Cibber, *An Apology for the Life of Mr. Colley Cibber, Comedian, and Late Patentee of the Theatre-Royal* (2nd ed.; London, 1740), p. 216; *London Stage*, I, 17. Date of premiere unknown, but play published on 20 December.

[3] *Plays*, p. 91.

to wring maximum profit from this success; as a beginning playwright he could expect little from the parsimonious Christopher Rich beyond the usual author's benefit of the third and sixth night's proceeds — after expenses had been deducted by the management.[4] Another potential source of indirect profit was the dedication of the printed play: Steele sorely needed influential patrons whether his career was to be literary or military, for Henry Gascoigne had long since retired. Steele was much in Congreve's company that year, but Congreve was only another Irish playwright and Steele, for all his gratitude, required a more important dedicatee. The dedication was discreetly addressed to the Countess of Albemarle, the Dutch bride of King William's trusted companion, Arnold Joost van Keppel, to whom the king had given large grants of land in Ireland. It was a conventionally florid dedication, politic in every sense of the word. The patriotic motif of the play itself was politic too. After several years of troubled peace, the powers of Europe were once more moving toward war. Louis XIV had aggravated a bad situation by meddling with the English succession, declaring on the death of James II in September, 1701, that he recognized James's Catholic son as King of England. Steele's satiric strokes at the French in the play and Lord Brumpton's patriotic resolution reflect the spirit of the times; Steele gave his audience what they wanted to see and hear.

There was a tangible reward. "Nothing can make the town so fond of a man as a successful play," Steele later said, "and this, with some particulars enlarged upon to his advantage . . . obtained him the notice of the King: and his name, to be provided for, was in the last table-book [i.e., notebook] ever worn by the glorious and immortal William the Third." [5] The army was to be augmented for the approaching war, and Steele was commissioned captain in the new Thirty-Fourth Foot, com-

---

[4] *London Stage,* I, c.
[5] *Tracts,* p. 339.

manded by Robert Lord Lucas, on 10 March 1702, just two days after the King's death. Perhaps, though this is very doubtful, it was the Earl of Albemarle who enlarged upon some particulars in his behalf; more probably Lord Cutts supplied the kind words; whoever did it had provided help in good time. Captain Steele's Williamite sympathies had been in no doubt since *The Procession* and *The Christian Hero*. There were few tears shed for the Dutch King in Oxford or Limerick, perhaps, but Steele had always recognized that King William, for all his obtuseness, for all his dour suspicion, was in some sense a deliverer. Steele had studied James's work at close hand. In January, 1702, buoyed up by high hopes, Steele borrowed £600 from an army friend, John Sansome, probably to help defray the expenses of recruiting his company of foot, since, as in Falstaff's day, army custom dictated that the company commander recruit his own unit. At full strength, Steele's company would consist of three officers and sixty-six men. We may imagine Steele traveling through the villages of Essex and Norfolk, his assigned recruiting territory, preceded by a recruiting sergeant pounding a drum, calling villagers who looked promising to the Queen's service, with a hint for the adventurous of sieges and booty; war could be profitable if one stayed alive.[6] That spring Steele's old commander, the Duke of Ormonde, was forming an army for the campaign in Spain.

Steele's company had no place so romantic as Spain ahead of them. He and his men were ordered to garrison Landguard Fort, overlooking one of the approaches to the important port of Harwich in Suffolk. By May the company was installed in the bleak, ill-equipped fort. Steele, though unwell, attempted to train his new recruits in their duties and found that the job required constant guarding of the guards themselves, who were dis-

[6] [Richard Cannon], *Historical Record of the Thirty-Fourth, or, The Cumberland Regiment of Foot* (London, 1844), pp. 9–10. See also Godfrey Davies, "Recruiting in the Reign of Queen Anne," *Journal of the Society for Army Historical Research,* XXVII (1950), 146–59.

posed to forget their mission in the biting wind off the Channel
and slip down the road to home. As he dragged himself from
his sick bed in the middle of the night to check the batteries in
the fort, Steele must have contrasted his position then with his
successful days in London scarcely six months before, when
The Funeral had made the town fond of him. London, where
Lady Mildmay had a good address in Bond Street, Piccadilly,
was a long way from Landguard, yet opportunities dwelt even
in Suffolk for an ambitious man and Richard Steele was ambitious.

Captain Steele's first duty was of course to get his men ready
to repel French privateers or even an invasion fleet. Besides the
troubles of training green recruits there was the added burden
of the fort itself. Windows were gone, the roof tiling was in such
condition that the rain poured onto the company's sick in their
beds. And there were plenty of sick. By September he had two
sergeants, two corporals, and nine sentinels unfit for duty, as
he indignantly reported to the Board of Ordnance in a request
for repairs to the fort.

But Steele now knew there were better occupations for a
captain of foot than repairing battlements. He had won success
in the literary world by writing a play; he would do it again.
Preferment had come to him through his politic dedications,
his strongly-announced Williamite sympathies. Politics could
bring preferment once more. For politics, like writing, was an
honorable occupation in Steele's England; almost everyone of
substance had a hand in politics, local or national: priests, poets,
bishops, brigadiers, squires, schoolmasters, all looked to their
interest and, despite occasional routine cries against "factional-
ism," everyone approved of their so doing. Furthermore, a man
who could combine writing and politics was an especially fortunate discovery; as England's literacy rate rose, the value of what
we would call propaganda rose likewise in the esteem of political
leaders. In 1699, for example, the Whig leaders Charles Mon-

tagu (later Lord Halifax) and John Lord Somers had plucked
Joseph Addison from his comfortable fellowship at Magdalen
College and sent him on a four year Grand Tour partly at public
expense, assuming that he would be of political value later, as
he indeed was. While Steele watched the chill rain drip through
the roof of Landguard Fort, Addison tramped through the Alps
near Geneva and was filled with "an agreeable kind of horror"
at the sight of the mountains.[7] However great the contrast of
their surroundings, each was readying himself for a place in
English public affairs.

The complexion of Great Britain's political life had changed
abruptly with the death of King William. If Steele obtained his
captaincy through the gratitude of the Dutch Earl of Albemarle,
he did so just in time, for as soon as the King was put away in
Westminster — after a private funeral — English politicians
sprang to regain the power they had given up on his accession.
A thoroughly English Queen Anne took the scepter and appointed Marlborough, of whom William had been suspicious,
Captain-General of all her armies. She made his fortune in the
bargain by naming him Quartermaster, one of those supply and
revenue-handling positions by means of which many private
fortunes were amassed in the eighteenth century. Marlborough's
trusted friend, Sidney Godolphin, became Lord Treasurer, and
a pro tempore ally, Robert Harley, of whom much more later,
was Speaker and leader of the House of Commons. None of
these men was of the true-blue Williamite Whig faction to which
Steele by education and previous association inclined. Though
Marlborough and Godolphin leaned to the Tory interest, party
divisions were in flux and Whigs abounded, of course, in the
boroughs. A man had to be nimble, but a nimble man could still
get ahead.

Richard Steele had learned something about politics as Lord
Cutts's secretary, for politics was next only to battle in Cutts's

[7] Peter Smithers, *The Life of Joseph Addison* (Oxford, 1954), pp. 73–74.

heart and he waged both with shrewdness and determination. In the summer of 1702 Steele's former patron was far away in the continental campaign, but other friends were nearer. Doubtless to Steele's satisfaction, Henry Gascoigne's erstwhile associate in the Duke of Ormonde's household, John Ellis, was elected a Member of Parliament for Harwich, the Fort's borough, in the House which met in October, 1702. John Ellis' brother, it will be remembered, was Welbore Ellis, "my ever honoured tutor," as Steele called him in the Preface to *The Christian Hero,* now in Ireland as chaplain of the Duke of Ormonde's household. John Ellis needed assistance and Steele was pleased to oblige. The captain acquired further experience in the business of sounding out electors, of keeping fences mended and key voters content, and it was important business. The ire of a handful of electors over the land tax or the game laws could cost a Member his seat in the next election. Perhaps Steele volunteered his services to Ellis; we do not know, but by early 1704 he was certainly well-instructed in Harwich politics, acting as Ellis' ears: "The Mayor is now at London, and not much inclined to you, but you perhaps have opportunity there of reforming him. . . ." "As to my own private opinion, as far as I can guess, I believe Sr Tho. Davall [another member from Harwich] aims for himself, and very coldly for any colleague, having thoughts for his son; and as to the other gentlemen it would be of use to you, when you come here, if it could be insinuated that serving you was obliging them, and would have the same effect for the town's interest. . . ." This was grassroots politics in Queen Anne's England: involved, personal, small-scale;[8] the convivial Steele found himself at home in politics from the outset.

Putting his experience to work as usual, and finding that garrison life in a coastal fort, despite occasional harassments, left

[8] J. H. Plumb, *Sir Robert Walpole: The Making of a Statesman* (London, 1956), pp. 37–78.

much time free, Steele began to write a new comedy, to be called *The Election of Gotham*. Christopher Rich, in an unwonted burst of confidence based on *The Funeral*'s success, advanced Steele £72 with the understanding, he later asserted, that the play would be provided for production in February, 1703. The play was never finished, Steele presumably applied the £72 against his other debts, and the transaction boiled over into a very complicated lawsuit in 1707 which was eventually dismissed without a finding one way or the other. Before feeling excessive sympathy for Rich, however, one may reflect that managing one of the monopoly theaters was a lucrative business and that Steele later supplied Rich with two other plays, compensation for which Rich was able to minimize by citing the £72 advance. Conditions were changing slowly, but the dramatic author was still in no very favorable position vis-à-vis bookseller and theater manager.[9]

Though little evidence survives to prove it, one may assume that Steele spent 1703 at Landguard, traveling to London when he could, carrying on the routine of an isolated command, reporting deserters, training recruits, paying off discharged soldiers, fighting the boredom such a command invariably breeds. In the fall of 1703 it was announced that the Duke of Ormonde was to raise a regiment of dragoons in Ireland. Steele was ready: service under his first commanding officer, the cavalry instead of garrison, more pay, the chance of action on the continent. He applied to John Ellis to seek him a troop in the new regiment. Apparently Ellis did so, for Steele thanked him and "desire[d] the continuance of your good inclination to me," but nothing came of it. Blenheim was fought and won while Steele watched the Channel from Landguard's gun emplacements.

But he continued to write. According to local tradition (and this agrees with what is known of the composition of *The Funeral*), Steele would from time to time withdraw to a farm-

[9] Suit summarized Aitken, I, 111–23.

house at Walton nearby or to the Queen's Arms at Harwich, there to work on his plays.[10] On 2 December 1703 his comedy, *The Lying Lover,* opened at Drury Lane and played for six nights, a successful run from the playwright's point of view, providing two benefit performances. The success was only apparent, however; few in the audience desired to see the play a second time. Steele had taken Collier's pronouncements and the general feeling of the time seriously. Queen Anne in January, 1704, was to issue an order to the playhouses prohibiting them from acting anything contrary to religion and good manners. In the Preface to the printed version, which appeared in January, 1704, apparently after Queen Anne's order, Steele clarifies his position on the question of stage reform:

> Though it ought to be the care of all governments that public representations should have nothing in them but what is agreeable to the manners, laws, religion, and policy of the place or nation in which they are exhibited; yet is it the general complaint of the more learned and virtuous amongst us, that the English stage has extremely offended in this kind. I thought, therefore, it would be an honest ambition to attempt a comedy which might be no improper entertainment in a Christian commonwealth.[11]

It is beyond the scope of this work to discuss at length Steele's many efforts for stage reform, and they have been well discussed elsewhere. In the case of *The Lying Lover,* however, a severe critic might judge that Steele was joining the side of the angels in order to cover the defects of a bad play. As its stage history confirms, *The Lying Lover* is the poorest of Steele's plays, not because it is, to use the term Hazlitt applied to Steele's comedies, a "homily in dialogue" — though there is moral instruction enough — it is the poorest not for this tendency to sermonize

---

[10] *Gentleman's Magazine,* LX (1790), part ii, 993; John H. Leslie, *The History of Landguard Fort, in Suffolk* (London, 1898), p. 59.

[11] Plays, p. 101; for an important discussion of Steele and dramatic reform, see John Loftis, *Comedy and Society from Congreve to Fielding* (Stanford, 1959), pp. 32–35.

but for the imprecise characterization and curious mixture of styles. Some of the plot is derived from Corneille's *Le Menteur* and the play is not well-integrated; we imagine Steele, pressed as he almost always was for time and money, hurriedly translating extended passages from Corneille, revising them quickly and copying onto manuscript. Despite some good sight comedy in the third act and some good dialogue (Steele had an excellent ear for comic dialogue), the play is an inferior effort, even judged by the most generous critical standards. It was not revived in Steele's lifetime. *The Lying Lover* was, however, adorned with good songs and music (Daniel Purcell composed some of the music for this and for *The Funeral*), and Drury Lane had excellent musicians on the payroll. Steele believed strongly in the importance of the incidental music; he was in touch with the foremost musicians of his day, and music undoubtedly contributed to the success which his plays enjoyed (though the theater manager, of course, was responsible for the actual planning and supervision of the accompaniment).

The play appeared, it will be recalled, during the winter in which the Duke of Ormonde was raising a new regiment of dragoons, and Steele dedicated the printed version to that noble lord. The dedication is close to being fulsome, but Steele was grateful to the House of Ormonde, as he had reason to be. "Out of gratitude to the memorable and illustrious patron of my infancy," Steele wrote, "Your Grace's grandfather, I presume to lay this comedy at your feet: The design of it is to banish out of conversation all entertainment which does not proceed from simplicity of mind, good-nature, friendship and honour. . . ." [12] As we have seen, the attempt for ducal preferment failed. The touchstones though are interesting: simplicity of mind, good nature, friendship, and honor; Steele's evolving personal ideals, dictated by his sunny nature. His writings and his biography are marbled with these ideals. Life is to be enjoyed. A friend is

[12] *Corr.*, p. 446.

a friend unless proven otherwise, and to be defended, as Addison had been defended in the Blackmore controversy. Honor: not the false honor of the dueling ring, but the honor of personal responsibility, of standing by one's decisions. These ideals gave Richard Steele's works their characteristic ring; one can almost always pick his essay out of a group of, say, *Spectator* papers because of his recurrent themes and the attitude of the author toward these themes. In an age which valued intellectual precision, Steele's emotional attachment to the simple virtues was unusual, and exposed him to much derision. And yet his work and life were bound together, interpenetrated in a way that is uncharacteristic of Queen Anne's Augustans who preferred to keep art at a certain distance from life, but which, perhaps, the present age would find more acceptable. At any rate, one must understand this interpenetration if one is to understand, to whatever degree a person can be understood, Richard Steele.

The year 1704 must have been a trying one for the Captain of Foot. Author of an unsuccessful play, mired in a dilapidated fort in Suffolk far from the London he loved and sought, swamped as usual with debts, Steele could have supposed that the world was passing him by like those ships outward bound from Harwich for the continent. The diversion of sniffing out John Ellis' political fortunes, though instructive, was only a diversion. Addison, by way of contrast, had concluded his extended Grand Tour with a visit to Holland, where he and Lord Cutts dined together. Then he returned to England via Harwich and in 1704 was admitted to the distinguished Kit-Cat Club, that powerful gathering of convivial Whigs, superintended by Jacob Tonson, who were to become in a few years the rulers of English politics: Lord Halifax, Lord Somers, the Earl of Wharton; plump with authority, their portraits by Kneller look down now from the walls of the National Portrait Gallery. It was a quasi-literary society, too; Congreve and Garth and Vanbrugh were members and Addison, the promising young

intellectual, no doubt rather as a matter of course took his seat
in the club room at Tonson's villa at Barn Elms. Steele's entry
was probably yet to come; though he was in and out of London
in 1704, he was, it seems, not yet distinguished enough for this
select group.[13] Addison himself was not particularly renowned
but great opportunity was at hand.

In August, 1704, Marlborough crushed the French and
Bavarian armies in his most famous victory, at Blenheim on the
Danube. Lord Cutts, Marlborough's Salamander, who opened
the attack, much later led the English troops into their final
assault using the method of combat he preferred, hand-to-hand.
Twenty-seven French battalions were captured, the army of
France was beaten, the balance of power in the world, though,
of course, this fact could not be known at the time, began to
shift from France to England. London was ecstatic; bonfires
flamed in the streets; Queen Anne in her joy gave the messenger
of victory a thousand guineas. And, amid all the excitement,
astute politicians knew that the war policy of Godolphin and
Marlborough had been vindicated. A fitting literary tribute was
in order; Lord Halifax suggested young Addison, who was experienced in the occasional vein (he had composed poems celebrating King William's Battle of the Boyne and the Peace of
Ryswick). Henry Boyle, Chancellor of the Exchequer and a
Kit-Cat was the intermediary; he formally approached Addison
and later delivered the first rough draft of the poem, *The Campaign,* to Godolphin for approval, in the time-honored manner
of bureaucracy. The approval was accompanied by an appointment as Commissioner of Appeal in Excise, a position that "required but little attendance." [14] In *The Diverting Post,* No. 2
(28 October to 4 November 1704), Richard Steele gave Addison's *magnum opus* a modest prepublication puff by way of *An*

---

[13] Rau (see chap. II, note 27 above).

[14] Smithers (see note 7), pp. 91–92. I follow Mr. Smithers' interpretation
of the conflicting account.

Imitation of the Sixth Ode of Horace . . . . Apply'd to his Grace the Duke of Marlborough. "Supposed," as the original version had it, "to be made by Capt. R. S.," the poem combines not only advertisement for Addison but proper compliment for the Duke and the Queen:

> Should Addison's immortal verse,
> Thy fame in arms, great Prince, rehearse,
> With Anna's lightning you'd appear,
> And glitter o'er again in war:
> Repeat the proud Bavarian's fall!
> And in the Danube plunge the Gaul!

Steele allots himself a lower place on Parnassus and perhaps refers to his own plays.

> In trifling cares my humble muse
> A less ambitious tract pursues,
> Instead of troops in battle mixt,
> And Gauls with British spears transfixt:
> She paints the soft distress and mien
> Of dames expiring with the spleen.

> From the gay noise affected air,
> And little follies of the fair,
> A slender stock of fame I raise,
> And draw from others' faults, my praise.[15]

Is there a muted note of discontent, even of envy in the poem? *The Campaign,* published in December, 1704, was a master-piece of tact and compliment and a sensational propaganda success, appearing no doubt by design on the very day the conquering Duke stepped ashore at Greenwich with sixteen captive French generals and the captured colors of the French army in his train. From the Whig point of view, the most gratifying

[15] *Verse,* pp. 14–15 and 78–79.

aspect of *The Campaign's* publication had been the fact that it was a propaganda success, thus separating to some extent the Toryish Marlborough and Godolphin — Queen Anne's favorites — from their natural Tory allies in the House of Commons, who advocated sea rather than land warfare against the French. As if invigorated by the victory, critic outdid critic in lauding Addison's effort. Jean Le Clerc, the Swiss theologian, reached praise's pinnacle, calling it "an incomparable piece in heroic verse. . . . We may justly affirm that . . . Mr. Addison, thus raised and supported by the nobleness of his subject, is as much superior to himself, as he is in all his other pieces to the greatest part of the other poets of what nation soever." [16] From this occasion Addison's political fortunes were made; by the following summer he had replaced John Ellis as Under-Secretary of State.

Richard Steele's prospects, on the other hand, did not appear to be improving perceptibly during the winter of 1704, but the following year was to be one of important changes in his life: by summer, 1705, he had left the army, had married, and had seen another of his plays produced at Drury Lane. The year began unfavorably. Lord Lucas, Colonel of the Thirty-Fourth, died in January, 1705, and was replaced by an officer from another regiment. Steele, the regiment's classicist, composed a Latin epitaph reflecting his admiration for the Whig veteran; his death may have been the impelling reason for Steele's decision to leave the army. With Lord Lucas dead, Steele had few resources left there. The efforts of John Ellis to obtain preferment for him with Ormonde had not succeeded and there was little expectation of promotion in a garrison post like Landguard, under a stranger's command. Without financial assistance — and none was in sight — he could expect to remain a captain for the rest of his life. The example, and the person, of Addison existed to remind him of the possibilities of a different

[16] As quoted in Smithers, p. 96.

career, of the fact that in his spare time, as it were, he had produced two literary works of quality and success, *The Christian
Hero* and *The Funeral*.

In late March or early April, 1705, Steele presented another
play to Christopher Rich, this one entitled *The Tender Husband*
or *The Accomplished Fools*. Steele, Rich later declared, knew
that April was an unfavorable month for openings, but according to Rich he nevertheless pressed for the play's production.
Opening on 23 April, it had an initial run of five nights, with
indifferent success. Steele thus missed his second benefit performance, postponed by agreement until November, by which
time Rich had somewhat skimmed the cream off the potential
audience by staging performances in May, June, and October.
In December both *The Funeral* and *The Tender Husband* were
presented at Drury Lane, without remuneration for the author.[17]

Despite the mediocre opening run, *The Tender Husband* was
a good play, the best-balanced of all Steele's dramas, tightly con-
structed and all in all one of the better comedies of the century.
Addison, Steele later recalled (in *Spectator* No. 555), contributed "many applauded strokes in it," though there has been
no agreement since as to which strokes were his. Years later,
Goldsmith and perhaps Fielding found the play a source of ideas;
Humphrey Gubbin, the loutish heir from the country, who discovers he is of age and conspires with his cousin against their
marriage, is certainly the lineal ancestor of Tony Lumpkin.
The play has, in fact, much of the spirit of *She Stoops to Conquer* and is little inferior to it.

A perennial favorite on the eighteenth-century stage, revived
almost every year for decades, it was performed more than sixty
times in Richard Steele's lifetime. Why, then, was its initial run
not better received? A professional actor, Colley Cibber, probably was near the truth when he noted that audiences are sometimes reluctant to accept the works that immediately follow an

[17] *London Stage,* I, 92–111.

author's initial success. "I am apt to believe that after the success of the *Funeral,* it was the same caprice that deserted the *Tender Husband. . . ."* [18] A good play will often attract its audience, however, and in a few months *The Tender Husband* was on its way to becoming a staple of the Drury Lane repertory: by then Steele had long since ceased to have any financial interest in the play. It is significant that he did not have another play produced until many years later when he was a partner in the management of Drury Lane and hence able to reap rewards both as author and manager.

From the beginning the play enjoyed a favorable critical reception. The printed version appeared in May, 1705, under Tonson's imprint, with a dedication to Joseph Addison which Steele began: "You'll be surprised, in the midst of a daily and familiar conversation, with an address which bears so distant an air as a public dedication. . . ." But, he continues, "I hope I make the town no ill compliment for their kind acceptance of this comedy, in acknowledging that it has so far raised my opinion of it, as to make me think it no improper memorial of an inviolable friendship." [19]

Steele, then, was in London in April, seeing Addison every day and enjoying the compliments of the town on his new play. The Thirty-Fourth Foot sailed for the Mediterranean in May without Captain Steele; [20] it appears certain that he left the army in this spring of 1705. The town's interest in the rising celebrity extended beyond his dramatic works to his personal life, for Steele, like his hero Captain Clerimont in *The Tender Husband,* was pursuing an heiress: "Captain Steele may make use of a widow's jointure to advance himself," Welbore Ellis commented with ungracious candor to his brother John, "but he's not a stake to be depended upon." [21]

[18] Cibber, Preface to *Ximena* (London, 1777), p. 9. Aitken, I, 108.
[19] *Corr.,* p. 448.
[20] [Richard Cannon], *Historical Record* (see note 6 above), p. 10.
[21] BM, Add. MSS. 28932, fol. 222, letter of 28 April 1705.

Unfortunately for the biographer, who should limn love's coming in appropriate colors, almost no recollection of Steele's first wife remains except that preserved in legal documents.[22] The story these documents relate, the tone of Welbore Ellis' remark, and Steele's own silence about the marriage together suggest a relationship altogether too patly like those scenes involving the aging widow in Restoration plays. The facts are these: his first wife was Margaret Ford Stretch, a widow formerly of Barbados. Margaret was herself the daughter of a prominent British landowner there, John Ford or Foord of St. Andrew's parish, who in 1680 had 280 acres, four menservants, and 120 negro slaves. By 1704 Margaret's brother, Major Robert Ford, a widower without children, had come into possession of the family holdings and in December of that year, preparing to go to England, Ford had made his will with Margaret as principal legatee. She was at this time living in England or Ireland (for Stretch or Stritch is an old Irish name), presumably a widow. Events followed with the compressed swiftness of a play: a French privateer took the ship on which Ford was coming to England and he died a captive on the high seas. By March Margaret Ford Stretch was a widow of considerable property, by April or May, 1705, she was Richard Steele's wife.

To the marriage Steele no doubt brought, as he brought to almost everything, great expectations. Margaret Stretch provided in real and tangible property a group of sugar plantations totaling some 700 acres, "mansions, windmills, boyling houses, copper stills, &c," white servants, and 200 negro slaves; the whole estate was let two years later for £850 a year, a handsome income for the time.[23] Whatever his personal feelings about the match, Steele had provided himself with a respectable fortune.

These fresh resources were called on immediately. In June

---

[22] Aitken, I, 127–45, summarizes these.
[23] Deed quoted in Rae Blanchard, "Richard Steele's West Indian Plantation," *Modern Philology,* XXXIX (1942), 282.

John Sansome, the friend who had in an unguarded moment three years earlier lent Steele £600, despaired of repayment and sued for recovery. With his usual candor in such matters, Steele admitted his obligation in court but refused to pay. He could not pay. His resources, the new play, the new wife, were genuine enough but not liquid; grasping for help anywhere he addressed Lord Cutts, now in Dublin, demanding further compensation for his service years before as Cutts's aide. Cutts, who watched his expenses closely, replied with proper hauteur:

SIR
I have received a letter from you, dated — Lady Mildmay's, Bond Street, Piccadilly; but without any mention either of the day of the month, or year of our Lord; so that I can't tell when it was wrote. You mention a former letter, which I never received, nor heard a word of before; so that I am totally a stranger to the hardships you say you suffer by my service; and I am the more surprised at this, because I have letters under your hand, that do implicitly if not expressly declare the contrary with a great deal of warmth.
You desire me to pay you for your long and chargeable attendance, which, since you demand it peremptorily as a justice, I must answer as plainly, that if you will make it appear to me, that I promised you any allowance in money, I shall be ready to take your demands into consideration. But I dare appeal to your cooler and more deliberate thoughts, whether I did not do you some services (however forgotten now) which at that time were understood by all the world to balance the service you had done me.

Steele complained to his friend Colonel Edmund Revett, who had married Cutts's niece, "Your uncle Cutts (who always thinks he has too many friends) has used me like a scoundrel." After several weeks he composed a reply to his former commanding officer's letter, enclosing a note of some expenses incurred in Cutts's service, and adding, as if in defiance, "I believe I shall soon be very well-employed." But then, rereading the letter, he struck through the optimistic forecast of employment to come. So ended the relationship between Cutts and Steele which had begun a decade earlier with the dedication of *The Procession*. Both were partly justified in their feelings at the end. Lord Cutts felt correctly that Steele's appointment in his household had been adequate compensation; Steele after all had spent some six or seven years there without complaint (and they were the years of his alchemical efforts). On the other hand, except possibly for the captaincy in the Thirty-Fourth, Cutts provided little in the way of tangible fulfillment of the promises he liked to make. Steele had entered the relationship expecting too much, as he was naturally inclined to do; Cutts also acting in character had no doubt held many things before Steele which he had no real intention of granting. And so it ended. As events were to show, Cutts, though not yet fifty, had fought himself out. He died suddenly in Ireland in 1707, where his two aides dug into their pockets for ten pounds with which to have his body embalmed, then waited for the instructions from England that never came. King William's Salamander, friendless at the last, was huddled into an unmarked grave at St. Patrick's.[24]

The acidulous exchange with Cutts marks, so far as we know, Steele's final link with the army. The market price for commissions was good after Blenheim; Steele presumably sold his during the first half of 1705 and left the profession which he had lightheartedly chosen more than a dozen years before, retaining his title in the manner of his Aunt Katherine.[25] But of course more clung than the appellation Captain Steele; twelve years of professional service could not simply be doffed like a dress uniform. Ireland earlier had stamped Richard Steele's character and provided him with friends. Later the British army did the

[24] HMC, *Egmont MSS.*, II, 215, and DNB.
[25] A correspondent of Robert Harley's about this year speaks of the transaction of a company in his regiment for 300 guineas and suggests that the price could have been double that. General William Steuart to Robert Harley, BM Loan MS. 29/158.

same. Unlike many, perhaps most, of his literary contemporaries, Steele never doubted the rightness of King William's and Marlborough's wars against France. Soldiers would appear as sympathetic characters in his writings, and highest among Steele's personal heroes was England's greatest soldier, now the Duke of Marlborough. Swift, in his distrust of redcoats and especially the senior redcoat, probably reflected the dominant national mood better than Steele; their diverging views on this subject were to have an important bearing on their relationship later.

Steele, it will be recalled, had promised Cutts that he would "soon be very well-employed." Exactly what he had in mind it is impossible to say, but it is reasonable to conjecture that Addison's success in securing political preferment impelled Steele in the same direction. Addison may well have encouraged the move; in May he lent Steele £400, prudently secured on Mrs. Steele's Barbados property. There was, of course, family precedent for service in the civil administration: Henry Gascoigne had prospered in governmental employment. And the Whigs of the Kit-Cat group were waxing; the parliamentary elections in May, 1705, had added strength to the Whigs in the Privy Council. Steele, now husband of an heiress and a fashionable figure along Piccadilly, probably became a member of the Kit-Cat Club himself about this time, but no preferment was forthcoming, for all his hopes.

What, then, was Steele doing with himself in 1705? He was presumably seeking employment, an occupation in itself, as readers of eighteenth-century literature know: sitting in great men's anterooms, associating with fashionable people at fashionable coffeehouses, saying the correct things and dressing in the correct manner, and, above all, cultivating one's patience. All these activities were involved in seeking employment, in getting a place. One could be unemployed but very busy. In December, 1705, Steele contributed the prologue to John Vanbrugh's new play *The Mistake,* acted at the new theater in the Haymarket which Vanbrugh himself had designed. The prologue is conventional — Steele's humble muse seldom soared — but Vanbrugh, playwright and architect, was an important Kit-Cat and Steele in the piece turns a handsome compliment to his versatility. This is what Steele was doing in 1705 and 1706.

His domestic life with the heiress is complete darkness. Certainly some of the romantic bloom must have faded, if it had ever been present, when Steele began straightway after their marriage to enmesh Margaret's estate in his tangled web of debts. The couple's only apparent source of income for more than a year was the estate, together with whatever small sums Steele could realize from his occasional writing and the reprints of his earlier works. With respect to duns and creditors, 1706 was if anything worse than the previous year. Steele lost two actions for debt, both with damages.[26] By August of that year, though, his star was definitely on the rise, however slowly. In June or July, his "Prologue to the University of Oxford" written for the opening of a series of dramatic performances at the University was read amid familiar surroundings: the Tennis Court near Merton.[27] Steele himself may have been present for the formal opening; if he was there, the occasion was appropriate, for from Merton some fourteen years earlier he had gone down to seek his fortune as a soldier. He had not found his fortune in the army. He had been a good soldier, but without money and family influence promotion was slow, even under Marlborough, except for the unusually gifted or fortunate. Now he had made his decision, his soldiering was done, he had embarked on a new way of life, that of courtier, writer, and politician. In August, 1706, Captain Steele was appointed Gentleman-Waiter to Queen Anne's husband, Prince George of Denmark, a position worth one hundred pounds a year, tax free.[28] It was his first civil preferment.

[26] Aitken, I, 149–50.
[27] *Verse*, pp. 45, 92–93.
[28] *Corr.*, p. 201.

CHAPTER IV

The Gazetteer

JUST HOW the political structure was held together, exactly
what were the groupings, who exercised the real power in Queen
Anne's England are knotty questions even now being vigor-
ously debated by historians of the period.[1] It is clear that a
simple naming of Whig and Tory shades the complexities, the
involved personal and family relationships which often produced
strange divisions in the House of Commons. The twisted in-
trigues of grass-roots politics in the boroughs, with which Steele
had become familiar in Cutts's constituencies on the Isle of
Wight and John Ellis' at Harwich, were further convoluted in
London where the rewards of political power were much higher.
Though some people disliked and decried the party labels of
Whig and Tory, others accepted them with pride. One group
that did so was the so-called Junto Whigs, and to this group
Richard Steele tied his political fortunes.

They were a skillful and aggressive assortment of men, these
Junto Whigs, with great collective experience in the game they
loved best. The leaders, each with a long train of kinsmen and
dependents of varying rank and influence, are usually taken to
be Charles Montagu, Lord Halifax; John, Lord Somers;
Thomas, Earl of Wharton; William, Lord Cowper; Admiral
Lord Edward Russell, Earl of Orford; and Charles Spencer,

[1] See Robert Walcott, *English Politics in the Early Eighteenth Century*
(Oxford, 1956); and J. H. Plumb, *Sir Robert Walpole: The Making of a
Statesman* (London, 1956), pp. 61–65.

Earl of Sunderland. The test of an effective political combination has always been the ability of such a combination to place its supporters in key positions of authority, and to secure the passage of legislation favorable to the interests of the combination. To this end Junto members in 1705 and the years following were striving to penetrate the Godolphin-Marlborough-Harley coalition which held the Queen's favor. As the case of Addison demonstrated, the Junto was beginning to succeed. In the parliamentary elections of May and June, 1705, many of their sympathizers were elected, but the preponderance of power was not yet the Junto's.

The social focus of this group of Whigs was the Kit-Cat Club, to which Steele presumably now belonged. At the weekly meeting of the Club, at gatherings on their great estates, the Whig lords appraised their followers with critical eyes, measuring them for future employment according to their abilities. In all probability one or another of them recommended Steele for his appointment as Gentleman-Waiter. Lord Halifax was of the Junto the member most familiar with writers and literature. As young Charles Montagu, he and Matthew Prior had composed the devastating parody of Dryden's *Hind and Panther;* he was affable, courtly, cultivated, shrewd. Perhaps he endorsed Steele. It was a good minor appointment. Steele knew well court life and the royal palaces, where he had served as a trooper, then as an officer of the Guards. He was convivial and friendly, and the phlegmatic Prince lacked both qualities. And as a member of the Household, Steele, with his sensitive ear for gossip, could ferret out information useful to his patron Whigs, who were at that time opposed in the Queen's favor by Sarah Churchill, the resourceful Duchess of Marlborough. The Junto needed friends in power, for all London knew that some of its members stood last in the Queen's grace. Sunderland, it was rumored, had flirted with republicanism; he was certainly blunt to the point of rudeness. The Earl of Wharton, humorous,

aggressive, profane, was a notorious rioter and some, including
Swift, told stories of his having once defiled a church. The
Church of England was the Queen's most cherished institution
and any sort of irreverence was certain to draw her wrath. But
the Junto had assets, too; Halifax and Cowper were gentlemen
of learning and refinement, full of charm and good talk. Russell,
the Admiral, had beaten the French at La Hogue in 1692. All
the leaders were experienced politicians, who fastened their gaze
resolutely on the main chance. But so did Sarah Churchill.

For the immediate horizon was as surely Marlborough's as
the Danube bank at Blenheim. With unflagging energy he reformed his armies after the great campaign of 1704, pressed the
war-weary Dutch to follow his lead, and cajoled support in
England for still another year's attempt to crush the power of
Louis XIV. At home patriots of every stripe joined with the
men of business (who saw new markets opening to British ships
and the pound sterling as a result of Marlborough's victories)
in fulfilling the Queen's wishes to honor her, and England's,
hero. The Royal Manor and Park of Woodstock, with lands
and revenues of some £6,000 per annum, was conveyed to the
Duke and his heirs, without opposition in the House. The Queen
awarded him a lifetime annual grant of £5,000 and appointed
him Colonel of his old regiment, the First Guards. And Sir
John Vanbrugh began building the great castle of Blenheim.
Worldly possessions no doubt pleased Marlborough — the
Churchills have never been ascetics — but he required political
control if he was to prosecute the war to the decision he wanted.
His faithful partners, Godolphin and Sarah, labored ceaselessly
toward this goal. The Junto was obliged, it became clear, to
work out some method of joining the Marlborough-Godolphin
coalition or to face being out of power for the foreseeable future,
that is, as long as Queen Anne lived. Robert Harley had already
forged such an accommodation, but in spite of occasional overtures, he was no friend of the Junto. A minor but hopeful augury
of Richard Steele's future usefulness, as the Junto lords doubt-

less saw it, was that he was a sincere, vocal admirer of the great Duke. He admired him as a gallant soldier, as, for so the world thought, a key figure in the displacement of James II by William, as one of the deliverers of Ireland, and as a successful man. Richard Steele, orphaned son of a chronic failure and now a former army captain and minor playwright, admired success extravagantly. Success signified living without the heartaches of the dunning creditor, enjoying the company of cultivated men and women, it signified conviviality and fine clothes; everything that was different from the stink of open sewers in crowded Dublin and the drip of rain down one's neck on the battlements of Landguard Fort. The Junto lords were, by Steele's definition, successful men; so, pre-eminently, was Marlborough.

Many of Steele's contemporaries succeeded in making more or less neat divisions of their lives; Addison, for example, could pursue a literary interest to its logical end without a diversion, and his courtship of the Countess of Warwick was to be a model of careful planning and judicious execution. Not so Richard Steele. He purchased life in the bulk and sorted it out as the occasion demanded. Now, while the Junto was struggling for power, was of course the time for Steele to devote himself exclusively to politics, to concentrate his energies on his political career. He did no such thing.

The opportunity for such a sustained concentration was his. By December, 1706, Steele's wife Margaret had passed away as conveniently as she had entered his life. One hopes that she was happy with Steele; certainly she seems to have had little effect on his imagination. A single reference to her in a letter from Steele to his second wife's mother contains all we know about Steele's feeling for her or hers for Steele: "My late wife had so extreme a value for me that she by fine conveyed to me her whole estate situate in Barbados. . . ."[2] There is something disquieting about Steele's first marriage; it seems an em

[2] *Corr.*, p. 201.

too convenient. It was formally regular, it helped him finan-
cially; the rest is forgotten. When Margaret Stretch Steele was
laid to rest, she left her husband in a comfortable financial situation; if he erected a memorial tablet with a proper Latin epitaph
for her, no one has been able to locate it.

Nor did he mourn long. Within a year he had remarried and
certainly there was nothing casual or perfunctory about his
second marriage. The bride-to-be he saw at Margaret's funeral,
in a curious re-enactment of the wooing of his "Wood Nymph"
at a funeral while an ensign in the army.[3] Evidently funerals
struck resonant chords in Steele's imagination; a psychologist
might trace the succession: the funeral of his father, the wooing
of the wood nymph, the dramatic examination of funerals and
grief, and finally the meeting of his second wife, "Dear Prue,"
at Margaret's last rites.

Mary Scurlock had known Margaret Steele well enough to
attend her funeral, though Mary was ill at the time. It is possible, then, that she and Steele were acquainted before his first
wife's death. Like Steele, she was not a native of England. Her
father, Jonathan Scurlock, was of an old Irish family, had
studied at Trinity College, Cambridge, and Gray's Inn, and
entered the law, finally serving in various legal positions in
Carmarthen, Wales. There he died in 1682, leaving a considerable estate to his widow and a daughter three years old.[4] Sometime in 1707, probably in July, with his first wife decently in the
grave but barely so, Steele decided to renew acquaintance with
the Welsh heiress. "Madam," he wrote Mary:

> Your wit and beauty are suggestions which may easily lead you
> into the intention of my writing to you. You may be sure that I
> cannot be cold to so many good qualities as all that see you must
> observe in you. You are a woman of a very good understanding,
> and will not measure thoughts by any ardour in my expressions,
> which is the ordinary language on these occasions.

[3] See above, chap. 2, p. 48.
[4] Aitken, I, 162–70.

I have reasons for hiding from my nearest relation [presumably his sister Katherine] any purpose I may have resolved upon of waiting on you if you permit it, and I hope you have confidence from mine as well as your own character that such a condescension should not be ill used by, Madam

Your most obedient servant
R. STEELE

This tactful letter with its shrewd emphasis on Mary's beauty and understanding — Steele always knew as if by instinct what ladies like to hear; the knowledge was a powerful ingredient of his literary success — impressed the young woman from Wales, who would be twenty-nine in November; she put it away to think it over without reply. Steele waited a few days and tried again:

MADAM

I writ to you on Saturday by Mrs. Warren, and give you this trouble to urge the same request I made then, which was that I may be admitted to wait upon you. I should be very far from desiring this if it were a transgression of the most severe rules to allow it; I know you are very much above the little arts which are frequent in your sex of giving unnecessary torment to their admirers; therefore hope you'll do so much justice to the generous passion I have for you, as to let me have an opportunity of acquainting you upon what motives I pretend to your good opinion. I shall not trouble you with my sentiments till I know how they will be received, and as I know no reason why difference of sex should make our language to each other differ from the ordinary rules of right reason, I shall affect plainness and sincerity in my discourse to you, as much as other lovers do perplexity and rapture. Instead of saying, I shall die for you, I profess I should be glad to lead my life with you; you are as beautiful as witty as prudent, and as good humored as any woman breathing, but I must confess to you I regard all those excellencies as you will please to direct 'em for my happiness or misery. With me, Madam, the only lasting motive to love is the hope of its becoming mutual; I beg of you to let Mrs. Warren send me word when I may attend you. I promise you I'll talk of nothing but indifferent things, tho' at the same time I know not how I shall approach you in the tender moment of first seeing you after this declaration which has been made by, Madam,

> Your most obedient & most faithful humble servant
> RICH^d STEELE

Here was a lover impetuous enough to warm the heart of the Sphinx. Sincerity shouts from every line. He would pursue; letter follows letter. He sought the lady at her house; she was not at home to him but promised to see him when he came next. On a Thursday the couple met; Steele's letter written the next morning breathes his happiness. Another rendezvous was planned for Sunday. In a passionate note he reassured Mary of the quality of his love:

> I have not a thought which relates to you that I cannot with confidence beseech the all-seeing Power to bless me in. May He direct you in all your steps, and reward your innocence, your sanctity of manners, your prudent youth, and becoming piety, with the continuance of His grace and protection. This is an unusual language to ladies, but you have a mind elevated above the giddy motions of a sex insnared by flattery. . . . Beauty, my fairest creature, palls in the possession, but I love also your mind; your soul is as dear to me as my own. . . .

Mary Scurlock was being forced to a decision. There was another man. Henry Owen, a widower who was a barrister and Justice of the Peace in Carmarthen, had been seeing her for years. Owen was persistent but tactless, to put the matter gently. In 1704 he sued Mary for breach of contract, alleging that she had agreed to marry him and had not done so. Nothing came of the proceedings of course, but Owen, incredibly, continued to press his personal suit with Mary, year after year. Disregarding, if she was able, the breach of contract suit, Mary could have been little impressed by this legalistic plodder. She was a young woman who had literary pretensions and who no doubt found

London days and nights more exciting than dull months in far-off Carmarthenshire.[5] Steele, on the other hand, was anything but a bore: thoroughly immersed in social London, a member of the Royal Household, a veteran of King William's army, a successful playwright, an impetuous lover. There were other points in his favor too. He was a widower with a fortune, as everyone knew, and, as will be seen, he had recently obtained a post in the government. Steele simply swept her away; the decision was made. Henry Owen's latest letter was consigned to the dustbin without her reading it, "he being beneath my scornful laugh." Anticipating the wagging tongues of London and Carmarthen, Mary wrote her mother, carefully avoiding proper names, asking her permission to marry the "survivour of the person to whose funeral I went in my illness." "I can't recommend the person to you as having a great estate, title &c," Mary explained "[which] are generally a parent's chief care, but he has a competency in worldly goods to make easy, with a mind so richly adorned as to exceed an equivalent to the greatest estate in the world in my opinion, in short his person is [what] I like, his temper is [what] I'm sure will make you as well as myself perfectly happy. . . ." Mary was certain. The marriage was a love match between two people old enough to know themselves and their partners.

Mrs. Elizabeth Scurlock did not feel the tender raptures in Carmarthen; as a good mother should, she wanted specific information on this "competency in worldly goods" her daughter mentioned so glibly. Steele accordingly sent her a candid statement of his income and urged haste in the decision, since "I am at a present juncture in my affairs, and my friends are in great power so that it would be highly necessary for us to be in the figure of life which we shall think convenient to appear in as soon as may be, that I may prosecute my expectations in a busy

---

[5] Suit summarized in Aitken, I, 179–82; verses in her handwriting, *ibid.*, p. 183.

way while the wind is for me, with a just consideration that
about a court it will not always blow one way." Since he was a
courtier, that is, the couple would have to live in a manner
befitting their station; like his aunt, Lady Mildmay, Steele was
concerned with the proper address, the proper occupation, the
proper cut of one's clothes. These were, he knew, part of the
successful man's success. Mrs. Scurlock delayed; the couple
took matters into their own hands, applied for a marriage license
and were married in St. Mary Somerset, one of Wren's garland,
on 9 September 1707. The new Mrs. Steele, whose understanding Richard admired, composed some verses having to do with
their relationship. They were probably written around the time
of their marriage; though slight they have feeling:

> Ah Dick Steele that I were but sure
> Your love like mine would still indure
> That time nor absence which destroys
> The cares of lovers and there joys
> May never rob me of that part
> Which you have given of your heart
> Others unenvied may possess
> What ever they think happiness
> Grant this O God my great request
> In his dear arms may I for ever rest.[6]

This wish was granted. Richard Steele remained Mary's devoted
husband until her death during pregnancy eleven years later.

The literary record of that devotion, Steele's famous letters
to "Dear Prue," constitute one of the most remarkable collections of its kind in literary history. Preserved with meticulous
care by Mrs. Steele, who evidently had a keener sense of literary
merit than she has been given credit for, these hundreds of
communications written at all hours of the day and night and
in every variety of emotional state reveal Richard Steele un-

[6] BM, Add. MSS. 5145 B. fol. 377, quoted in *Corr.*, p. 207n.

laced with somewhat disquieting thoroughness; at times one
has the feeling of being an uninvited guest in the conjugal bed-
room. On the whole, though, the notes show Steele's best qualities: his humor, his candor, his kindness, his well-developed
sense of fun, all salted with a certain marital irony, as in this:

Hide-park Corner, 9 in the morning
Wednesday, Oct^{br} 13th, 1708

DEAR PRUE
The bearer is one I propose to be our footman. He is as you
see very queer, and fit for what I often heard you call it, a thor-
ough servant, besides which he speaks the Welch tongue fluently.
. . . I hope he will be approved by you; if he is the livery shall
be fitted for his shape against the time that he and I can attend
the chariot to bring Mrs. Binns and you to town, which shall be
done with all suitable ceremony. In the mean time, I am busy
about the main chance. . . .

Or this:

Augst 28th, 1708

DEAR PRUE
    The afternoon coach shall bring you ten pounds. Your letter
shows you are passionately in love with me. But we must take
our portion of life as it runs without repining and I consider that
good nature added to that beautiful form God has given you
would make an happiness too great for human life.

Yr Most Oblig'd Husband & Most Humble Ser^{nt}
RICH^d STEELE

Ne'er so well expressed! And so the dialogue, for such it was,
continued year in and year out until Mrs. Steele's death wrote
a full stop to the memorable record.

    But in the autumn of 1707 the couple was faced first of all
with the necessity of informing and mollifying Mrs. Scurlock.
Richard Steele addressed a warmly respectful letter to that lady,
reporting the event and soliciting her blessing. The couple would
occupy Mrs. Scurlock's house in Swallow Street, Piccadilly,

until December, when they would move into a house on Bury Street, very near St. James's Square and a few hundred yards from Whitehall, where Steele was now employed. He had been sharing Addison's bachelor lodgings.[7]

As he had hinted to Mrs. Scurlock, Steele's friends were coming into power. On 3 December 1706 Addison reported without comment to George Stepney, fellow Kit-Cat and envoy to the Imperial court at Vienna, that Lord Sunderland had been sworn into the office of Secretary of State for the Southern Department.[8] Thus did the discreet Addison let Stepney know about an event both realized to be of highest importance to the Whigs, for Sunderland's appointment in the place of Hedges was the first substantial success in the Junto's struggle to seize control of the Ministry. The Queen disliked Sunderland; his appointment was a palpable hit for the Junto. Addison was, of course, retained as Under-Secretary, and in late April or early May, 1707, his old schoolmate and friend Richard Steele was appointed writer of *The London Gazette,* the official government news medium.

Exactly who was responsible for Steele's appointment is not certain, but one may safely assume that Addison had a good deal to do with it and that the Junto approved, knowing Steele's literary qualifications and his political fidelity.[9] This is all logical

---

[7] *Corr.,* p. 212.

[8] *The Letters of Joseph Addison,* ed. Walter Graham (Oxford, 1941), p. 62.

[9] The water has been muddied by too much reliance on Swift's statement to Stella that Harley, as one of the two Secretaries of State, had appointed Steele (*Journal,* I, 67–68). But Swift himself qualified this flat assertion in *The Importance of the Guardian Considered,* and both statements are those of an embittered friend. Addison, as Under-Secretary, had general supervision of office routine (see Mark A. Thomson, *The Secretaries of State, 1681–1782* [Oxford, 1932], pp. 134, 148). In all probability Addison suggested Steele's name to Sunderland, who approved and sent the nomination via Mainwaring to Harley, his colleague, as a tactful gesture. Harley, trying to build a delicate coalition at the time, would scarcely have risked an open break with Sunderland and the Junto by exercising a veto over a relatively trivial appointment. Cf. Godfrey Davies, "The Fall of Harley in 1708," *English Historical Review,* LXVI (1951), 254.

enough; the Junto was striving to place its people not only at the top but throughout the ranks of government. The Whigs were quick to recognize the importance of having a group of good writers at their service; this was a great age of political pamphleteering, and party leaders needed writers to help them into office and to defend them when they got there. Robert Harley, no less astute than the Junto, was collecting his own circle of writers; eventually both Defoe and Swift were to be in his employ.

Steele wrote the paper in Lord Sunderland's office in the Cockpit, under the general supervision of Sunderland's Under-Secretary, Addison. Ostensibly at least, the paper was non-partisan. In his *Apology* (1714), Steele recalled his duties as Gazetteer, "where he worked faithfully according to order, without ever erring against the rule observed by all Ministries, to keep that paper very innocent and very insipid." The statement, a study indicates, is somewhat disingenuous; there is reason to believe that Sunderland intended to influence public opinion in favor of the Junto's policies by adroitly suppressing some news items and magnifying others.[10] He would have been a poor politician if he had done otherwise.

Politics or no politics, the post of Gazetteer was by its nature no sinecure. Two years earlier de Fonvive, editor of the newspaper *The Postman,* had refused Harley's proffer of the position, calling it "no way of preferment." "The writing of the *Gazette,*" he reminded Harley, "though judged trifling by such who never tried the difficulties thereof, requires more learning than some imagine, and a great deal of care to avoid blunders and contradictions. . . ." [11] As the official newspaper, the *Gazette* used domestic news sources and, especially, dispatches from envoys

---

[10] *Apology: Tracts,* p. 339; Sunderland's activities: Robert W. Achurch, "The Literary and Historical Relations of the *Tatler* to Defoe's *Review* and the *London Gazette*" (unpublished dissertation, University of North Carolina, 1943), p. 244.

[11] HMC, *Portland MSS.,* VIII, 187–88.

overseas, which came into the office to Addison's desk and were supplied by him to the Gazetteer. Steele then selected the more important ones for his paper, which appeared twice a week. For this work Steele received £300 a year, an increase from the former Gazetteer's stipend of £60.[12]

His troubles commenced immediately. The *Gazette* early in May reported that a supply fleet had arrived at Ostend "to the great satisfaction and advantage of the people there." Prince George himself expressed his regal displeasure through an intermediary: the wording, he felt, made it appear that the Dutch had not had a supply convoy for a long time. Thus, the Prince thought, the paper reflected on England's treatment of her ally Holland. Steele got wind of the Prince's displeasure and attempted to explain the heinous deed, pleading that he had noted the event on Sunderland's own direct orders as transmitted by Addison and furthermore that he had used the reporting ambassador's very words in the account.[13] Such, he found, were the troubles of the Gazetteer.

Despite *contretemps* like this, the new Whig journalist, plying his quill in the Cockpit during the winter of 1707–1708 could have felt that, taking things all in all, the preceding twelve months had been extraordinarily promising. "Expectations" was the word he had used in discussing his business affairs with Mrs. Scurlock, and it represented a concept never far from Steele's mind. His letters, especially those to Mrs. Steele, glitter with forecasts of impending wealth, of higher place. Always to be blessed, Steele seldom looked back; creditors were forced to hale him into court to restore the defective memory of his debts. Too much has been made of Steele's financial improvidence and too little of his *futurus* sense. They are two sides of a single human phenomenon, a not unusual one: the spendthrift always looking for something to turn up. Contrary to fable and Sunday

---

[12] Letter to Mrs. Scurlock (n. 2 above).
[13] *Corr.,* pp. 21–22.

School lesson, for the clever spendthrift like Steele something often does, but when it turns up it usually is insufficient to maintain the spendthrift in the style to which his vaulting imagination has already carried him — hence, greater expectations. And so it was with Steele. Though, of course, he regretted the inconvenience of debt (the lawsuits, the threats of repossession and jail), his thoughts of future fortune did not include paying off all debts and settling down to a restricted, frugal life, as his friend Addison advocated. Steele's vision was more expansive than that. "I desire of you," he wrote Prue from the Cockpit one day, "to get the coach and yourself ready as soon as you can conveniently and call for me here from whence we will go and spend some time together in the fresh air in free conference. Let my best periwig be put in the coach box and my new shoes for 'tis a comfort to [be] well dressed in agreeable company." To be well dressed in agreeable company was an expectation Steele was ready to wait and work for, and the devil take the creditors.

In 1707 Steele could exercise his penchants for company and dress. His new employment put him where he rejoiced to be, near the center of government business. Much of his time was spent conferring with friends and political cronies; Steele used taverns like the Devil, Temple-Bar, and the George, Pall Mall, for this half-business, half-recreation characteristic of Queen Anne London. "I'le come within a pint of wine," he promised Mrs. Steele one night. Of this tavern-Court-business life Steele had for years been an attentive observer, an enthusiastic participant. All this was grist for the politician's mill, of course, but it was also the source of his most original work, *The Tatler,* which Steele may have been meditating as early as 1707.

His finger always on the public pulse, Steele proposed to Lord Sunderland that the ambassadors be required to send reports to the Gazetteer every post and that the paper appear three times instead of twice a week in order to raise the prestige of the

Gazette and diminish that of the many competing newspapers. This was a news-hungry public. Nothing came of his suggestions and one may imagine Steele dreaming of the way he would direct a periodical. Matters looked up. In May, 1708, Addison stood for Member of Parliament for the traditionally Tory borough of Lostwithiel, Cornwall, and was declared elected. Though the election was disputed and eventually Addison declared not elected, he was plainly making his way in the political world. He was courting Charlotte, the widowed Countess of Warwick and his future wife, that summer, by way of the friendship of her young son.[14] A summer haven from London heat and smells was the hamlet of Sandy-End near Fulham, conveniently close to the Countess' residence, Holland House. There Addison was joined by the Steeles from time to time. Richard Steele had lived at Fulham when a boy and was lyrical at the prospect of going back. "I love the country most mightily indeed I do. . . ."

Mrs. Steele was not so lyrical. That summer she was experiencing the new bride's customary return to reality. Her husband dined on business with important men like Lord Halifax, while she sat at home and fended off creditors. There were quarrels; Steele asked forgiveness, pointing out what she undoubtedly knew, that he had "made myself liable to impatient people who take all advantages." Now these impatient people seemed likely to be satisfied. During the summer he began to receive money at last from the settlement of Margaret's Barbados estate. He had, it is true, borrowed liberally against this settlement, but by 20 August he was able to report every creditor "except one" paid, including Addison, whom he owed £1,000. Money was forthcoming from other sources: early in the summer Mrs. Scurlock proposed to settle £160 on the Steeles. Per-

---

[14] Peter Smithers, *The Life of Joseph Addison* (Oxford, 1954), pp. 130–35; and A. L. Cooke, "Addison's Aristocratic Wife," *Publications of the Modern Language Association of America,* LXXII (1957), 379–82.

haps on the basis of these expectations Steele rented or bought a second residence in addition to the Bury Street lodging: this one nearer the country which he loved most mightily, at Hampton Wick. The bickering continued. "Know," he advised his wife, "that 'tis the glory of a woman to be her husband's friend and companion and not his sovereign director." Mary Scurlock had other concerns; she was pregnant. Marriage Steele defined about this time as a "snug, if not a rapturous, condition." [15]

[15] *Corr.*, p. 25. The cottage at Hampton Wick is the residence usually singled out as the one sold by Addison to recover a loan. I do not believe the incident took place as related by Samuel Johnson. Johnson's story about Addison, "as well known as that he wrote *Cato*," he received twice, both times at second hand: from Savage who had it from Steele, and from Benjamin Victor, who heard it from Robert Wilks, co-manager with Steele of the Drury Lane Theatre. The gist, as everyone knows, was that Addison had the Hampton house and furniture sold to recover a debt, sending the balance to Steele with a monitory letter. Like Mr. Smithers, in his *The Life of Joseph Addison,* I believe Addison capable of such an action but there is no first-hand evidence at all of its having taken place. Furthermore, the circumstances of the law suits of 1708 are such that oral accounts by Steele might have been misinterpreted by both Wilks and Savage. The case is indeed complicated. Simplified, it might be seen this way: Steele sold the Barbados estates, against which a £1,000 loan from Addison had been secured, for £9,300 less various encumbrances — of a considerable total. The trustees, to whom the estate had been voluntarily delivered to facilitate the very complex transaction, refused on various legal grounds to repay Addison immediately, though that had been part of the understanding by which he surrendered his share (i.e., £1,000 plus interest) in the estate. Addison in October, 1708, brought a friendly suit against Steele and the trustees (with, Smithers feels, Steele's collusion) to recover the sum owed, which Steele had in fact apparently repaid (*Corr.*, p. 229) the previous August. Thus the suit would get from the estate the £1,000 balance which was Steele's, though legally — until the estate was settled — still part of the estate itself. In a sense, then, Addison was seeking to sell Steele's property and give him the balance, though the property was in Barbados rather than Hampton. The proceedings certainly invite misconstruction, and unless new evidence is forthcoming I believe that Johnson's story should be held not true, based on Wilks's and Savage's understandably inaccurate oral retelling of Steele's memory of the 1708 proceedings. It is, of course, possible that the story applies to circumstances of a different date, but no evidence has come to light to warrant such a supposition. For a fuller presentation, see Smithers, pp. 136–139; Arthur L. Cooke, "Addison vs. Steele, 1708," *Publications of the Modern Language Association of America,* LXVIII (1953), 313–20; and Rae Blanchard, "Richard Steele's West Indian Plantation," *Modern Philology,* XXXIX (1942), 281–85.

While Mrs. Steele stayed at Hampton Wick in the cottage Steele later called "The Hovel," the Gazetteer remained at work in London. Jonathan Swift was in town on business for the Church of Ireland; he called his association with Addison and Steele the "Triumvirate." [16] William Congreve was of their group and so was Ambrose Philips, an officer in the army still, but looking to better things as all of them were. They were, that summer of 1708, still young men of promise, glimpsing from without the circles of real fame and power but not yet admitted. Life permitted these friendships; a year later responsibilities, rising upward like plants between paving-stones, would be forcing them apart. But in the summer of 1708 they could agree on the pleasures of a bottle, a good book, of good talk with old friends each involved in an increasingly interesting occupation. Richard Steele's skin was thickening. He no longer took every criticism of the *Gazette* personally; "I take my employment in its very nature to be what is the object of censure. . . ." Even the war news was good; Marlborough had won again. Steele's "Imitation of the Sixth Ode of Horace," dedicated in 1704 to the victor of Blenheim, had reappeared in January with the author's name in full.

One minor matter vexed Steele that summer, as it always would: the rising English taste for Italian opera. His resentment was both patriotic and personal. As a trueborn Englishman, with a Whig's suspicion of foreign imports, he regarded the Italians as a decadent people; witness their use of *castrati,* symbolic as he put it in a poem later, of "luxury and loose desires." [17] Addison's attempt at English opera, *Rosamond,* had failed resoundingly the year before. Furthermore, the Italian opera drew the public away from native English drama and here

---

[16] *The Correspondence of Jonathan Swift, D.D.,* ed. F. Elrington Ball (London, 1910–1914), I, 100.
   [17] *Verse,* p. 65.

Steele was personally concerned, for he had acquired what public reputation he possessed by way of his three plays. The drama appeared to him as a source of future fame and revenue now threatened by emasculated foreigners. Another way had to be found to please the public taste and at the same time reform it. But what was the way?

Steele's Junto superiors were busily pressing their advantage in the summer and autumn of 1708. Robert Harley had been temporarily discredited by the conviction of his secretary for treason; he was out of action. Henry St. John's Tory followers had lost ground to the Whigs in the spring election.[18] Every victory by Marlborough was, or was made, a victory for the Whigs; the Junto had in Marlborough a winning horse and backed him, publicly, to the limit. Nothing could have better pleased Steele, but for reasons different from those of the Junto. Captain Steele's attitude was, as we have seen, personal rather than political; Marlborough was every soldier's dream of himself, a military genius, conqueror of the French, savior of his country, and rewarded by that grateful country with ducal wealth. The Junto regarded Marlborough with cool objectivity as a former Tory who had been forced by circumstances into an alliance becoming very much to their advantage.

In October, 1708, Queen Anne's husband, Prince George, died. One of Steele's duties as Gentleman-Waiter was to guard the catafalque, sitting up all night every third day for more than two weeks while the unbeloved Dane lay in state. At home, creditors pressed on every side; Prue was besieged and begged Steele for money to fend them off. By November one of Steele's more persistent adversaries, John Huggins, high bailiff of Westminster, had entered an execution for arrears of rent on the Bury Street house. "I doubt not," Steele wrote Prue from the Garter Tavern, "but we shall have our money, which will be

[18] Walpole's letter to Marlborough in Plumb (n. 1), p. 138.

the introduction into that life we both pant after with so much earnestness." [19] Steele's hopes were as nearly unquenchable as a man's can be, but his wife could not help being acutely aware of Huggins' officer standing outside the door of their house. Steele solved the problem as he often did, by finding someone who would pay the creditor, thus buying trouble for the future.

Captain Steele's instincts were correct: better days were ahead. Weakened in her resistance to the Junto by the death of Prince George, the Queen consented to accept Wharton as Lord Lieutenant of Ireland and Somers as President of the Council. Addison was thereupon appointed Wharton's Secretary and Steele envisioned himself as the new Under-Secretary of State for the Southern Department. For some time the appointment of Addison's successor remained a mystery; Steele built his hopes high. But they were doomed. By 28 December the ubiquitous Peter Wentworth heard that Sunderland had put the Gazetteer off with promises.[20] A Scot, Robert Pringle, was made Under-Secretary.

Easy come, easy go; Steele was not crushed by his disappointment. *The Gazette,* for all its insipidity, was an influential publication; people read it, talked about it, *bought* it. For a year and a half he had sweated in the nameless notoriety of the Gazetteer. His rewards, so far, had been exactly equal to his salary. Addison had been appointed to one of the most lucrative posts in the British Isles. There must be, Steele might have thought, an easier route to fame and fortune than the one he had been traveling. In the spring of 1709 he began publishing a new periodical.

---

[19] *Corr.,* p. 245. Huggins was a determined Tory; see *A Letter to Sir Miles Warton* in *Tracts,* p. 77, where Steele compares him with the inflammatory Sacheverell. Not that Steele let party deter him in his borrowing.

[20] *The Wentworth Papers, 1705–1739,* ed. James J. Cartwright (London, 1883), p. 68.

CHAPTER V

Isaac Bickerstaff's *Tatler*

THOSE LONDONERS of coffeehouse and salon who stumbled all
unknowingly into literary history by reading the first issue of
The Tatler that April day (the twelfth, old style, precisely) in
1709 found themselves looking at a folio half-sheet, printed on
both sides and resembling, for twentieth-century eyes, an over-
sized handbill. It bore a proper Latin motto (but no English
translation) from Juvenal's First Satire: *Quicquid agunt homi-
nes . . . nostri farrago libelli:* Whatever men do is grist for
our mill. If the readers therefore expected scandal and Juvenalian
satire they were misled, for the anonymous author who called
himself Isaac Bickerstaff was not of Juvenal's satiric school.
Though the prevailing tone of pamphlet and periodical was
rancorous in those days, this Bickerstaff seemed downright good-
humored. The paper, he announced, was "principally intended
for the use of politic persons, who are so public-spirited as to
neglect their own affairs to look into the transactions of state."

Now these gentlemen, for the most part, being men of strong
zeal and weak intellects, it is both a charitable and necessary work
to offer something, whereby such worthy and well-affected members of the commonwealth may be instructed, after their reading,
what to think; which shall be the end and purpose of this my
paper; wherein I shall from time to time report and consider all
matters of what kind soever that shall occur to me, and publish
such my advices and reflections every Tuesday, Thursday, and
Saturday in the week. . . . I have also resolved to have some-

thing which may be of entertainment to the fair sex, in honour of
whom I have taken the title of this paper.

It was an age which savored tone and the tone of this was just
right. The time — April in wartime — was right. The price,
free for the first four issues and thenceforth a penny, was attractive. Even the narrator or *persona* was right, for Londoners still
laughed about the discomfiture of the wealthy and obtuse almanac maker, Partridge, the year before. One Isaac Bickerstaff
had issued his own set of almanac predictions, which included
the death of Partridge; on the appointed day Partridge had indignantly denied that he was dead, whereupon elaborate reports
of his last moments, death, and funeral were circulated by the
engineer of the plot, Swift, and his enthusiastic collaborators.[1]
Bickerstaff redivivus promised more of the hoax and half-hoax
dear to eighteenth-century Englishmen. All in all, matters
seemed hopeful for the new paper.

"Do not cast [your]self down," Steele exhorted his wife at
the beginning of the second week of publication, "but depend
upon it that I shall bring you home what will make things have
a cheerful aspect. . . ." Poor Prue had heard sentiments of the
sort often enough before, but this time her husband was not
exaggerating the prospects. The paper was a great success. Let
us give Richard Steele his due. He had gauged his audience
shrewdly, planned the debut carefully, and produced something
new. There had been predecessors, of course. There were newspapers of various sorts, public like the *Gazette,* and privately
owned like the *Daily Courant.* Some periodicals, the *Athenian
Mercury* was one, were devoted entirely to questions and an-
swers. Defoe was in the fifth year of his *Review,* which carried
both news and editorial opinion. It was a new era of journalism;
Richmond Bond has estimated that seven hundred newspapers
and periodicals of various sorts had appeared between 1620 and

[1] For a full account see R. P. Bond, "Isaac Bickerstaff, Esq.," in *Restoration & 18th Century Literature,* ed. C. Camden (Chicago, 1963), pp. 103-24.

1700.[2] A new paper could not survive on novelty alone, a thousand had fallen at Bickerstaff's side. Steele identified and combined the appeals of various periodicals in one. The question-and-answer and the hoax letter, for example, appeared, sometimes separate, sometimes combined, transfigured as the letter to the editor, a device which Steele exploited; shrewd editors have done the same ever since. News was included to attract readers; Steele felt that as Gazetteer he had access to superior news sources: the diplomatic reports. For various reasons this expedient did not work and the news sections gradually disappeared from *The Tatler*.[3] The principal appeals, however, were just those Bickerstaff had announced in the first issue: variety, entertainment for the ladies and information for the men, and actually both for both. This is Horace's *prodesse aut delectare,* instruction and entertainment, in a new format attractive to the widest audience. Ostensibly the audience addressed was the inner circle of wit and learning, those who knew of and laughed at the Partridge-Bickerstaff hoax. But Steele was speaking over the heads of these to the vastly larger circle in London and the provinces and even the colonies (William Byrd in Virginia was a faithful reader of *The Tatler*) who wanted to be told how to act, what to read, what, as Bickerstaff had put it, to think; who wanted to learn these things outside of church or chapel and yet who were suspicious of the libertinism associated with the literary life since Charles II's reign. A recent student of the rise of fiction, Mr. Ian Watt, has put the matter this way:

This compromise, between the wits and the less educated, between the belles-lettres and religious instruction, is perhaps the

[2] *Studies in the Early English Periodical,* ed. Richmond P. Bond (Chapel Hill, 1957), p. 4. Professor Bond's Introduction, really a monograph in itself, is a useful commentary on the early periodicals.
[3] Principally because of competition from himself, as gazetteer. *The Gazette,* also a thrice-weekly after June, 1709, apparently proved too severe a competitor as a newspaper. See R. W. Achurch, "Richard Steele, Gazetteer and Bickerstaff," in *Studies in the Early English Periodical* (note 2), pp. 49–72.

most important trend in eighteenth-century literature, and finds
. . . expression in the most famous literary innovations of the
century, the establishment of the *Tatler* in 1709 and of the
Spectator in 1711.[4]

The compromise, of course, was an effect. When Steele began
The Tatler, he was simply following his nose, combining his
strong inclination to ethical instruction (as displayed earlier in
the plays and *The Christian Hero*) with the knowledge of
audience tastes and popular interest he had acquired at first
hand over the years in the taverns and theaters of London. As
an Irishman he knew the excitement fashionable London life
awakened in the outsider, like the country wife in Wycherley's
play. But though these outsiders were attracted by London
society, they were suspicious of it; the country squire, the merchant, the Dissenter, the parson, all these stock butts of the
comedy in Restoration plays must be mollified and transformed
into subscribers to a London periodical, for the inner circle was
too small. Bickerstaff proceeds to this directly by way, significantly enough, of a review of *The Country Wife,* recently revived. "As I just now hinted," he writes in *Tatler* No. 3, "I own
myself of the Society for Reformation of Manners." This, one
might think, would be exactly designed to drive the London
audience away. Not so; Steele knew that the London *beau
monde,* and every other *beau monde,* liked best of all to read of
itself. He followed the declaration of his membership in the
SRM with the warning, "After this . . . if a fine lady thinks
fit to giggle at church, or a great beau come in drunk to a play,
either shall be sure to hear of it in my ensuing paper : for merely
as a well-bred man, I cannot bear these enormities." [5] There

---

[4] *The Rise of the Novel* (London, 1957), p. 50.

[5] Steele was no doubt also gently satirizing here the excessive zeal of the
many Societies for the Reformation of Manners, then at the height of their
activities. Swift and Defoe also protested the zeal of these reformers. See
Maurice J. Quinlan, "Swift's *Project for the Advancement of Religion and
the Reformation of Manners," Publications of the Modern Language Association of America,* LXXI (1956), 201–12.

would always be, he knew, giggling ladies and drunken beaux.

Modern literary criticism is ill-equipped to deal with essays and periodical publications; categories that operate well enough with lyric poetry appear meaningless when applied to newspapers and magazines. Some theorists, indeed, are quite willing to conclude that the periodical is not a literary form at all and therefore, presumably, should be avoided by anyone having a due concern for his sensibilities. Over against such a conclusion, however, are generations, now centuries, of readers and, recently, scholars like Mr. Watt who have recognized that the better eighteenth-century periodical was, if not literature, certainly a powerful literary force. And of course, the medium in which at one time or another almost every significant writer of the century chose to work. If one then decides to defend the periodical, the nearest way out for the critic is to select a part which can be analyzed and to ascribe the quality of the whole to that part: thus *The Spectator* is good because it contains Addison's series of essays on the imagination, a subject that fits modern critical categories precisely. This approach evades entirely the question of the cumulative effect of a good periodical; why does one agree that the *American Mercury* was a good magazine in the nineteen-twenties? It was not solely because it included within its pages *Rackety-Rax.*

Steele's *Tatler* and its successor, *The Spectator,* proved to be revolutionary departures in English literature principally, perhaps, because of their tone, the attitude toward the audience, rather than their specific content. Almost everything *in* both papers had been anticipated somewhere, in some periodical, even the famous club motif. Steele had the instincts of a great editor, it is true, and the combination of ingredients, the pleasing variety, had and still has much to do with *The Tatler's* success. But it may have been the tone, lightly learned, good-humored, confident, a bit patronizing, sometimes pedantic, that, early arrived at and consistently maintained, gave the papers their true character and authority. Bickerstaff and Mr. Spectator would tell the world — and the world would listen!

Part of *The Tatler*'s quick success was due to Steele's earlier literary experience, to his knowledge of the audience, to his innate sense of the dynamics and fascination of life itself. And a large part was due no doubt to instinct or luck, for Steele, after years of searching for work, was fully employed that spring of 1709. Still Gazetteer, he had now committed himself to three extra deadlines a week and was in full charge, willy-nilly, of writing, editing, and seeing the paper through the press. Two friends, he wrote Prue one day, "having desired to meet me at three o'clock and the Gazette being not quite finished, though now near two I have not time to dine. Therefore can only wish you a good stomach and not come myself." Addison, with whom he may have talked over the new project, had left London just before the first issue appeared, following the new Lord Lieutenant to Ireland. Ambrose Philips was gone also to Copenhagen as secretary to the British envoy. Jonathan Swift was in London, the object of a certain amount of pulling and tugging between Tory and Whig factions but still a good friend of Steele's. He was duly laid under contribution and for the ninth *Tatler* provided his "Description of the Morning" under the name of Humphrey Wagstaff, "an ingenious kinsman of mine," as Bickerstaff described him. By 19 May Addison could report that the Irish capital was much pleased with the new paper.[6]

Steele's hazard of distributing the first four numbers free had succeeded and well that it had. On 26 March Mrs. Steele, with appropriate congruence, had given birth to their first child, a daughter, Elizabeth. No pleasure for Steele could ever be un-

---

[6] *The Letters of Joseph Addison,* ed. Walter Graham (Oxford, 1941), p. 140. Though Tickell later stated that Addison had no knowledge of the paper's authorship before reading in No. 6 a critical remark of his own, it seems unlikely that this was literally true. See Smithers, p. 160. See also Swift's *Bickerstaff Papers,* ed. Herbert Davis (Oxford, 1940), pp. xxiv–xxxv.

alloyed; on 2 May the editor and father was arrested, and apparently imprisoned briefly, for debt, of course.

That spring Steele's government employers were having troubles aplenty, only a few months after the Junto had consolidated its alliance with the Godolphin-Marlborough ministry, and Steele immediately lent his new paper to the support of the government. The troubles were of two sources, natural and man-made, that is, the weather and the war. This had been the legendary winter of the Great Frost, the coldest in many years all over Europe, the winter during which the Rhone and even the canals of Venice froze and a fair (immortalized by John Gay in *Trivia*) was held on the ice-covered Thames. The late spring brought no relief, but prolonged rains and crop failure; the price of grain doubled in some parts of England.[7] And after the weather, there was the war, interminable war. Richard Steele had marched off behind the Duke of Ormonde against Louis XIV in 1692 — seventeen years had passed and the Allies despite many victories were little nearer Paris than they had been in 1692. In this miserable spring of 1709 the British people contemplated the campaign ahead, rising taxes, and the mounting national debt, this last a phenomenon hitherto unknown to them. Though the government, a war ministry, would not admit it, the greater part of the British people high and low had had enough of war.

Marlborough knew it; he had already opened his own private negotiations with Louis, through Marlborough's nephew, the Duke of Berwick, envisioning a sizable, secret financial settlement from the Sun King for his co-operation. Fortunately for Richard Steele's peace of mind, he never learned of these conversations. Public peace negotiations, in the meantime, were inhibited by the Whigs' strong stand on the Spanish question; the Junto found itself saddled with a policy which was finally to

[7] *The Wentworth Papers, 1705–1739*, ed. James J. Cartwright (London, 1883), pp. 68, 84.

bear the Whigs down. For a number of years the Allies had been engaged in two series of campaigns, both directed ultimately at reducing the power of France. The first was the series masterfully fought by Marlborough in the Low Countries and often known as Marlborough's War. The second was the endless Peninsular War, designed to set a safe Hapsburg, Charles III, on the Spanish throne in the place of Louis XIV's suspect Bourbon grandson Philip V. In this theater British invasion had, in spite of some major successes, resulted in forcing the Spanish people to rally around Philip. The Junto Whigs clung resolutely to the belief, however, that Louis could withdraw Philip from the throne by a simple command if he thought it desirable: "No peace without Spain" became their rallying cry. On this rock peace negotiations foundered.

Steele rallied to the government's support without a week's hesitation. In *Tatler* No. 4 he described the political leaders of a blissful island named "Felicia" whose influence, Bickerstaff asserts as syntax wavers beneath his weight, "makes the people enjoy the utmost tranquility in the midst of a war, and gives them undoubted hopes of a secure peace from their vigilance and integrity." In No. 5 Marlborough is cited as a "man formed by nature to lead a nation of heroes." In No. 8, using the hoary Chaucerian device of a dream vision, Steele presents the Junto position on Spain in Vergilian allegory. And in No. 10 he comforts hungry Britons by printing accounts (derived from diplomatic dispatches at the office no doubt) of famine in France where, he declares, the frost had been even worse than in England.

Into these early instances of Bickerstaff in the Junto's service is written a good deal of Steele's political future. He was, above all, a journalist in politics, yet he liked to think of himself as a politician in journalism. The distinction is clearer than at first appears. For Robert Walpole, even for Joseph Addison, writing was a useful adjunct to politics, that is, to the securing and application of power. Steele had no very clear idea of this definition of politics: he was much more the political amateur, his habit of thought was in terms of ideology rather than power, of slogans and issues rather than elections. In this respect he is to be distinguished from his greater opponent and sometime friend, Jonathan Swift, who realized once for all that though "all government, without the consent of the governed, is the very definition of slavery . . . in fact eleven men well-armed will certainly subdue one single man in his shirt." [8]

As a politician Steele was not notably inconsistent. On the contrary, he tended to be all too consistent, in the manner of a newspaper nowadays which will support an editorial policy to the end because the paper has adopted it. Like most journalists he was more effective on simple issues and matters reducible to slogans, and he was especially talented in opposition. Not accidentally his greatest prestige as a political journalist accrued between 1712 and 1714, in the period before the Whigs acquired undisputed control of the government. After 1714 Steele's adherence to principle became troublesome to the ruling circles of the Whigs; they could no longer afford to accept what a realist like Walpole could only regard as Steele's sentimental vagaries.

No doubt the Junto was acquainted with Steele's weaknesses as a politician by 1709. Judging men was after all their principal business in that day of political combinations, factions, and family groups. The Junto was playing for the highest stakes, and they surely acted correctly in sending Joseph Addison to Ireland for further training and keeping Richard Steele at his journalist's desk. But in spite of his defects as a statesman, Steele had ability as a journalist and the Junto recognized this too. He could turn a phrase or a slogan with the best and he knew his audience, from whom many of the electors of Parliament were drawn. And he was certainly faithful to the Junto.

Not the least among Steele's recommendations, from that

[8] *The Drapier's Letter,* No. IV.

group's point of view, was his very wide circle of acquaintance. Fellow Irishmen, army comrades, wits of the tavern, theater people, clergymen, philosophers of both the genuine variety, like George Berkeley, and the alchemical variety — Steele knew them all. Very soon the new paper began to display this acquaintanceship. Swift we have seen as an early collaborator (though the total of his contributions, contrary to popular legend, did not amount to much). Ambrose Philips mailed a much-admired "Winter Piece" from Copenhagen. By late May, Addison was sending material from Ireland, excellent material like the definition of a "Very Pretty Fellow" in No. 24. In the early autumn Addison returned to London and the great partnership began in earnest. Throughout the lifetime of this paper, and of the original *Spectator* as well, Steele continued as managing editor; this pressing responsibility must have had a good deal to do with the slap-dash quality some of Steele's essays display.

From the beginning a major theme of *The Tatler,* as it was to be of *The Spectator,* was the reform of manners, a subject difficult to treat without appearing either pedantic or obvious. The virtues Steele advocated in this reform are the ordinary, homely ones he speaks of elsewhere: good sense, decency, kindness, simple generosity; and his tone is good-natured, often jocular. As here, in an early defense of the pedestrian (*Tatler,* No. 144), he writes:

> Thus, in spite of all order, justice, and decorum, we, the greater number of the Queen's loyal subjects, for no reason in the world but because we want money, do not share alike in the division of her Majesty's highroad. The horses and slaves of the rich take up the whole street, while we peripatetics are very glad to watch an opportunity to whisk across a passage, very thankful that we are not run over for interrupting the machine that carries in it a person neither more handsome, wise, nor valiant, than the meanest of us. For this reason, were I to propose a tax, it should

certainly be upon coaches and chairs: for no man living can as-
sign a reason why one man should have half a street to carry him
at his ease, and perhaps only in pursuit of pleasures, when as
good a man as himself wants room for his own person to pass
upon the most necessary and urgent occasion.

This is clear enough, but what is one to add? Are we to trace
the echo to its classical source and ascribe the sentiment to
Steele's reading of Juvenal in his schooldays? Or place this essay
in the history of ideas and show how advocacy of the homely
virtues is related to the rise of benevolism, the ethic of the good-
willing man, in European Protestantism? Or trace Steele's call
for decency, good sense, and fair play back to his orphaned
childhood? Such comments seem relevant but superfluous in
The Tatler's clear light. So it was with dueling. Steele, his
memory of the grim business with Kelly still vivid, wrote as well
as anyone has on the subject of this curious mole of nature and
probably contributed to the eventual elimination of dueling in
the English-speaking world. His essays on dueling were often
quoted by later reformers. But the elimination of dueling was,
after all, only a half-skip in civilization's grand march. One can
comment a minor virtue into extinction, or even maintain that
the virtues Steele advocates, generosity, kindness, decency, and
the rest, are not to be dignified by the term. But their presence
or absence in the so-called human may be more significant than
we have realized; George Orwell, at any rate, has thought so
in our time.

In *The Tatler* Addison and Steele found a wider audience for
their views on dramatic reform, the same views they had been
expressing by precept and example for several years. The Italian
opera is no better than it should be. Immorality, Restoration
style, has no place on the London stage. "It is not the business
of a good play to make every man a hero; but it certainly gives
him a livelier sense of virtue and merit than he had when he
entered the theatre. This rational pleasure (as I always call it)

has for many years been very little tasted; but I am glad to find, that the true spirit of it is reviving again amongst us. . . ." [9] Addison and Steele seem to array themselves on the side of Collier and Defoe against "profaneness and immorality" but, as John Loftis has pointed out, Collier and Defoe were interested in the abolition of the stage, while the essayists sought to reconcile the newly powerful mercantile community with the theater.[10] Some reform was certain to come; it was a question of whether the theaters would be closed altogether or would set a reformed middle course. Addison and Steele were concerned that the latter counsel prevail, as it did. Some part of the space given over in literary histories to belaboring Steele for perverting the drama and introducing "sentimental" comedy might better be devoted to an examination of the social situation in which those plays were produced.

During the spring and summer of 1709, Steele and *The Tatler* were involved with two of the century's most volatile characters, in separate controversies. Much has been made of Steele's geniality and good humor. He was indeed personally genial and good-humored, a delightful companion, but the fact remains that he had an Irishman's nose for a fight and was swamped in controversy, public and private, personal and legal, from the beginning of his literary career to the end. Dispute was rooted in his character. The controversies of 1709 are typical. In *Tatler* Nos. 44 and 50 Steele took up the cause of a friend, the doughty Benjamin Hoadly, then merely rector of St. Peter-le-Poor in London, but later a veritable connoisseur of mitres because of his aggressive Low-Church Whiggery. Hoadly, who evidently had read, marked, and inwardly digested John Locke's *Second Treatise of Government* at Cambridge or afterward, had only one theme for his frequent political sermons: arbitrary author-

---

[9] No. 99.
[10] *Comedy and Society from Congreve to Fielding* (Stanford, 1959), pp. 31–32.

ity, and one attitude: he was against it. By arbitrary authority he meant non-legislative authority, the authority of the executive uncontrolled by the legislature. Given the age and the party situation, this single theme was enough to bring Hoadly four successive bishoprics after the Whigs came to power, each more lucrative than the last (two of which dioceses he never set foot inside). He was, from Robert Walpole's point of view, a splendid bishop, who could be relied on to vote properly in the House of Lords.

In the spring of 1709 Hoadly was as usual hotly engaged in a politico-theological dispute, in this case with Offspring Blackall, the Bishop of Exeter, who had preached a sermon before the Queen (on Romans 13) and seen it published, in which he averred that the authority "exercis'd by the Magistrate is a ray or portion of the Divine authority." Man is naturally born in a state of subjection, the Bishop contended, following Filmer's classic presentation of society under divine-right rule. The magistrate, therefore, has absolute authority and may do anything, even seize clerical prerogatives; the subject's only recourse is to "remonstrate to the Prince in the most decent and respectfull manner." [11]

Hoadly's replies do not concern Steele; suffice it to say that they were thoroughly Lockean. In *Tatler* Nos. 44 and 50 Steele joins the fray, using one Christopher Powell, a real puppet-maker of London to represent Blackall. "Powell" writes a hoax letter to the editor in No. 50 in which he asks: "whether I have not an absolute power, whenever I please, to light a pipe with one of Punch's legs, or warm my fingers with his whole carcass? . . . whether the devil would not be in Punch, should he by word or deed oppose my sovereign will and pleasure?" "Powell's" letter is a *reductio ad absurdum* of the divine-right position, but these were dangerous matters for discussion so

[11] *A Sermon Preach'd Before the Queen at St. James's, on Tuesday, March 8, 1708* [/9] (London, n.d.), pp. 2, 13.

long as Queen Anne lived, who valued the Stuart prerogative and High Churchmanship. Indeed, these two papers seem to have caused Steele more trouble than any other issues of the periodical. In the preface to Volume IV of the first collected edition, published in April, 1711, which was a disclaimer of political partisanship, Steele discusses the contributions of his collaborators. "But all the credit of wit which was given me by the gentlemen above mentioned (with whom I have now accounted) has not been able to atone for the exceptions made against me for some raillery in behalf of that learned advocate for the episcopacy of the Church, and the liberty of the people, Mr. Hoadly."

Theological arguments, one remembers, were not taken lightly in Anne's England; a few months later, the government fell largely because of a single sermon. Skilled disputants on both sides of any question were always at hand and the controversy generally became a party matter. Steele knew all this, but joined the dispute nevertheless and lived to regret doing so.

The other controversy of that year, more personal and less damaging, points forward to his later quarrel with Swift, in that Steele's wrath was roused, as it afterward was, by criticism of his supreme hero, the Duke of Marlborough. The critic in this case was his erstwhile associate in alchemy, Mary Delarivière Manley. Their friendship, it will be recalled, had gone aground some years earlier, apparently upon Steele's refusal to lend her money. Since that time Mrs. Manley had found her true métier as a scandalmonger, a talent in considerable demand then and now. She was a Tory, or as she put it, "a perfect bigot from a long untainted descent of loyal ancestors," and suspicious of Marlborough who had, she thought, gone over to the other side. Her first work, *The Secret History of Queen Zarah and the Zarazians* (1705), was an unrestrained denunciation of Sarah, Duchess of Marlborough, set forth in allegory thin as gossamer. But the time was not then right for her complete success; this came in May, 1709, when the first volume of her *magnum opus* was published, *Secret Memoirs and Manners of Several Persons of Quality, of Both Sexes, from the New Atalantis, an Island in the Mediterranean. The New Atalantis,* as the work came to be called, was a mélange of scandalous stories, under another meager allegorical disguise, about prominent politicians, most of them Whigs. The Marlboroughs were given special attention.

This was no mere pinprick; Mrs. Manley was intelligent and had good sources, for, if the *New Atalantis* contained many mistakes or plain lies, it also contained uncomfortably much truth. Furthermore, Mrs. Manley had a racy narrative style, and, finally, the general public was ready to hear something scandalous about Marlborough, whose victories it liked but of whose war it had tired. When the second volume appeared in October, 1709, the government ordered her arrested and interrogated, though the charges against her were eventually dismissed.[12]

Steele was involved not only because the *New Atalantis* defamed the characters of Marlborough and of his Junto superiors but because he himself was caricatured by his erstwhile friend, who described him so:

> I shall burst with laughter; these are prosperous times for vice; d'ye see that black beau, (stuck up in a pert chariot) thick-set, his eyes lost in his head, hanging eye-brows, broad face, and tallow complexion; I long to inform my self if it [i.e., the chariot] be his own, he cannot yet sure pretend to that. He's called *Monsieur le Ingrate,* he shapes his manners to his name, and is exquisitely so in all he does; has an inexhaustible fund of dissimulation, and does not bely the country he was born in, which is famed for falsehood and insincerity. (2nd ed. [1709], I, 187.)

[12] Mrs. Manley's Toryism: cf. her *The Adventures of Rivella; or, the History of the Author of the . . . Atalantis* (2nd ed.; London, 1715), p. 116; arrest: *ibid.,* p. 113.

Mrs. Manley continues in the same vein for several pages, telling of Steele's alchemy and her efforts to help him care for one of his illegitimate children. The ordinary reader looking for bigger game must have been puzzled by these details of Steele's peccadilloes.

Monsieur le Ingrate was not amused. *Tatler* No. 63 tells of a projected college for young damsels, where the young ladies are to have a "tincture of the ancient and modern Amazonian tactics" of which "the direction is undertaken by Epicene, the writers of Memoirs from the Mediterranean, who, by the help of some artificial poisons conveyed by smells, has within these few weeks brought many persons of both sexes to an untimely fate. . . ." Mrs. Manley protested the treatment; Steele replied with frosty dignity that "your sex, as well as your quality of a gentlewoman (a justice you would not do my birth and education) shall always preserve you against the pen of your provoked most humble servant." The reflections on his birth and education had, typically, stung most sharply. *Tatler* Nos. 88 and 92 continue the attack on libelers.

Mrs. Manley was not easily put down. When her next lubricious volume appeared on the stalls the following spring, with its innocent title, the *Memoirs of Europe, toward the Close of the Eighth Century,* it bore a richly ironic dedication to Isaac Bickerstaff. About that time she was formally recruited for Tory propaganda work; her quarrel with Steele was to continue for years.

These two controversies of 1709, the one public, the other private, and both partly political, foreshadow the larger controversies of later years in which Steele was so often embroiled. During the next decade he took a public stand on almost every issue of any importance that arose in the nation. Indeed, one rereads his writings with the feeling that this predilection for committing himself amounted to a compulsion. It may have been in a sense the recreation in the moral sphere of the dueler's stance and it may represent, as dueling sometimes did for others, a morality of exuberant growth, an idealism larger than life. Even the personal quarrels with Mrs. Manley, with Swift, with Addison, have some of this quality, of an offense against Steele's image of himself — one recalls his reproaching Mrs. Manley for not doing justice to his birth and education. But as in the actual duel with Kelly, Steele generally came to regret the personal aspects of the quarrel and ordinarily took the initiative in seeking reconciliation.

The coolness with Swift was still some months off. In the fall of 1709 Steele planned to see a volume of Swift's miscellaneous writings through the press and perhaps to write an introduction for it. At Addison's instance, Lord Halifax, the Junto's expert in dealing with writers, was dangling a prebendary of Westminster before Swift's interested eyes. It seemed reasonable to believe that Swift might end in the Whig camp if in either; probably neither Steele nor Halifax knew that Swift early in 1709 had received what he took to be a personal affront from the new Lord Lieutenant, the Earl of Wharton. Swift nursed his wound; when a division occurred, Swift was unlikely to be on Wharton's side.

In November, 1709, an apparently trivial issue forced the country toward such a division, generating excitement far out of proportion to the issue's importance, and shaking the very citadel of the government. The crux was religious. On 5 November, with ironic appropriateness Guy Fawkes Day, one Henry Sacheverell, Fellow and Bursar of Magdalen and a friend of Addison's Oxford days, preached a sermon before the Lord Mayor at St. Paul's in which he affirmed the absolute power of the monarchy and attacked the government as corrupters of the Church, alluding to Godolphin as "Volpone." Here was the Hoadly-Blackall controversy revived and magnified. The attack was so pointed and public that the government decided it must reply; its prestige had been shaken earlier in the fall by Marlborough's Pyrrhic victory at Malplaquet. Sacheverell was brought to trial and every opponent of the government in the land exulted. Sacheverell wore the cloth; the reliable slogan of the century before, "The Church in danger," was raised, and all England rallied to one side or the other. Sir Christopher Wren himself was commissioned to design the trial chamber in Westminster Hall, and exasperated diplomats complained to their governments that "people here will see or hear nothing but the Sacheverell trial." [13] Most unfortunately for the government, Queen Anne's sympathies were well-known to be High Church; overnight the Junto found itself cast in the role of persecutor of religion.

Steele must have been sorely tried by this turn of affairs, but there is scant evidence of any strong feeling in *The Tatler.* Addison, who had already begun exercising a restraining influence, was in Ireland; someone else, probably Sunderland or Halifax, may have issued specific orders to Steele that he keep out of this increasingly delicate business. At any rate there are brief, humorous references to the excitement of the trial in Nos. 140, 141, and 142 — nothing else. Steele had another reason for being concerned about the fate of his party and government. In January, 1710, he acquired a new sinecure, a Commissionership of the Stamp Office "for the duties upon stamped vellum, parchment, and paper." The stipend was £300 a year. Debts kept several paces ahead of his income as usual; in April George Doddington brought him to court to recover a debt of £1,000 and Steele spent time in a spunging house, an institution where debtors could cool their heels and reflect on their misfortunes.[14] On 25 May 1710, Steele's second child and first son,

[13] Joh. Phil. Hoffmann, Imperial envoy, as quoted in Onno Klopp, *Der Fall des Hauses Stuart* (Vienna, 1875–1888), XIII, 383.

[14] Appointment: Aitken, I, 271; Doddington, *ibid.,* 277. My assumption is that this was the case for which Steele went to the spunging house, as reported by Swift in *Journal,* I, 127. A judgment for £140 plus damages was also given against him in July (Aitken, I, 279). The exact date of his incarceration is uncertain.

Richard, was born into an environment not much less distressed than that into which his father had been born. The child's prospects were good, however; Lord Halifax stood as a godfather for the youngest Richard Steele at St. James's, Piccadilly.

The lengthy Sacheverell trial, into which the government poured every resource, had ended in late March with a bare conviction and a token sentence. Sacheverell was barred from preaching for three years and the offending sermon was ordered burned by the public hangman. The incendiary cleric traveled through England, greeted everywhere by bonfires and wild acclamation; the Junto was in serious trouble. Robert Harley began to assemble dissidents, working astutely behind the scenes with a view to securing the White Staff of office.

Perhaps exhilarated by the Stamp Office appointment, perhaps trying to strengthen the Junto's wavering supporters, Steele indulged his taste for extravagant praise of the government in *Tatler* No. 130, singling out each member for special citation much as he had the previous year in No. 4. "Such a constellation of great persons, if I may so speak, while they shine out in their own distinct capacities, reflect a lustre upon each other, but in a more particular manner on their Sovereign. . . ." This was going a bit far, for all the world knew that the Queen regarded the Junto with mingled suspicion and alarm and preferred to acquire her lustre from other sources. Furthermore, Tory strength was growing and Isaac Bickerstaff risked much by becoming identified too closely with the Whigs, as the new Tory paper, *The Examiner,* reminded him a few months later, referring to this same *Tatler:*

My advice to you is only this, that you would still appear in your proper sphere; and not quit a character which has given you some credit, to take up another that does not in the least become you. Give me leave to tell you, you mistake your talent, whenever you meddle with matters of state. . . . Don't magnify your constellation of worthies to that degree, as if the world were to be left in darkness, if any of these shining lights should be with-drawn. . . . Begin to take care of your self; remember the fate of one of your predecessors, and don't gaze at your stars 'till you fall into a ditch. No more of your politick lucubrations; put out your candle; favour your age and go to bed sooner.[15]

Mrs. Manley based her main attack on Steele in the *Memoirs of Europe* (published May, 1710) on *Tatler* No. 130. The theme of her accusation in the *New Atalantis* had been personal: Steele's supposed ingratitude. The later book portrays Steele in the character of a hack apologist for the Whigs. The Earl of Wharton, Swift's special bête noire in the Junto, whom Mrs. Manley calls "Cataline," discusses the stratagems of the party in the trial of Plato, the Patriarch of Constantinople (Sachev-erell), and cites the "witty Stelico":

Has he not made a very deity of me, and given me and some of my fellow patricians such gay clothing that I defy our best friends to know us in his garb? He had almost persuaded me to believe (did I not feel the contrary) that I am just! Courageous! Reli-gious! and very near, Merciful! and I have rewarded him for it, and would have done more, but that 'tis not politick, being too liberal, lest the poor rogue should get above his necessities, and grow too great for business, or else indulge too far his native genius to laziness and being governed by his wife.[16]

Mrs. Manley's talent for the personal thrust is evident enough here. This was the line the organized Tory writers were to adopt and repeat, year after year, times without number: that Steele was a spendthrift hack who wrote for his bread, a weak-minded, unprincipled rogue whom the electorate should never trust. Part of the Tories' effectiveness was due to the fact that Mrs. Manley and Swift knew Steele so well, knew every gap in his armor. Naturally they always adopted the *ad hominem* technique. A more circumspect man than Steele might have read

[15] Vol. I, No. 5 (31 August 1710).
[16] 1st ed. (London, 1710), pp. 235–36.

in the *Memoirs* and *The Examiner* a warning, even an ulti-
matum. If Steele did so, he chose to ignore it.

Harley's strength increased as that of the government waned.
In April Queen Anne broke finally and irrevocably with her
friend and confidante, Sarah, Duchess of Marlborough. In-
trigues began to replace Sarah's husband with the Duke of
Ormonde. In spite of the limitations imposed by the Revolution
of 1688, the sovereign possessed crucial power and Harley was
succeeding in attracting that power to the Tory side, where the
Queen's sympathies naturally lay. Dissatisfaction with the war
throughout the country was high: rioting, commonplace anyway in eighteenth-century England, became more frequent and
more violent; in June three army regiments mutinied in York-
shire. Marlborough's succession of victories were shaded in the
public mind by memories of almost twenty years of intermittent
fighting on the Continent and in the colonies. In June, 1710,
the Queen, with Harley's approval, dismissed Marlborough's
son-in-law, the Earl of Sunderland from his post as Secretary
of State for the Southern Department. The Junto's fate was
sealed.

It was, of course, a crisis in Richard Steele's small world, too.
Sunderland was his immediate superior in the government, but
Steele was a very minor functionary, editor of the *Gazette* and
holder of a pair of modest sinecures. By adroit maneuvering a
civil servant in his position could easily hold on through a
change of ministry, especially inasmuch as Robert Harley was
known to be attempting to form a center party, attracting support from both Whig and Tory elements. Jonathan Swift, who
had associations with the Junto, maintained an attitude of detachment in Ireland; in June he ordered the arrangement can-
celed under which Steele was to publish his volume of miscellanies.[17] Caution was proper for the circumspect.

[17] *The Correspondence of Jonathan Swift, D.D.,* ed. F. E. Ball (London,
1910–1914), I, 185.

The least circumspect of men had made his choice. A series of violently partisan *Tatlers* in late June and early July announced to London that Richard Steele's fortunes were tied to those of the Junto Ministry. Addison was in Dublin, unable to impose caution if he had been willing to do so. No. 187 was given over largely to a letter from "Pasquin," Bickerstaff's spy in Rome, who reports that the situation in England is there being compared with that of Hannibal and his enemy Hanno in Carthage: Hannibal, after conquering Rome, was recalled by the Senate through the connivance of a faction at home. Bickerstaff's readers could derive the analogy between Hannibal and Marlborough, and a faction and the Tories. Two issues of the Tory periodical *The Moderator* deplored this *Tatler,* firing, as it were, warning shots across the bow. Even at that late date, however, much of *The Tatler*'s political maneuvering was concealed by the paper's bland façade. By this time *The Tatler* had settled into the format of the periodical essay; instead, that is, of several separate sections in each issue, as originally planned, Steele would present an essay on one subject or a few subjects, using the mask of Isaac Bickerstaff. News reporting as such was almost completely gone; No. 210 contains the last bit, a report of the Whig Stanhope's victory in Spain, and the partisan motivations for this inclusion are so obvious as not to require comment. Steele's essays are almost always purposive; he has a rhetorical object in mind, if not the righting of the political scheme of things, then the reform of manners, or of the drama. In No. 182, for example, Bickerstaff discusses the pleasures of theater-going, the high quality of Cibber's and Wilks's acting, and the proper subjects of drama, alluding to the forthcoming dramatic work of a "young poet" under his tutelage. There is reason to believe that Bickerstaff's young poet is Richard Steele and the drama *The Conscious Lovers,* not actually produced until 1722.[18] This *Tatler* may then properly be called a *ballon d'essai.*

[18] Cf. John Loftis, *Steele at Drury Lane* (Berkeley, 1952), pp. 186–88.

Literature was second, but only second, in Richard Steele's public life: politics was first. By this time *The Tatler* had become so engulfed in controversy that readers scrutinized each issue for partisan content when it came off the press. Sometimes an allegory or a personal application was discerned where none existed. No. 191, containing the notorious "Polypragmon" portrait, may be a case in point. Though widely given out to be a satirical character of Harley, internal evidence for such an interpretation is at best doubtful, and Steele later (in *Guardian* No. 53) specifically denied having Harley in mind when he wrote it. No. 193, however, was a forthright and effective blow in the Whig cause, calculated to rally the wavering and forestall Harley's attempts at a coalition. As a turning point in Steele's life it deserves some attention.

Steele begins the essay by defending himself against the accusations of those who said his motive in taking sides on political questions had been money (this, it will be recalled, had been Mrs. Manley's point in the first volume of her *Memoirs of Europe* and Swift was to use the idea frequently too), pointing out that "when a man declares himself openly on one side" neither side will reward him, the one being hostile, the other sure of him. "For which reason, I thought it was the shortest way to impartiality, to put myself beyond further hopes or fears, by declaring myself. . . ." He then writes briefly about the theater and proposes to introduce a letter from old John Downes, prompter for many years at Lincoln's Inn Fields and author of *Roscius Anglicanus*, a book well known to students of eighteenth-century drama. The letter is, of course, not by Downes but by some Whig correspondent, perhaps by Steele himself. Downes recalls how a "deep intriguer" had earlier "worked himself into the sole management and direction of the theatre," though it was obvious that his plans were harmful to "the good old British actors" and tended to the "introduction of foreign pretenders." Downes doubts that the new company will succeed:

[T]he actors having a great mind to play 'The Tempest,' there is not a man of them, when he is to perform anything above dumb show, is capable of acting with a good grace so much as the part of Trinculo. However, the master persists in his design, and is fitting up the old 'storm'; but I am afraid he will not be able to procure able sailors or experienced officers for love or money.

Besides the reference to Harley's difficulties in getting experienced men to replace those employed by Godolphin and the Junto, the phrase about "able sailors or experienced soldiers" has to do with the expectation that Marlborough would not serve under the new government, and the allusion to Trinculo possibly recalled Harley's notorious fondness for the bottle.

All this is delightful eighteenth-century pamphlet warfare at its best, but from Steele's point of view singularly ill-timed. Nothing could stop the fall of the old ministry; less than a month later Lord Treasurer Godolphin at the Queen's request broke his White Staff of office. Even the most sanguine Whig recognized the inevitability of a dissolution and a new election. The Tories were meanwhile gaining powerful new voices in the propaganda battle, including a new periodical *The Examiner,* the first number of which appeared in early August. When Henry St. John wrote *A Letter to the Examiner* in August, he associated the Censor, Bickerstaff, with Defoe and others serving a "Factious Cabal." [19]

Thus identified as a Whig, Steele could look only to that party for support and it was forthcoming. Lord Cowper, Lord Chancellor until September and an able and moderate Junto member, drafted and published an anonymous reply to St. John's *Letter* under the title *A Letter to Isaac Bickerstaff, Esq.; Occasioned by the Letter to the Examiner.* He praises *The Tatler* generously, for showing how "simplicity of nature and common

---

[19] Reprinted in Swift, *The Examiner and Other Pieces Written in 1710–11,* ed. Herbert Davis (Oxford, 1940), p. 221. Defoe was at the time in Harley's pay, a small commentary itself on early eighteenth-century politics.

reason" necessarily conduce to form the "best servants of a prince, and the truest patriots." "But . . . in doing this," Cowper writes, "you took a proper season to expose some of those brutish notions of government, and vile arts of wretched pretenders to politicks. . . ." When Volume III of the collected *Tatler* appeared in April, 1711, included in Steele's dedication to Cowper was the sentence: "Forgive me, My Lord, when I cannot conceal from you, that I shall never hereafter behold you, but I shall behold you, as lately, defending the brave and the unfortunate."

It is somewhat unclear whether Steele places himself here, along with Marlborough, in the category of the brave or the unfortunate. Cowper's bold words may have revived Steele's spirits; they were otherwise of little value except as an indication that better things were ahead for Steele when the Junto returned to power; that day, however, was four long years off. Addison had returned from Ireland, his eyes badly overstrained but the heir of his brother Gulston's considerable estate. From mid-summer on, with the return of Addison and the appearance of *The Examiner,* Isaac Bickerstaff took a more cautious line in political matters. There was good reason: alert Tory editors were dogging his footsteps. It was better policy to dwell on happier topics, subjects more in keeping with the image of the good-natured Isaac Bickerstaff, such as No. 242:

> This accidental talk of [Horace and Juvenal] runs me from my design, which was to tell some coxcombs that run about this town with the name of smart satirical fellows, that they are by no means qualified for the characters they pretend to, of being severe upon other men, for they want good nature. . . . There is a certain impartiality necessary to make what a man says bear any weight with those he speaks to. This quality, with respect to men's errors and vices, is never seen but in good-natured men.

No critic, Tory or Whig, could take exception to this sentiment, except perhaps to observe that Bickerstaff was coming to impartiality rather late in the season.

In spite of these amends, Steele's position as an employee of the government was parlous and growing worse. He had committed himself too far to survive under a Tory ministry. Jonathan Swift returned to London in September, not a little carried away by the blandishment of politicians. He expressed his belief to Stella that Steele would lose his place as Gazetteer, "all the world detesting his engaging in parties." His predictions were fulfilled sometime shortly before the middle of October, when Steele resigned from the *Gazette,* keeping, however, the Commissionership of Stamps. Swift's remarks to Stella have provided the evidence for the statement repeated through the years that Steele lost his post because of *Tatler* No. 193, the Downes *Tatler.*[20] Actually the Gazetteership was by its very nature a post requiring someone whose predispositions were at least not hostile to the ministry in power. The opportunity, the necessity for editing the news in a manner favorable to the government was part of the job. Hence, Steele's loss of the editorship was foreordained; his principles would not have let him take part in the propaganda effort for Harley's government. The Tories would, he knew, set about discrediting the Junto and Marlborough forthwith.

Though the *Gazette* was lost, the Commissionership of Stamps was not. This position was not politically sensitive, and in plain truth Steele needed the income from the post. Robert Harley knew he needed it, for Harley was a master politician who always, as if by instinct, tried to build support wherever he thought it possible; negotiations behind the scenes were his special talent. No man knew better the value of the confidential aside, the well-timed minor favor. A conference was scheduled, with Swift as intermediary, between Harley and Steele. The Treasurer told Steele that he could continue in the Stamp Commission and even hinted of further employment if all went well; what Harley doubtless had in mind was neutralizing Steele's

---

[20] *Journal,* ed. Williams, I, 67.

propaganda.[21] The evidence is not decisive but it seems likely that the price the Treasurer exacted in return for the Commissionership was ending *The Tatler*.

At first this must have seemed a high price. In a year and a half, Steele could reflect, the paper had established itself as far and away the outstanding periodical in English. No other editor had such talented contributors; Steele himself was writing better than he ever had and Addison was at the peak of his powers. In eighteen months Steele's image had been transformed in the London mind from that of a minor playwright and Kit-Cat follower to that of Isaac Bickerstaff, Censor of Great Britain, editor of the best-known paper in the land. All this was hard to give up.

On the other hand, Steele's incursions into politics, though always a part of the paper, had become more frequent and annoying to Tory readers; circulation may have declined. By the time of the meeting with Harley, Steele was certainly aware that the paper was suffering from its identification with the Whigs. Perhaps the discreet Addison suggested that it was time to retire Isaac Bickerstaff in favor of someone new, someone not so closely associated with the fallen Junto as the Censor of Great Britain.[22]

On 2 January 1711 Steele published *Tatler* No. 271, ending the series without warning and with only the unsatisfactory explanation that "The printer having informed me, that there are as many of these papers printed as will make four volumes, I am now come to the end of my ambition in this matter, and have nothing further to say to the world under the character of Isaac Bickerstaff." The last *Tatler* finds Steele meditating on

[21] Cf. *Corr.*, pp. 43, 268. John Gay, writing the next year, guessed that the paper may have been ended "as a sort of submission to, and composition with the Government. . . ." See his *The Present State of Wit*, ed. Donald F. Bond in The Augustan Reprint Society, Series One (Ann Arbor, 1947), No. 3, p. 3.

[22] Though Swift (*Journal*, I, 151) maintained that Addison was as surprised as he at the sudden ending.

the disparity between professions and actions, conscious as in the days of *The Christian Hero* of his own shortcomings.

> The general purpose of the whole has been to recommend truth, innocence, honour, and virtue, as the chief ornaments of life; but I considered, that severity of manners was absolutely necessary to him who would censure others, and for that reason, and that only, chose to talk in a mask. I shall not carry my humility so far as to call myself a vicious man; but at the same time must confess, my life is at best but pardonable. And with no greater character than this, a man would make but an indifferent progress in attacking prevailing and fashionable vices, which Mr. Bickerstaff has done with a freedom of spirit that would have lost both its beauty and efficacy, had it been pretended to by Mr. Steele.

A graceful compliment to Addison, a brief statement acknowledging the paper's politics ("I could not be cold enough to conceal my opinion"), a few random remarks, Richard Steele signs his name and *The Tatler* is done.

Richard Steele had thus revealed himself as the author of the most popular periodical in the English-speaking world; what would its readers have known about the author himself? Though of course long known to the intimate London world of court and coffeehouse as the author of amusing comedies and the creator of Isaac Bickerstaff, Richard Steele himself was a stranger to most of his readers in the provinces and colonies. As Gazetteer he had acquired important experience in editing and writing, but because of the nature of the position he had written anonymously; anonymity, he explained in the last issue of *The Tatler,* had also seemed proper in the conduct of that periodical. Isaac Bickerstaff's tastes, opinions, and crotchets were quoted, imitated, and discussed on all sides, but the person and personality of Richard Steele were little known to most of *The Tatler's* subscribers. This fact must have been borne in upon him as he contemplated the approach of his thirty-ninth birthday in March, 1711, and noted the remorseless progress of

Harley's followers at the expense of the Junto Whigs. Beyond the London literary world, Richard Steele as Richard Steele was a minor figure once again.

Something like this doubtless concerned him, for within the next twenty-four months he had sat for no less than three portraits, by Richardson, Thornhill, and Kneller,[23] as if to insure that his likeness, as distinct from that of Bickerstaff, become known. The portrait by Kneller, done for the Kit-Cat Club, is clearly the best as one would expect, but all agree in general outline: the round face, the alert brown eyes set well into his head, the bee-stung lips curled as if ready to smile. His skin was olive in an age that valued pallor and his "dusky" or "tallow" complexion was often used by foes as evidence of his humble origin. Beginning to go fat in 1711, Steele was still a powerful man, with large chest and shoulders; he was still possessed of much of the physical strength and energy which had been demanded by his army service.

Those who knew him were fond of him. Steele was to make many political enemies in his lifetime, but few who were well acquainted with him, with the significant exception of Jonathan Swift, retained their ill will very long. He was pre-eminently the good-natured man, rejoicing in the company of friends and family, quick to dispute but also quick to forget the dispute, the soul of conviviality in a convivial society, "born," as Lady Mary Wortley Montagu said of him years later, "for happiness."

Though he had been a reckless financial investor since his army days, with a special affection for the scheme for instant wealth, he had little or no interest in cards or gambling as a social activity, beyond that of their being popular in his society and hence topics for his plays and periodicals. Nor did hunting and riding appeal to him, at least in his maturity; perhaps the years on a cavalry horse had exhausted his interest in the pleasures of the chase. By 1711 he was enjoying the rewards of

[23] Cf. *The Theatre,* ed. John Loftis (Oxford, 1962), pp. 51, 131.

a settled domestic existence, and if he was not at the theater, or conversing in a coffeehouse, or dining at the estate of a wealthy politician (all of which activities were in a real sense, business), he was at home. Mrs. Steele was a woman of good common sense and the children were a continuing pleasure to him; his home was a source of comfort and stability not available in 1711 to Addison or Pope or Gay or Swift. Steele was resolved to work out a mode of living which included his wife and children; a few years later he was to astound Augustan London by dedicating a book to Mrs. Steele. "That I think them," he wrote there, "preferable to all other children, I know, is the effect of passion and instinct. That I believe you the best of wives, I know proceeds from experience and reason." [24]

In addition to his city home, however, Steele seemed to require a place in the country, a hideaway as distinguished from an estate; he was to own several in his lifetime like the Hovel in Hampton and the cottage on Hampstead Heath. These retreats reflected the contemplative aspects of his character and, judging by what is known about the way he composed his plays, they were where he planned his literary activities and, in all probability, wrote many of his essays, several at a time.

For a few weeks in December and January that winter there were no essays to be written, but much to be planned.

---

[24] *Correspondence,* p. 489.

CHAPTER VI

The Years of
The Spectator

THE MONTHS BETWEEN March, 1711, and December, 1712, when the original *Spectator* appeared represent the high tide of Addison's and Steele's literary careers. As no one had earlier produced a periodical that was *The Spectator's* equal, so none of the many that appeared in the century following ever quite came up to its high standard, its varied excellence, its multiplicity of good things. And neither of the collaborators was able afterward to command the time and energy required for such a large effort. It was a large effort: five hundred and fifty-five numbers on folio half-sheet appearing six days a week, each with extensive new advertising; collected the paper ran to seven good-sized octavo volumes.

A periodical of these dimensions needed a good editor and *The Spectator* had two, both now experienced in every phase of journalism, both shrewd judges of their audience's taste and wishes. *The Tatler* had been of Steele's creation and nurture but the new paper was from the beginning a joint enterprise. Though operating with considerable freedom in 1711 and 1712 through the use of the convenient narrator, Mr. Spectator, the neutral onlooker, Addison and Steele were nevertheless faced with the political situation: they were members of the opposition and party feelings were bound to rise eventually as long as the problem of Queen Anne's successor remained unresolved.

By December, 1712, Richard Steele was about ready to commit himself to propaganda warfare; in March, 1711, a certain pose of detachment was still possible. For Steele, at least, it was always a pose.

Mr. Spectator had many things to observe and comment on besides politics; all the variety of London life which had fascinated the Irish co-author these twenty years also appealed to the reading public, it soon appeared. *The Tatler* was both a model and a source, especially with respect to tone. Mr. Spectator spoke like Isaac Bickerstaff: learned, witty, affable, faintly pedantic, slightly patronizing, like some well-bred uncle addressing his nephews — and nieces — who appeared to need instruction but who also must be humored in their youthful desire for novelty.

The paper was a runaway success. Circulation figures rose and kept rising; by mid-March, 1711, in the tenth number, Addison could report a daily distribution of three thousand and, with humorous exaggeration perhaps, a readership of sixty thousand. It seems probable that circulation remained above three thousand until the imposition of the Stamp Tax in August, 1712, at times considerably above.[1] The paper was, then, grossing at a penny per copy more than £300 a month for most of its original life, not including reprints or advertising revenue. Even allowing for the expenses involved in printing and distribution, *The Spectator* must have brought its authors greater direct financial rewards than any other enterprise in literary history to that time.

The operation of such an enterprise required, of course, more organization than even a prosperous periodical like *The Tatler* had demanded. Two printing shops, presumably those of Jacob Tonson and Samuel Buckley, alternated in printing the press

---

[1] Information on printing and circulation derived from Donald F. Bond, "The First Printing of the *Spectator*," *Modern Philology*, XLVII (1950), 164–77.

runs and were assisted at various times in the distribution by at
least a dozen other establishments. Steele was the general editorial supervisor, responsible for seeing the paper through the
press, while both Addison and Steele wrote papers — and wrote
papers. With its six-a-week publishing schedule and ascending
circulation, *The Spectator* must have consumed inordinate
amounts of Steele's time, even though the authors, with two
printing shops at their disposal, were now able to submit copy
for three or more essays in advance to the compositor. The train
of editorial assistants developed later, though by mid-summer
1711 Addison's cousin Eustace Budgell was beginning to bear
a hand occasionally. In order to get some time away from the
lurking deadline, no doubt, the pair agreed to put in monthly
stints during that summer, Addison contributing most of the
July numbers and Steele all but two of those in August, doing
twenty-five papers in thirty-one days. Dredging for subjects
came hard. In June Steele penned his wife a note of apology.

> Madam,
>   I heartily beg your pardon for my omission to write yesterday.
> It was no failure of my tender regard for you; but having been
> very much perplexed in my thoughts on the subject of my last
> [paper], made me determine to suspend speaking of it until I
> came myself. But, my lovely creature, know it is not in the
> power of age, or misfortune, or any other accident which hangs
> over human life, to take from me the pleasing esteem I have for
> you. . . .

By August the desperate editor was printing this letter and
several others to Prue (with addressee anonymous of course)
as "Images of a Worthy Passion."

    To attract new readers, Addison and Steele provided plenty
of novelty and also used features carried over from *The Tatler*.
Reform, the reformation of manners and of the drama, continued, with a light touch, but fundamentally serious in intention. Addressing the female audience directly, Mr. Spectator

declared in Steele's No. 4 that "I shall take it for the greatest glory of my work, if among reasonable women this paper may furnish tea-table talk." And the letters-to-the-editor feature which had been successful in the earlier paper was revived. Addison called for correspondents in the first issue; the response was so great that by late March he had appointed the perfumer Charles Lillie to act as the Spectator's deputy, receiving all letters and advertisements for "the City of Westminster and the Dutchy of Lancaster," while Buckley, the printer, continued to handle mail for the City of London.[2]

Dramatic reform often occupied Steele's thoughts; *The Spectator* carried on *The Tatler's* crusade, always a losing one, against imported operas, especially Italian. Everything was wrong: the translations, the use of recitative, the scenery. Young Frederick Handel's first venture in the English theater, his opera *Rinaldo,* had opened in February, 1711, to enthusiastic audiences. Addison, who associated Handel with the Italians, calling him "Seignior," dissented. "If the Italians have a genius for music above the English, the English have a genius for other performances of a much higher nature. . . ." The criticism smacks of sour grapes in view of Addison's own abortive experience with opera, but the editors were consistent if wrongheaded in their disapproval of Italian opera. They had positive ideas on the subject. Addison's and Steele's objections, like those of many other Englishmen including John Dennis, were based on what they regarded as the subordination of words, that is, poetry, to music in the Italian opera. The sister arts in the eighteenth century, Jean Hagstrum has reminded us, were poetry and painting; music was considered a lesser art.[3] Thus Addison's remarks in *The Spectator* (No. 18) concerning the absurd effects of rec-

[2] For interesting examples of the editor's use of letters, see Richmond P. Bond, *New Letters to the "Tatler" and "Spectator"* (Austin, 1959).
[3] Hagstrum, *The Sister Arts* (Chicago, 1958), *passim.* See also Siegmund A. E. Betz, "The Operatic Criticism of the *Tatler* and *Spectator,*" *Musical Quarterly,* XXXI (1945), 318–30; *Spectator,* Nos. 5, 29.

itative, especially in translation ("I have known the word 'and' pursued through the whole gamut, have been entertained with many a melodious 'the'. . . .") were related to his statement about the English genius for "other performances." These other performances dealt principally with words, poetry, and put music in its proper secondary place.

Steele's answer to the menace of Italian opera was a project not fulfilled until years later, a project so redolent of the man's character that it deserves some attention at this point. He proposed a series of entertainments or performances which would include music but would also embrace poetry readings, lectures on learned subjects, and scientific demonstrations. "All works of invention," as he was later to write, "all the sciences, as well as mechanick arts will have their turn. . . ." [4] The series was to be held in some permanent hall, would be in certain respects like a repertory theater, and would be known as the Censorium, a name recalling Isaac Bickerstaff's title and also, as Steele explained it rather obscurely, by reference to Newton's *Optics,* alluding to the "organ of sense, as the eye is of sight. . . ." Though the project's fulfillment was several years off, Steele made a beginning in early 1711 by soliciting the help of John Hughes, a Whig friend and minor poet, in revising Dryden's *Alexander's Feast* for a new setting by the composer Thomas Clayton. Clayton had experienced a limited success with his opera *Arsinoe* in 1706 and had written a poor setting the next year for Addison's single operatic attempt, *Rosamond,* which had failed resoundingly, frightening, according to one contemporary, "all England with its abominable musick. . . ." [5]

Undeterred by Clayton's record, Steele set about organizing the recital, striking a blow, as he must have felt, for English poetry and English music while pursuing his goal of the refor-

<hr>

[4] MS. note quoted in John Loftis, "Richard Steele's Censorium," *Huntington Library Quarterly,* XIV (1950), p. 57. My discussion relies on this article.
[5] Smithers, p. 118.

mation of manners and the correction of public taste. Hughes examined Clayton's score and concluded mildly that "upon the whole, as far as I am able to judge, the music . . . tho' in some places agreeable, will not please masters." [6] After lavish advertising in *The Spectator,* the performance took place in a hired hall in York Buildings during a driving rainstorm on 24 May 1711.[7] The first performance and a second on the twenty-ninth seem to have stirred little comment; Steele persevered. *The Spectator* advertised a concert at the same location for 16 July, where poetry would be sung to Clayton's setting, good poetry: Dryden's *Alexander's Feast* again and Matthew Prior's song "If Wine and Music have the Power," as well as a poem by Swift's protégé, William Harrison. Later that month Steele was planning bigger and better performances for the following winter; he enlisted the help of young Alexander Pope, whose recently published *Essay on Criticism* had attracted much favorable attention. Pope, a little embarrassed, perhaps, but flattered too, wrote his friend Caryll:

> I have two letters from Mr. Steele, the subject of which is to persuade me to write a musicall interlude to be set next winter by Clayton, whose interest he espouses with great zeal. His expression is, Pray oblige Mr Clayton, that is me, so far as, &c. The desire I have to gratify Mr Steele has made me consent to his request; tho' 'tis a task that otherwise I'm not very fond of.

Steele's zeal was not as Pope believed directed toward Clayton's relief but to the fulfillment of his dream of the Censorium, a dream still unformed. Later he was to return to the project with concrete plans for the further reformation of English taste.[8]

Educational reform had its proper place in *The Spectator* too. Steele's interest in children seems somehow out of keeping with

[6] *Corr.,* p. 46.
[7] *Journal,* ed. Williams, I, 279; *London Stage,* I, 251, 253.
[8] *The Correspondence of Alexander Pope,* ed. George Sherburn (Oxford, 1956), I, 132; and John Loftis, *Steele at Drury Lane* (Berkeley, 1952), pp. 102–4.

his age, vaguely un-Augustan, perhaps because so many of the great eighteenth-century writers like Swift, Pope, and Johnson were childless. The proper rearing of children was a central concern of Steele's as his essays, plays, and criticism attest, and one does not have to relate the concern either to Steele's own difficult childhood or to his burgeoning family, though both probably had something to do with it. Mr. Spectator's educational suggestions were practical and specific; in February, 1712, and again in May of that year he appealed for support of the charity schools. This movement to provide primary education for impoverished children had been started by the Society for Promoting Christian Knowledge in the first meeting of 8 March 1699; eight years later 216 such schools were in operation, by 1714, over a thousand. The permanent secretary of the S.P.C.K. during the years of *The Spectator* was an American, the Reverend Henry Newman of Harvard College and Massachusetts, who had come to London under the sponsorship of Steele's old friend Colonel Joseph Dudley. For years Steele and Newman carried on an intermittent correspondence and the essayist was always happy to oblige his friend with a word of praise for the charity schools. "It is monstrous," he wrote in No. 294, "how a man can live with so little reflection as to fancy he is not in a condition very unjust . . . while he enjoys wealth, and exerts no benevolence or bounty to others. . . . Would you do an handsome thing without return? Do it for an infant that is not sensible of the obligation. Would you do it for public good? Do it for one who would be an honest artificer. Would you do it for the sake of heaven? Give it to one who shall be instructed in the worship of him for whose sake you gave it." Remembering his own boyhood on charitable foundations at Charterhouse and Oxford, Steele always cheerfully repaid this sort of debt.[9]

[9] Newman and Dudley: Yale Univ. Library MS. 45M–580 (9), letter of Newman to Dudley. See also Leonard Cowie, *Henry Newman: An American in England, 1708–43* (London, 1956), *passim,* and the MS. Letterbooks at the Society's headquarters in London.

Neither manners nor dress nor education wanted reformation so much, according to Steele's way of thinking, as politics, but in 1711 he was not able to take his accustomed place in party controversy: *The Spectator* drew readers from all sides. Nevertheless, something could be done under the cover of neutrality. Addison, writing as Mr. Spectator in the first number, declared that "I never espoused any party with violence, and am resolved to observe an exact neutrality between the Whigs and Tories, unless I shall be forced to declare myself by the hostilities of either side." This passage is often quoted to illustrate Addison's moderating influence, and the inference is generally drawn that Steele was responsible for any partisan coloration the paper may have acquired from time to time. Actually the passage is a standard disclaimer of the sort prefaced to partisan sermons, pamphlets, and dedications without number; Defoe, to cite a prominent example, begins his *Review* with a similar statement. Decrying party and faction was one of the great clichés of the age; the most orthodox party hacks did it as a matter of course.

But Addison was a subtle man, and he knew that Harley's ministry was strong and growing stronger. He had learned directly of Steele's troubles with *The Tatler;* restraint was in order, political matters must be handled gingerly. Thus in the third *Spectator,* for example, Addison returns to the dream vision, presenting an allegory of "public credit," a beautiful young lady threatened by a young man. While he threatens, the bags of gold which she guards disappear. This not very complicated allegory refers to James the Pretender, whose approach, Addison shows, diminishes the credit of England. As the principal objectives of the Tories during the next four years would be to secure the peace and to discredit Marlborough and the fallen government, so the task of the Whigs, looking to Queen Anne's eventual death, would be to identify the Tories with the Roman Catholic Pretender. Economic theory took on political coloration as well, of course. The very notion of credit was anathema to many Tories, to whom it represented machinations of the moneyed interests. Pope gives this view final expression in *Moral Essay* No. III:

> Blest paper-credit! last and best supply!
> That lends Corruption lighter wings to fly!
> Gold imp'd by thee, can compass hardest things,
> Can pocket States, can fetch or carry Kings. . . .[10]

Whig and Tory; the moneyed and the landed interests; these are the traditional divisions. But if an analysis of the politics of Queen Anne's reign demonstrates anything, it demonstrates that too much reliance must not be placed on such easy labels. Members of Parliament voted together for various reasons: connections with or dependence on the Court or the Treasury or trade, place of residence, family relationship, attitude toward the Church and Church policy, and so on. It was an age of shifting loyalties, and party lines could not be rigidly held despite the best efforts of party leadership. Nevertheless, these two terms "moneyed" and "landed" were often employed by speakers and writers of the time and have some value in determining political sympathies. The two interests were represented by some writers as the great divisions of the economy, the landed Tories and the moneyed Whigs. In actuality, of course, the labels were often reversed; there were moneyed Tories in great numbers and as many landed Whigs: Robert Walpole, the arch-Whig himself, was a fox-hunting, hard-drinking country squire if one ever existed. The terms do have value, however, at least to students of propaganda, because of their currency as labels; however far they were from fact, they were believed in by some as signifying a genuine difference between Tory and Whig. Jonathan Swift, for example, used the distinction repeatedly and to great effect, as in his *Some Reasons . . . in a Letter to a Whig-Lord*

---

[10] "Epistle to Bathurst" in *Epistles to Several Persons,* ed. F. W. Bateson (London, 1951), p. 90, lines 69–72.

(1712) : "A standing senate of persons, nobly born of great patrimonial estates, and of pious learned prelates, is not easily perverted from intending the true interest of their prince and country; whereas we have found by experience, that a corrupt ministry, at the head of a monied faction, is able to procure a majority of whom they please, to represent the people. . . ." [11] Swift refers specifically to the House of Lords here, but the allusion to "patrimonial estates" is meant to stir visions of honest men and good land, contrasting neatly with the avaricious "monied faction."

One of *The Spectator*'s main motifs — and it was a theme of which Richard Steele never tired — was the sympathetic representation of those "trading interests" which did, in truth, represent a large part of the Whig strength. This, Addison no doubt emphasized to his unruly partner, could be done subtly, while, indeed, the editors proclaimed the paper's nonpartisan stand and cried down faction. Thus the Spectator could view the Royal Exchange with English pride (No. 69) : "It gives me a secret satisfaction, and, in some measure, gratifies my vanity, as I am an Englishman, to see so rich an assembly of countrymen and foreigners consulting together upon the private business of mankind, and making this metropolis a kind of emporium for the whole earth." Who could object? This is no mere partisan rhetoric. It is patriotism; trade benefits everyone. "Trade, without enlarging the British territories, has given us a kind of additional empire: It has multiplied the number of the rich, made our landed estates infinitely more valuable than they were formerly. . . ."

More effective and subtler than the essays extolling moneyed values was the presentation of those values dramatically in the club itself. The club device as such was not entirely new; Defoe had employed the motif in his *Review;* Addison had used some-

[11] *Political Tracts, 1711–1713,* ed. Herbert Davis (Princeton, 1951), p. 125.

thing similar in his unpublished "Dialogues upon Medals." [12]
And Steele, of course, had written plays in which certain favorite
ideas of his were represented. Like the dialogue and the play, the
club kept the authors safely removed from their materials. If
Sir Roger de Coverley, the country squire, emerged from his
arguments with the merchant Sir Andrew Freeport rather the
worse, one could hardly maintain that Addison and Steele were
defaming Tories for the benefit of Whigs, even if this was
psychologically true.

From the beginning the authors diminish the reader's respect for Sir Roger's abilities even as they accent his good
personal qualities. He wears clothes that are out of date (as out
of date as his ideas, the reader is intended to infer), is a landlord "rather beloved than esteemed" whose tenants grow rich,
presumably by cheating their rentor. Sir Roger is a Justice who
fills his chair with "great abilities, and three months ago gain'd
universal applause by explaining a passage in the Game-Act."
The game laws with their heavy penalties for poaching had always been the special province of the squire, for whose benefit
they were passed, but were considered a nuisance or bore by the
merchant and downright tyranny by the hungry rural poor, as
Fielding shows in *Tom Jones.* Glossing the Game Act was
scarcely a demonstration of legal ability.

In sharp contrast with Sir Roger is Sir Andrew Freeport.
"His notions of trade are noble and generous. . . . He is
acquainted with commerce in all its parts, and will tell you that
it is a stupid and barbarous way to extend dominion by arms;
for true power is to be got by arts and industry." Freeport is
diligent, frugal, yet companionable; altogether a formidable
person, one far better qualified to govern the affairs of the country than a Sir Roger, we are intended to gather. Unfortunately
Sir Andrew is dead dramatically; he is as colorless as a clean

[12] Cf. Smithers, pp. 203–4.

sheet of ledger filler; he bores readers, who have always therefore ignored the hero of the club. But one should not make too
much of the club's politics. Dr. Johnson observes in his "Life
of Addison" that the Tory squire Sir Roger de Coverley became
that writer's favorite club member, as he has been for almost
every reader since. The political coloration of *The Spectator* is
true-blue Whig, but it is according to Addison's judicious hand.

Mr. Spectator threaded his politic way cautiously in 1711;
even so Steele's disagreement with Swift, noticeable the year
before, was widening as it must. During the winter of 1710–
1711, Swift had assumed the direction of *The Examiner* and
under his guidance the Tory periodical had acquired strength
and point. Mrs. Manley served an apprenticeship on the paper
and succeeded Swift as editor in July, while he turned his energies to completing his great political pamphlet, *The Conduct of
the Allies.* In late July the triumvirate of Addison, Swift, and
Steele met for dinner at Jacob Tonson's. "Mr. Addison," Swift
reported to Stella, "and I talked as usual, and as if we had seen
one another yesterday, and Steele and I were very easy, although
I writ him lately a biting letter, in answer to one of his. . . ." [13]
The principal source of friction between Swift and Steele was
still Marlborough; stripped of political support at home, the
Duke continued to win, brilliantly, on the Continent.

Another friend of the old days was falling away from Steele
in 1711, though not because of politics. John Dennis was a convinced Whig; he had known Steele at least since the days of their
association with *Commendatory Verses* at the turn of the century, and like Steele had enjoyed the patronage of the great
Whig politicians, especially Lord Halifax. His reputation as a
critic has suffered unduly from the controversy with Pope about
the *Essay on Criticism;* Dennis was a learned man and most of
his important works have a saving stratum of insight. His concern for theatrical reform no doubt helped form a bond of friend-

[13] *Journal,* ed. Williams, I, 321.

ship with Steele, whose views were similar. But Dennis had a temper always near the flash point and in 1711 it was somehow ignited. Some jocular allusions to critics and criticism in *The Tatler* had first stirred Dennis; his livelihood, after all, depended on the public's taking criticism seriously. Harder for Dennis to swallow, no doubt, was Steele's success; here was an old friend with intellectual gifts no better than his own, if as good, who had gained fame and fortune almost overnight and who could now afford to indulge in pleasantries about grubbing critics. Had pride perhaps changed Steele?

In the summer of 1710 Dennis' suspicions had apparently been confirmed. He had directed a letter to Steele seeking an appointment; Steele had failed to reply. Furious, Dennis had written, asking that an advertisement be inserted in the next *Tatler,* "by which the world might be inform'd that the Captain Steele, who lives now in Bury-Street, is not the Captain of the same name, who lived there two years ago, and that the acquaintance of the military person who inhabited there formerly may go look for their old friend, e'en where they can find him." [14] Perhaps Pope's *Essay on Criticism* revived the smoldering quarrel in 1711; Dennis may have discovered that Pope and Steele were on good terms. At any rate, Dennis dispatched a series of letters to Steele, protesting what he took to be slights in *The Spectator;* later in the year he selected some of these letters for publication with his *Essay on the Genius and Writings of Shakespear.* They are extreme, of course, full of the muscular personal attack which the Augustans deplored but delighted in: "I cannot but congratulate your incomparable felicity, it being plain that you have got more reputation in three years' time than Milton has done in fifty years, or than Shakespear has in an hundred." [15] Steele said nothing, turned the other cheek and was rewarded with

[14] *Corr.,* p. 42.
[15] *The Critical Writings of John Dennis,* ed. E. N. Hooker (Baltimore, 1939–1943), II, 28.

many years of critical attack; what Dennis did not know was
that the papers to which he took exception (Nos. 40, 42, 70
and 74) were all written by Addison. Is it not strange that Addison never bothered to let Dennis know this fact?

The year closed on a happier note. Addison called Pope's
Essay on Criticism "a masterpiece in its kind" in the issue of
20 December and the young poet wrote a graceful note of thanks
(to Steele whom he took to be the author), declaring that he
would "in good earnest be fonder of your friendship than the
world's applause." [16] The year 1711 had indeed been a year of
literary achievement for Addison and Steele; their friendship
was worth cultivating. *The Spectator* had become a large business operation, and a uniquely influential paper. If all had not
been well, to use Steele's phrase, all had certainly not been ill.

The year 1712 opened ominously for the Whigs. Swift's
pamphlet, *The Conduct of the Allies,* a devastating examination
of Marlborough's war, had become a major publishing success.
Between first publication in November, 1711, and the end of
January some eleven thousand copies were sold and a new
seventh edition was being readied.[17] Worse still, Robert Harley
had cracked Whig control of the House of Lords by inducing
the Queen to create twelve new peers, all safely Tory. When the
dozen took their place in the House, the Whig Earl of Wharton
inquired sarcastically if they voted by their foreman. Everywhere Tories flexed their muscles: Robert Walpole was accused
of corruption as Secretary-at-War, expelled from the Commons
(though by a narrow margin) and committed to the Tower in
January.[18] In the midst of Whig gloom, Richard Steele chose
to fly his colors, dedicating the first two volumes of the collected

[16] *Corr.,* p. 52. Steele thanked Pope but promised to make him acquainted
with the true author.

[17] Swift, *Political Tracts* (see note 11), p. ix.

[18] J. H. Plumb, *Sir Robert Walpole: The Making of a Statesman* (London,
1956), pp. 178–80. For a detailed account of the Swift-Steele quarrel at this
time see Bertrand A. Goldgar, *The Curse of Party* (Lincoln, Neb., 1961),
pp. 91–98.

Spectator (which appeared on 8 January) to the Junto lords, Somers and Halifax. "I should not act the part of an impartial Spectator," he began the dedication to Somers, "if I dedicated the following papers to one who is not of the most consummate and most acknowledged merit." The pose of impartiality is like Addison's a few days earlier in *Spectator* No. 262: "[M]y Paper has not in it a single word of news, a reflection in politicks, nor a stroke of party. . . ." The year 1712 must have seen a sort of tug-of-war between the editors: Addison, who wanted to maintain the impression of impartiality while advancing the paper's political interests, and Steele, who chafed under the disguise of disinterestedness, even when neutrality was profitable. The old cavalryman always preferred the frontal assault.

That spring Addison was indulging his penchant for civilized talk among friends at a coffeehouse recently opened in Russell Street by his former servant Daniel Button. Most of the friends as it happened were rising literary Whigs like Edward Young and John Hughes; years later Pope was to recall Addison's "Little Senate" as an assembly of sycophants, but in 1712 Pope's relationship with Addison and Steele was entirely harmonious. Steele gave over No. 378 to the first publication of Pope's "Messiah," introducing it with the statement that it was "written by a great genius, a friend of mine in the country, who is not ashamed to employ his wit in the praise of his maker." Later in the year Pope contributed several letters and a translation of Hadrian's verses to his soul. The relationship was cordial, complimentary, literary, but formal; it was to the advantage of both Mr. Spectator and the young genius in the country.

Such Addisonian efforts to keep friends all around had a sound economic basis. As the paper's circulation increased so did the advertisements, and the editors there maintained a fine impartiality, accepting advertisements from Whig and Tory alike, helping sell Swift's *Conduct* and Whig replies to the *Conduct,* Dennis' criticism and Pope's poetry; not to mention claret and canary, Poussins and Tintorettos, and "A Treatise of the Hypochondriack and Hysterick Passions, vulgarly call'd the HYPO in Men and VAPOURS in Women; in which the Symptoms, Causes and Cure of those Diseases are set forth after a Method entirely new." [19] The treatise was a bargain at three shillings sixpence. By July, 1712, at the height of the paper's circulation, the editors were running ten or even twelve of these advertisements in each number. Modern advertising, for better or for worse, was fully fledged.

That spring *The Spectator* provided extensive advertising of a different sort gratis for a member of Addison's Little Senate, Ambrose Philips. Philips, returned from his diplomatic mission in Denmark, was working on a play based on Racine's *Andromaque,* to be called *The Distressed Mother.* Philips was a protégé; furthermore, the play itself agreed with Steele's idea of reformed drama. The characters, he noted in early February (No. 290) almost six weeks before the play opened, "are all of them laudable, and their misfortunes arise rather from unguarded virtue than propensity to vice." Steele well realized that laudable characters do not make for lively dramatic action; he and Addison virtually took over the play's promotion, even contributing the prologue (Steele) and the epilogue (Addison and Budgell). The prologue's claims are modest enough. Steele tells of Shakespeare's genius, then turns to poor Philips, much as an anatomy instructor displays a subject to his class:

> Our author does his feeble force confess,
> Nor dares pretend such merit to transgress;
> Does not such shining gifts of genius share,
> And therefore makes propriety his care.
> Your treat with study'd decency he serves;
> Not only rules of time and place preserves,

---

[19] Quotation and information in this paragraph from Lawrence Lewis, *The Advertisements of The Spectator* (Boston, 1909), p. 202 and *passim.*

> But strives to keep his characters entire,
> With French correctness and with British fire.[20]

Philips was the sort of plodding journeyman to set Pope's teeth on edge, but what he lacked in talent, Addison and Steele determined to make up with publicity. *The Distressed Mother* opened to a good house — including, presumably, every literary Whig able to walk — and received favorable notices in *Spectators* 335, 338, and 341. After twenty years' absence Sir Roger de Coverly returned to the theater and was pronounced "fully satisfy'd with his entertainment." In fact, the teary drama appealed to the audience, as Rowe's she-tragedies did, as Steele's own *The Conscious Lovers* was to do. Addison's and Steele's patronizing tone with respect to their captive author may be significant in assessing their part in the controversy between Pope and Philips the following year.

The simple life had only a literary or theoretical attraction for Steele (as for most of the Augustans); always his bent was toward complication. If he had chosen, in the spring of 1712 he could have relaxed for a while: with Philips' play safely launched, with *The Spectator's* circulation and advertising holding up well, with a second son in the house (born on 4 March and defiantly christened Eugene, in honor of Marlborough's fellow-soldier, Prince Eugene) — now was the time, one would have thought, for drawing rein. As if he had some such action in mind, he had acquired another rural retreat, the cottage on Haverstock Hill painted in the nineteenth century by Constable, the approximate site of which is, appropriately, marked in the present day by a public house, the *Sir Richard Steele*. He was to spend little time there that year; by the end of the summer he had become embroiled with the government on three separate occasions, had borrowed money, bought a house, been sued for debt, and borne a hand in an elopement.

---

[20] *Verse*, p. 46.

The first contretemps with the Tories was entirely of Steele's doing, and involved *The Spectator* in politics most directly. William Fleetwood, the Bishop of St. Asaph, had published a little book of collected sermons in early May, with a Whiggish preface in which he pointed out the dangers of dealing with the Pretender and looked forward to the succession of the Hanoverians after Queen Anne's death. As Hoadly had before him in the Blackall controversy, Fleetwood asserted the supremacy of the legislative power, even over that of the sovereign. These were fighting words to the incumbent legislative body; the Tory majority in Commons passed a resolution in June stating that the preface was "malicious and factious," and ordered it burned by the public hangman. Steele, in the meanwhile, had published the offending preface on 21 May with the bland statement: "I should be thought not able to read, should I overlook some excellent pieces lately come out. My Lord Bishop of St. Asaph has just now published some sermons, the preface to which seems to me to determine a great point." The hue and cry was raised, of course, and Tory satirists, including Swift himself, were soon on Mr. Spectator's track.[21]

At almost the same time Steele had offended the House of Commons in another matter, this one quite unwittingly. In debt as usual despite his higher income, he introduced a new lottery scheme in *The Spectator*. As he explained in No. 413 (24 June), this was to be called "The Multiplication Table," and anyone with a half-guinea was exhorted to enter for "when these little parcels of wealth are, as it were, thus thrown back again into the redonation of Providence, we are to expect that some who live under hardship or obscurity, may be produced to the world in the figure they deserve by this means." A wholly typical enterprise: the vision of quick wealth and an exalted "figure" in the

[21] Cf. John C. Stephens, Jr., "Steele and the Bishop of St. Asaph's Preface," *Publications of the Modern Language Association of America*, LXVII (1952), 1011–23. Swift: *A Letter of Thanks* . . . , in *Political Tracts* (see note 11), pp. 147–55.

world. Unfortunately, an Act of Parliament against unlicensed lotteries went into effect that very day; Steele had given a handle to his enemies this time. Swift reported the Multiplication Table difficulty to Stella, adding "I believe he will very soon lose his employment, for he has been mighty impertinent of late in his *Spectators*," alluding presumably to the Fleetwood preface.[22]

The employment Swift mentions was the Commissionership of Stamps, and Steele needed its stipend that summer. He was at almost the same time being sued for debt and borrowing £3,000 from a friend,[23] all the while negotiating for a new home in Bloomsbury Square, the very best of addresses, or as he told Prue, "the prettyest house to receive the Prettyest Woman." Fortunately for Steele, Robert Harley (now the Earl of Oxford) could forgive when forgiving suited his ends, and Harley never ceased attempting to bring over good writers to his cause. The lottery affair was overlooked and Steele informed Prue on 28 June that his employment was assured. About this time, apparently at Oxford's behest, overtures were made to Steele concerning the patent for the Drury Lane Theatre.[24] Nothing came of this wooing; Steele was firmly in opposition, but in August he felt able to send the Lord Treasurer from his new house in Bloomsbury Square a plan for improving the state (i.e., legal) lottery as recompense for the "generous treatment which I have had from your Lordship. . . ."

In the midst of all this official hurly-burly, an affair of the heart in which both the Steeles had been involved came to a crisis that August. Steele's friend and fellow Whig politician Edward Wortley-Montagu summoned up his courage and eloped with Lady Mary Pierrepont on the eighteenth, thus ending a court-

---

[22] *Journal,* ed. Williams, II, 546.
[23] Aitken, I, 341, 352.
[24] John Loftis, *Steele at Drury Lane* (Berkeley, 1952), pp. 25–33. The date of the overtures is uncertain, but probably between June, 1712 and May, 1713. I am inclined to feel Loftis' conjecture (April, 1713) is too late and that the offer was made when Steele was most prominent and least factious, as Mr. Spectator.

ship opposed by Lady Mary's father, Lord Dorchester, and
hindered by the chronic indecision of both principals. A year and
a half earlier the hesitant lovers had used the Steeles' house in
Bury Street for their rendezvous, and some of the problems of
courtship and marriage in the eighteenth century, typified by
their own problems, found expression in both *Tatler* and *Spectator.*[25] The second volume of the collected *Tatler* had been dedicated to Edward Wortley-Montagu, a gentleman extravagantly
admired by both Addison and Steele but now forgotten except
as the husband of one of literature's great letter writers and
peppery females.

Steele's third and most serious brush with the law that year
was not of his own doing except, perhaps, indirectly. On 1
August the government staggered Grub Street by imposing a
half-penny per sheet duty on all printed periodicals and a shilling
tax on every advertisement. The Tories thus acknowledged, as
many other ministries have, the power of the pen, but journalists could have spared the compliment. "Do you know," Swift
wrote Stella, "that Grub Street is dead and gone last week?
. . . The *Observator* is fallen; the *Medleys* are jumbled together with the *Flying Post;* the *Examiner* [which Swift no
longer edited] is deadly sick, the *Spectator* keeps up and doubles
its price. I know not how long it will hold." [26] This was a seriously repressive measure : a superior paper could still survive, like
The Spectator, or a heavily subsidized paper, like the Tory *Examiner,* but the general and quite remarkable freedom of the
English press in the early eighteenth century was diminished,
crowded by politics. When the Whigs returned to power they
applied repressive measures too ; politicians are often fonder of
a free press in theory than in practice.

Addison had informed his readers of the bad news on 31

[25] Robert Halsband, *The Life of Lady Mary Wortley Montagu* (Oxford,
1956), pp. 10–28.
[26] *Journal,* II, 553–54.

July, the day before the tax: "This is the day on which many eminent authors will probably publish their last words." Though circulation fell (by more than half at first, according to Steele's statement in the final paper), readers continued to buy *The Spectator* at the doubled price and in September Addison jocularly suggested some expedients (in No. 488) by which the price of the paper might be saved out of other household expenses: ladies could sacrifice one ribbon in their toilette, or a family burn one fewer candle a night. Or, best of all, readers might buy the collected papers, ten thousand volumes of which, he declared, had already been sold.

If he meant ten thousand copies of each collected volume, Addison was probably exaggerating, but he had good reason to inflate the total a measure. In November Addison and Steele sold their rights to the collected volumes (which they had wisely retained), a half-share each to Samuel Buckley and Jacob Tonson, Junior, for £575 the half-share. This was almost double the sum Dryden had reportedly received some twenty years earlier for his translation of Vergil; a very considerable payment,[27] for a valuable property. Two years later Tonson was willing to pay Buckley £500 for his half-share and doubtless found it a profitable investment; at least eight authorized editions had appeared by Steele's death, and scores more by the end of the century.[28] In Virginia William Byrd was still reading *The Tatler* regularly, along with holy writ and *The Whole Duty of Man*. *The Spectator* was salable enough separate or collected, but the authors had already decided to end it when the agreement with Tonson and Buckley was transacted. The first step was to break up the club. The issue of 23 October sent

[27] Dryden payment: Charles E. Ward, "The Publication and Profits of Dryden's *Virgil*," *Publications of the Modern Language Association of America*, LIII (1938), 811.

[28] *Corr.*, pp. 461n–462n; Fritz Rau, "Texte, Ausgaben und Verfasser des *Tatler* und *Spectator*," *Germanisch-Romanische Monatsschrift*, Neue Folge, VIII (1958), 126–44; and Donald F. Bond, "The text of the *Spectator*," *Studies in Bibliography*, V (1952–1953), 109–28.

Sir Roger to his long home, and Captain Sentry succeeded to his estate. On 7 November the marriage of the club's perennial bachelor, Will Honeycomb, to a farmer's daughter was announced, and Sir Andrew Freeport retired to the country (No. 549), acquiring a landed estate in fiction as many of his fellow merchants were doing in fact. On 1 December Mr. Spectator spoke of "being very loquacious" in a new club and forecast his reappearance "on the twenty-fifth of March next." With No. 555 of 6 December 1712 the original series ended, Steele acknowledging over his signature those who had helped or, as he put it, balancing "my accounts with all my creditors for wit and learning." In a properly reminiscent mood, he recalled his long friendship with Addison: "I remember when I finished the *Tender Husband,* I told him there was nothing I so ardently wished, as that we might some time or other publish a work written by us both, which should bear the name of *The Monument,* in memory of our friendship." It is in the realm of speculation, but one may guess that the authors ended *The Spectator* because both wanted to move on to something new, to end the game while they were ahead. The new taxes, to be sure, had sliced into their revenues, but perhaps their chief consideration was artistic. Years later Addison wrote (in *The Freeholder* No. 40), "It would be well for all authors, if . . . they knew when to give over, and to desist from any farther pursuits after fame, whilst they are in the full possession of it." The paper's fame was bright and crescent, even on the Continent, where Jean Le Clerc in the *Journal Littéraire* declared that "The finest writers in England have executed, in the *Spectator,* all the force of their reflections, all the delicacy of style and all the fire of imagination that can be conceived." [29] Extravagant praise, but eighteenth-century Americans gave *The Spectator* the sincerer compliment of careful reading and imitation. Its mixture of piety, mild Lockeian Whiggery, and good sense was welcome

[29] As quoted in Smithers (note 12), p. 245.

in a trading nation; its advice on gentle conduct was valued on the rustic shores, and *The Spectator's* style was answerable to American needs. One of the greatest of Americans, Benjamin Franklin, recalled his boyhood encounter with the paper:

> About this time I met with an odd volume of the *Spectator*. It was the third. I had never before seen any of them. I bought it, read it over and over, and was much delighted with it. I thought the writing excellent and wished if possible to imitate it. With that view, I took some of the papers, and making short hints of the sentiment in each sentence, laid them by a few days, and then without looking at the book tried to complete the papers again, by expressing each hinted sentiment at length and as fully as it had been expressed before, in any suitable words that should occur to me. Then I compared my *Spectator* with the original, discovered some of my faults, and corrected them.[30]

If Addison and Steele decided on artistic grounds to end the paper, political considerations were operative too. Steele wanted a vehicle in which he could throw off the nonpartisan guise and participate more directly in the propaganda battle ahead. That fall he had been in touch with Halifax and Somers; the Whigs were gathering their forces for the debate over the Peace Treaty, negotiations for which, everyone knew, were progressing. It may be that the Junto lords themselves suggested the end of the paper, as their rival Harley for different reasons may have called for the end of *The Tatler*. Whatever the reason, the great partnership ended with the year and the authors went their separate ways.

[30] *The Autobiography of Benjamin Franklin*, ed. Max Farrand (Berkeley, 1949), pp. 18–19.

CHAPTER VII

The Guardian
and the Peace

IN JANUARY, 1713, a young Irishman came to London carrying the manuscript of a book with him. Though only twenty-eight, George Berkeley was a fellow of Trinity College, Dublin, and already the author of two books of philosophy, but Irishmen needed entrees in London. Casting about for acquaintances, Berkeley found one of his eminent fellow-countrymen, the former editor of *The Spectator,* living in what seemed to his dazzled eyes nothing less than splendor. "[T]here appears in his natural temper," Berkeley reported of Steele to his Irish friend Sir John Percival, "something very generous and a great benevolence to mankind."

> I have dined frequently at his house in Bloomsbury Square, which is handsome and neatly furnished. His table, servants, coach and everything is very genteel, and in appearance above his fortune. . . . His conversation is very cheerful and abounds with wit and good sense. Somebody (I know not who) had given him my treatise of the *Principles of Human Knowledge* and that was the ground of his inclination to my acquaintance. For my part I should reckon it a sufficient recompence of my pains in writing it, that it gave me some share in the friendship of so worthy a man.[1]

[1] *The Works of George Berkeley, Bishop of Cloyne,* ed. A. A. Luce and T. E. Jessop (London, 1948–1957), VIII, 61.

All this attention was delightfully flattering to the future Bishop of Cloyne and patron of Yale University, and Steele no doubt found Berkeley's regard pleasant too, but his principal interest in the young academic was professional: Steele was thinking of the next periodical, examining Berkeley as a possible contributor. Many other things, as we shall see, clamored for his attention that winter and spring; politics, personal concerns, money — always money — but foremost was the new paper, *The Guardian.*

On Thursday, 12 March, the first number of the periodical appeared, bearing that title. A reader inclined toward symbolic interpretation might have traced the increasing seriousness of Steele's periodicals by their titles: from *Tatler* to *Spectator* to *Guardian.* And the *persona* or narrator of the most recent paper seemed one who would brook no nonsense. Mr. Spectator's successor was Nestor Ironside, his name conveying impressions of elderly wisdom and toughness, his purpose properly exalted:

> My design upon the whole is no less than to make the pulpit, the bar, and the stage, all act in concert in the care of piety, justice, and virtue; for I am past all the regards of this life, and have nothing to manage with any person or party, but to deliver myself as becomes an old man with one foot in the grave, and one who thinks he is passing to eternity.

It is Steele rather than Addison who writes; politics will be admitted. "The parties among us are too violent to make it possible to pass them by without observation. As to these matters I shall be impartial, though I cannot be neuter. . . ."

Readers may have found Nestor's distinction between impartiality and neutrality a little hard to grasp, but otherwise he seemed on familiar ground. Reform and entertainment as usual, the mixture of enlightenment and chit-chat which had been proven in *The Spectator* were to remain the staple of *The Guardian.* There was a club of sorts for an organizing motif, various members of the Lizard family, friends of Ironside's, serving the function of Mr. Spectator's club, though not developed to anything like the same extent. The six-issues-a-week pace of *The Spectator* was continued and Steele quickly taxed literary friends for contributions. Of some 175 numbers, Steele himself wrote all or most of eighty-odd, accepting aid from Pope, among others, and various members of the Little Senate such as the faithful Budgell, Hughes, and Thomas Tickell. Addison was busy readying a play for production during the early days of the periodical but later wrote frequently and well for his old collaborator. George Berkeley soon justified Steele's hopes with a sprightly series against freethinkers; by the paper's end the young philosopher had written some dozen papers. All these helped make *The Guardian* the third most popular, after *Tatler* and *Spectator,* of Steele's periodicals, but Nestor Ironside showed signs of weariness from the outset: the truth was that most of the paper's subject matter appeared somewhat shopworn after 271 numbers of *The Tatler* and 555 *Spectators.* Ironside's admonitions on dress or dueling or fornication ring a bit dully, coming as they do for the tenth or the twentieth time.

Though the overall literary quality of *The Guardian* may be somewhat below that of the earlier papers, *The Guardian* for that very reason better illustrates one important aspect of Addison's and Steele's literary activities: that of being spokesmen for what would later come to be called the Enlightenment, especially with respect to interest in the new science. It is, of course, not suggested that Addison and Steele were anything but amateurs in either philosophy or science, but their standing as journalists, their wide acquaintanceship among the serious thinkers of the day, and the continuing sympathetic presentation in their papers of philosophic and scientific matters made them important — and very early — focal points in the dissemination of ideas. It is true that, as they said in various places in various ways, their hope was to bring about recognition of the fact that science and philosophy were united in the promotion of virtue, but against this rather tendentious program should be balanced their assumption that science had a place of its own in intellectual life; this assumption itself was a step forward in a period when many literary and clerical figures regarded scientists as at best mere meddling virtuosi and as at worst underminers of the social and religious order. Defoe shared their liberal views toward the new science, and was himself perhaps a more original thinker than Addison and Steele, but he could not supply the cachet of social acceptability which publication in *The Spectator* or *The Guardian* provided, nor was the circulation of *The Review* anything like that of Addison's and Steele's papers, especially when reprints are considered.

A case in point illustrative of Addison's and Steele's sympathies was that of William Whiston, the mathematician. Whiston had a genuinely creative mind and was most scrupulous in maintaining the purity of his personal life, but his pronounced views on the necessity for reviving primitive Christianity had made him something of a social pariah in Cambridge, where he taught, and elsewhere, and resulted finally in his expulsion from Cambridge on charges of heterodoxy. In 1713, now in desperate straits, he was recommended to Steele by Henry Newman, the American secretary of the Society for Promoting Christian Knowledge; Steele published a letter from Whiston in *Guardian* No. 107 about Whiston's scheme for determining the longitude, and in the summer of that year he and Addison arranged for Whiston to give a series of lectures on mathematical subjects at Button's Coffee House, for which help Whiston was ever afterward grateful.[2] This was the way Addison and Steele used their

[2] *Memoirs of the Life and Writings of Mr. William Whiston . . . written by himself* (London, 1749–1750), I, 182, 302–4. The date of Whiston's lectures, hitherto unknown, appears to be established by Newman's letter of thanks to Steele, dated 10 August 1713, in which he asks Steele to "conjure him silence upon all topicks foreign to the mathematicks in his conversation or lectures

papers and their influence for the advancement of science and philosophy. If they brought little about, they at least helped make the climate of opinion somewhat more favorable to the reception of new ideas. And, of course, they contributed most directly to the physical maintenance of George Berkeley, William Whiston, and others.

Steele's contribution to the new learning was perforce sporadic in 1713; he had even less time to spend on *The Guardian* than on the earlier papers. Family business, commitments to friends, political journalism, all these filled his days, and as always his mind abounded with projects that served further to dissipate his energies.

At the turn of the year Steele's mother-in-law arrived in London, ostensibly to be with her daughter during her approaching accouchement but actually to see the family for the last time. Though she and Steele had preserved a correct, rather than a warm, relationship, both conspired to conceal Mrs. Scurlock's illness from her daughter, and after some considerable discussion and vacillation they were able to reach an understanding on that matter of such total importance in the eighteenth century: the question of her estate. About the end of January or beginning of February Mrs. Scurlock died, and Prue was brought to bed of her fourth child, her daughter Mary.

Steele was now supporting five children, Prue's four and his illegitimate daughter, Elizabeth Ousley. Forty years earlier his father had voiced a complaint which Richard could echo of his

---

at [the] coffeehouse." (S.P.C.K. MS. Letterbooks, CS 2.) Evidently the talks were then about to take place. Later Newman recommended the work of his friend William Derham, author of the influential *Physico-Theology,* to Steele. (*Ibid.,* letter of 24 Sept. 1713.) Bertrand Goldgar, *The Curse of Party* (Lincoln, Neb., 1961), pp. 7–9, makes the interesting suggestion that Steele's and Swift's differing attitude toward science, as exemplified by Steele's help for Whiston whom Swift detested, was a factor in the dissolution of their friendship. See also my article, "Addison and Steele in the English Enlightenment," *Studies on Voltaire and the Eighteenth Century,* ed. T. Besterman (Geneva, 1963), XXVII, 1901–1918.

"great charge of children," but the younger Steele had the consolation, Berkeley heard, of some £500 a year from Mrs. Scurlock's estate, and could fancy that he was a member of the
landed gentry again: "Mr. Steele of Llangunnor in the county
of Carmarthen," he called himself in the Preface of the collected
Guardian.[3] As if celebrating Steele's broadened horizons, Nestor
Ironside gravely declared himself (in No. 76) determined "to
the utmost of my power, to reconcile [the landed and the trad-
ing] interests to each other, and to make them both sensible that
their mutual happiness depends upon their being friends."

Another of Steele's projects was nearing completion in early
1713. His idea for an answer to the fad for Italian opera, first
appearing two years before in Clayton's concerts, had ger-
minated. Berkeley reported Steele

> proposing a noble entertainment for persons of a refined taste.
> It is chiefly to consist of the finest pieces of eloquence translated
> from the Greek and Latin authors. They will be accompanied
> with the best music suited to raise those passions that are proper
> to the occasion. Pieces of poetry will be there recited. These in-
> formations I have from Mr. Steele himself. I have seen the place
> designed for these performances: it is in York Buildings, and
> he has been at no small expence to embellish with all imaginable
> decorations. It is by much the finest chamber I have seen, and
> will contain seats for a select company of 200 persons of the best
> quality and taste, who are to be subscribers.[4]

By late March the Censorium was almost ready for the first
performance; Steele complained to a friend that the project had
cost him a thousand pounds. The Censorium was to be above
party; Lord Treasurer Oxford himself he approached, and for

---

[3] Berkeley, *Works* (note 1), VIII, 60. Berkeley refers to a son; the assumption has always been that this is a mistake since Mary was certainly
born within the year 1713.

[4] *Works*, VIII, 62. See also Chapter VI above and John Loftis, "Richard
Steele's Censorium," *Huntington Library Quarterly*, XIV (1950), 43–66;
Corr., p. 113.

a time Steele had hopes of somehow including that statesman in his project, as a token of its comprehensiveness. But not until 1715 apparently, after Queen Anne's death and the fall of the Tory Ministry, did Steele entertain a select company in the finest room Berkeley had ever seen.[5] In 1713 party strife was rising, not abating.

And Steele himself was fanning the fire of party. Debate on the peace treaty approached in Parliament. A year earlier the Tories had persuaded Queen Anne to create a dozen new peers, with the intention of securing thereby a tractable majority in the House of Lords. The Lords have, it seems, seldom been tractable, however, and it was rumored that the Ministry intended to repeat the stratagem of creating (or having created) "occasional" peers. A single folio broadside dated 5 March 1713 appeared on the streets of London, bearing the title *A Letter to Sir M. W. Concerning Occasional Peers* and signed "Francis Hicks." Later Steele acknowledged authorship of this, his first extended piece of political writing not bound by the restrictions imposed by the periodical form. The Sir M. W. was Sir Miles Warton, a squire who had refused one of the dozen peerages of the year before. All in all, the tract is a creditable piece of journalism, the gist being that the creation of "occasional" peers would upset the constitutional balance, created after the Revolution of 1688 and based on English tradition much older than that revolution. "This fatal novelty," he writes, affects all three constituents of the balance: "the Queen's most excellent Majesty, the House of Peers, and the whole people of England." This is the familiar separation of legislative and executive powers which Americans are disposed to think invented by the Constitutional Convention but which was, of course, a commonplace of political theorists, especially Whig theorists, in the early eighteenth century. The truly supreme power, however, and here he shows his Whiggish inclination, is the legislative: "While the laws are in

[5] John Loftis, *Steele at Drury Lane* (Berkeley, 1952), pp. 106–10.

being, I am safe; and no man can be safe who out-lives them. . . ." Little or nothing is new here, but Steele presents his argument clearly and forcefully; the tract is a foreshadowing of his ability as a pamphleteer. He would write a number of single tracts like this one in the years following, though his instinct always was toward the periodical.[6]

Everyone knew that Addison had a play in progress and Steele, like the rest of the *beau monde,* looked forward to its opening in April; no one who planned to be at the first night could realize, of course, that they were to be present at one of the great occasions in theatrical history. *Cato* had been a long time coming. Apparently Addison had a rough draft prepared when he left Magdalen on the grand tour in 1699. By the end of 1704 it was near enough completion to show to Colley Cibber and Steele; Steele remarked to Cibber, knowing Addison's scrupulosity, that he would never submit it to the judgment of an audience. But Addison was older in 1713 and more self-assured, and, after all, the Whigs had managed to huff and puff Ambrose Philips' feeble vehicle off the ground. Addison asked Pope to show the script to Harley and Bolingbroke to assure that it did not offend Tory feelings; then, apparently satisfied, consented to its production but supervised the rehearsals himself. On the evening of 14 April the play opened to a full house, many of the audience there at Steele's solicitation. The opening turned quickly into a Roman holiday.[7] Addison sat nervously in a box, fortified by applications of burgundy and champagne; to his growing dismay he saw that the audience was divided into Whig and Tory and that each side fancied, or affected to fancy, that Cato's noble struggle against tyranny was analogous

---

[6] *Tracts,* pp. 72–79; and Caroline Robbins, *The Eighteenth-Century Commonwealthman* (Cambridge, Mass., 1959), p. 102. Steele had published in January, 1712, the short *The Englishman's Thanks to the Duke of Marlborough* (*Tracts,* pp. 69–71).

[7] Malcolm G. Goldstein, *Pope and the Augustan Stage* (Stanford, 1958), pp. 5–9; Smithers, pp. 250–55.

to their own. Pope, who had contributed the prologue, described the scene to a friend:

> The numerous and violent claps of the Whig party on the one side the theatre, were echoed back by the Tories on the other, while the author sweated behind the scenes with concern to find their applause proceeded more [from] the hand than the head. This was the case too of the prologue-writer, who was clapped into a stanch Whig sore against his will, at almost every two lines. I believe you have heard that after all the applauses of the opposite faction, my Lord Bullingbrooke sent for Booth who played Cato, into the box, between one of the acts and presented him with 50 guineas; in acknowledgment (as he expressed it) for [his] defending the cause of liberty so well against a *perpetual dictator:* the Whigs are unwilling to be distanced this way, [as 'tis said,] and therefore design a present to the said Cato very speedily. . . .[8]

Bolingbroke's reference to a "perpetual dictator" applied to the Whig's hero Marlborough; despite Addison's precautions — or was it because of them? — *Cato* became a party play. One never knows about Addison; at any rate he had, in today's jargon, a hit on his hands. *Cato* ran for twenty-five performances (a record number) and the printed play, snapped up by the fore-handed Tonson, had gone through eight editions by the end of the year.[9] On 18 April Steele devoted an issue of *The Guardian* (No. 33) to the play and carried the prologue and epilogue to "gratify the impatience of the town." With the seventh edition of the play appearing in June of that year, Tonson printed a garland of congratulatory poems by Hughes, Tickell, and others, including some limping but obviously sincere lines by Steele. Steele was no poet.[10]

April was a lively month for Richard Steele. With the *Cato*

---

[8] *The Correspondence of Alexander Pope,* ed. George Sherburn (Oxford, 1956), I, 175.
[9] Smithers, p. 256.
[10] *Verse,* p. 15.

excitement diminishing and the paper selling comfortably, young Alexander Pope exploded a bomb in *Guardian* No. 40, as if to keep the editor from lethargy.[11] Pope's victim was another contributor, Ambrose Philips, and the case shows to good advantage the young satirist Pope trying his powers. Philips had made a modest reputation in the preceding few years, with many a hand-up from Addison and Steele. Aside from whatever luster he derived from *The Distressed Mother,* his renown was mainly as a pastoral poet, a somewhat restricted field in which Alexander Pope also had ambitions: in fact their work had been published together in Tonson's *Poetical Miscellanies: The Sixth Part* (1709). "Pastoral Philips," as he was referred to in the eighteenth-century manner, was a faithful member of Addison's Little Senate at Button's and secretary of the newly-formed Hanover Club, a sort of lesser Whigs' Kit-Cat Club. Praise for Philips' pastorals had become an avocation among Addison's group, and in early April *The Guardian* devoted a series of issues (Nos. 22, 23, 28, 30, 32) to analysis of the eclogues, praising them especially for their use of native English scenes, characters, mythology, and diction — in implied contrast to Pope's works in the same genre, which had followed another theoretical course and presented classical characters in a severely correct classical setting.[12] These *Guardians* may have been by Thomas Tickell; their somewhat precious and feminine style is not Steele's. Whoever the author, he lavished praise on Philips, concluding the last essay in the series by deriving the true genealogy of pastoral poets from Amyntas through Theocritus, Vergil, Spenser; "and Spenser was succeeded by his eldest-born Philips."

[11] Controversy summarized in George Sherburn, *The Early Career of Alexander Pope* (Oxford, 1934). See the article by William D. Ellis, Jr., "Thomas D'Urfey, the Pope-Philips Quarrel, and *The Shepherd's Week,*" *Publications of the Modern Language Association of America,* LXXIV (1959), 203–12.

[12] Cf. Pope, *Pastoral Poetry and An Essay on Criticism,* ed. E. Audra and Aubrey Williams (London, 1961), pp. 15–20.

This absurd overpraise was too much for Pope's skin, never
very thick. There were, moreover, in the opinion of the disputants important critical issues at stake; Philips' case was quite
as good in theory, if not in practice, as that of Pope. Pope dispatched an essay to *The Guardian* which purported to praise
Philips' work but actually demonstrated with ironic gravity that
the pastorals, with their rustic dialect and realistic detail, were
after all very like the popular Grub Street ballads of Tom
D'Urfey. Readers of *The Guardian* rejoiced or were dismayed
at Philips' discomfiture according to their literary (and political) sympathies. Steele found himself in the embarrassing position of responsibility for having printed Pope's ironic analysis,
and Philips was naturally furious. One story tells of Philips'
keeping a switch on the bar at Button's, for use if Pope happened by. A year later John Gay was to continue the attack on
realistic pastoral poetry and Philips' work with his burlesque
eclogue series, *The Shepherd's Week*. Beyond the publication
of the *Guardian* essays, Steele had little or no part in the pastoral controversy, and remained on excellent terms (presumably after some apologies to Philips) with Pope and Philips.
Both continued to contribute to the paper.

The question remains, why did he allow Pope's analysis to be
printed? Though his attitude toward Philips was patronizing,
he certainly would not knowingly have permitted this embarrassment. Probably the explanation lies in Steele's method of
working. He wrote very quickly and had a large head full of
ideas, but he was unmethodical and careless in the final degree.
There was much to be done in life, deadlines always rose ahead
— six a week — and Richard Steele took short cuts where he
could, printing contributions sometimes that were below the
mark or dull or indiscreet: it was his way, the way of a journalist rather than a scholar. And during that last week of April,
politics was very much on Steele's mind — the beginning of a
controversy which was to bring a final end to the friendship

with his fellow-Dubliner, Jonathan Swift. Pope, in fact, does not establish his ironic intent in the essay for some several hundred words; to a hasty reader the piece seems innocent enough at first. Steele probably glanced at Pope's communication without reading it through and sent it to the printer, thankful that he had hurdled a deadline.

The Guardian had kept clear of politics during a brief era of good feeling in March and early April, preceding the signing of the Treaty of Utrecht on April 11. For a while it seemed as if the old triumvirate of Swift, Steele, and Addison might be reunited. True, a chill yet hung over the relationship between Swift and Steele, but Steele was on friendly terms with Swift's superior Oxford, telling young Berkeley that he no longer believed Oxford intended to bring over the Pretender as Queen Anne's successor.[13] Swift unbent to the extent of persuading Bolingbroke, leader of the more extreme Tories and real architect of the Treaty, to invite Addison to dinner before *Cato* opened. But these gestures betokened a truce among the triumvirate of Swift, Steele, and Addison, not peace: the Tories would press their advantage. Some measure of their confidence and jubilation may be gathered from the circumstances of *Cato*'s opening night. Swift had access to the highest Tory councils: he had corrected the Queen's Speech to Parliament (prepared, of course, by the Ministry) announcing the Treaty and had written the Lords' "Vote of Address of Thanks." The Treaty was, as his editor remarks, "the justification of all his efforts, the end for which he had worked. . . ."[14] It was the Tory Ministry's triumph.

Perhaps the clarity of the triumph made Whig wounds smart more sharply. At any rate, when in April *The Examiner* attacked Daniel Finch, the Earl of Nottingham, Steele decided the time had come to confirm Ironside's statement that he could

[13] Berkeley, *Works* (note 1), VIII, 63.
[14] Herbert Davis in *Political Tracts, 1711–1713* (Princeton, 1951), p. xxviii.

not be neuter. On the following Tuesday, in *Guardian* No. 41 he replied, using a cherished motif, the letter to the editor. "If life be . . . less valuable and dear than honour and reputation," he declared, "in that proportion is the *Examiner* worse than an assassin." All Steele's repressed grievances, all his resentment at the *Examiner*'s treatment of Marlborough and the fallen Whigs bubble up: "We have stood by and tamely heard him aggravate the disgraces of the brave and the unfortunate. We have seen him double the anguish of the unhappy man, we have seen him trample on the ashes of the dead. . . ." Ironside throws off the mask of neutrality.

It is tolerably certain that Steele thought Swift the source of the offending paper, an idea not so illogical after all. Though Swift did not edit *The Examiner* after 1711, he continued to be closely associated with it ("I will now and then send hints," he wrote Stella when he gave up the editorship) and he had contributed to it from time to time, writing among others a paper on the Bishop of St. Asaph's preface in July, 1712, which contained a passing stroke at Steele. Nottingham, furthermore, was a favorite target of Swift's. An unprepossessing man personally, he had extensive family connections in both houses of Parliament: some thirty-one Members of Parliament and fourteen lords. A High Churchman, Nottingham had been won over by the Junto, partly because of his resentment toward Oxford, and had supported the slogan "No Peace without Spain." [15] After this he became a favorite quarry for the Tory journalists, who generally referred to him by his nickname, "Dismal." To Swift especially he was anathema. "Nottingham has certainly been bribed," he wrote Stella after the Earl's defection; he soon brought out a ballad on the subject, and a Grub Street half-sheet, called *A Hue and Cry After Dismal*.[16]

Not surprisingly then, when *The Examiner* began to attack

[15] Family: Robert Walcott, *English Politics in the Early Eighteenth Century* (Oxford, 1956), pp. 59–60. See also HMC, *Portland MSS.*, V, 101.
[16] *Journal*, II, 432; pamphlet in *Political Tracts* (note 14), pp. 137–41.

"Dismal" in early 1713, Steele suspected that Swift was behind the campaign. Swift was in the course of being named Dean of St. Patrick's Cathedral, Dublin, and was finishing work on his account of the peace negotiations, later known as *The History of the Four Last Years of the Queen;* if he supplied anything to the offending paper it was probably only one of his promised hints. The *Examiner* editor, William Oldisworth, was fully capable of defending himself, asking "Have you [i.e., *The Examiner*] forgot Old Downs . . . Powell of the Bath . . . with at least fifty more sufferers of figure under this author's satire, in the days of his mirth, and when he could shew his teeth to advantage?" This reminiscence of the old *Tatler* days probably confirmed Steele's suspicions that the author was either Swift or Mrs. Manley. He addressed another letter to Nestor Ironside in *Guardian* No. 53 for 12 May over his own signature and prefaced it with a paragraph naming himself author of No. 41.

> I will give myself no manner of liberty to make guesses at him, if I may say him: for though sometimes I have been told by familiar friends, that they saw me such a time talking to the Examiner; others, who have rallied me upon the sins of my youth, tell me it is credibly reported that I have formerly lain with the Examiner. I have carried my point, and rescued innocence from calumny; and it is nothing to me, whether the Examiner writes against me in the character of an estranged friend or an exasperated mistress.

The "estranged friend," of course, could refer only to Swift, the "exasperated mistress" to Mrs. Manley.

Swift answered quickly, by way of a letter to Addison dated 13 May, that is, the day after *Guardian* No. 53 appeared. He complains that Steele has "abused me in the grossest manner he could possibly invent, and set his name to what he had written." [17] "Is he so ignorant of my temper, and of my style?" asks

[17] All extant correspondence in this quarrel is conveniently reprinted in *Corr.,* pp. 70–81.

Swift, not flattered at having Oldisworth's work mistaken for his own. He concludes, "Have I deserved this usage from Mr. Steele, who knows very well that my Lord Treasurer has kept him in his employment upon my intreaty and intercession?" Swift, note, does not directly deny his connection with the Tory paper, except to say (what was not, by the way, true) that he was "altogether a stranger" to the editor.[18]

In his letter of reply dated 19 May, Steele deals first, as one might expect, with Swift's charge of ingratitude. "They laugh at you," he writes, "if they make you believe your interposition has kept me thus long in my office." He voices his belief in Swift's complicity in the *Examiner*'s publication: "If you have spoken in my behalf at any time, I am glad I have always treated you with respect: though I believe you an accomplice of the Examiner's. . . . You do not in direct terms say you are not concerned with him: But make it an argument of your innocence, that the Examiner has declared you have nothing to do with him."

An important date in the dispute is 23 May 1713, which with its analyses of motives, claims, charges, and denials begins to resemble a courtroom cross-examination. On that day Steele published a bitter letter in *The Guardian* over his own signature complaining of *The Examiner* and began a letter to the Earl of Oxford resigning the Commissionership of Stamps. That day, too, Swift replied to Steele, rehearsing in his letter the efforts he had made to persuade Oxford to retain Steele in the Commissionership. He evades the question of his *Examiner* connection with a question of his own, which he suggests Steele ask himself, "If Dr. Swift be entirely innocent of what I accuse him, how shall I be able to make him satisfaction? and how do I know but he may be entirely innocent?" Swift repeats the assertion made earlier that he had caused the printers to delete

---

[18] See *Journal,* II, 637, entry of 12 March 1713 for proof that he knew the editor ("I dare not let him see me. . . .").

uncomplimentary references to Steele in *The Examiner* (no very good argument for his innocence, one would think, of any connection with the paper).

Steele wrote his final letter to Swift with a rhetorical flourish or two, in the tone of a man who has made up his mind. He focuses on what for him was the real center of the quarrel, Marlborough:

> . . . I would not conceal my thoughts in favour of an injured man, though all the powers on earth gainsaid it, to be made the first man in the nation. This position, I know, will ever obstruct my way in the world; and I have conquered my desires accordingly. I have resolved to content myself with what I can get by my own industry, and the improvement of a small estate, without being anxious whether I am ever in a Court again or not.

The reply dated 27 May, with which Swift ended this phase of the quarrel, is temperate. "As to the great man whose defense you undertake," he writes, "though I do not think so well of him as you do, yet I have been the cause of preventing five hundred hard things being said against him." And so the matter rested between the two former friends until the Dunkirk controversy, a few months later. But events and their own choice were driving them apart. The character of neither, certainly, appears to very great advantage in this phase of their disagreement; both are too ready to deal in equivocations. It is certain that Swift's regard for Steele had diminished almost to the vanishing point; whatever efforts he made on his behalf with Oxford were surely half-hearted. His statements to both Addison and Steele, moreover, concerning his connection with *The Examiner* are at best disingenuous and at worse, falsehoods. On the other hand, Steele certainly had no idea of retiring to the "improvement of a small estate"; this was simply dishonest rhetoric.

In the meantime Steele had decided to close out the controversy with *The Examiner,* which had been conducted on an increasingly personal basis and must have begun to bore his readers. In No. 63 (23 May) he invited the writer of the Tory paper to make himself known, as well as "any gentleman who wrongfully lies under the imputation of being, or assisting the Examiner," that is, Swift; and affirms that the report that he had lain with the editor of the paper was false, making ironic reparations to the lady (Mrs. Manley) by "begging her pardon, that I never lay with her." For a while after this Steele kept his paper non-political.[19]

As his last letter to Swift indicated, he had decided to sever all ties with the Ministry and to run for Parliament in the general elections which were approaching in the fall. On 4 June 1713 he sent Oxford a much revised final draft of the letter of resignation that he had originally dated 23 May. Steele assured the Earl that whatever he had said or written had "proceeded from no other motive, but the love of, what I think, Truth," and complimented him for his generosity. He expressed his misgivings at the course of events, alluding to Whig fears for the Protestant succession on the death of the Queen, whose health had been failing for some time.

> I am going out of my particular dependance on Your Lordship, and will tell you with the freedom of an indifferent man, that it is impossible for any one who thinks and has any public spirit, not to tremble at seeing his country . . . in the hands of so daring a genius as yours. If incidents should arise that should place your own safety and . . . greatness in a balance against the public good, our all depends upon your choice under such a temptation.

Within a few weeks, before or after, of his resignation from the Stamp Commission, Steele also gave up his earliest civil

---

[19] Except for printing a letter criticizing *The Examiner,* in No. 90. In this number, incidentally, he printed a handsome letter of thanks to Berkeley for his contributions, which might be included in future editions of Steele's correspondence.

preferment, the pension as Gentleman-Usher to Queen Anne's late husband.[20] For the first time since 1706 he was entirely dependent upon his own efforts, a condition that discomposed Prue. There is a note (dated 22 July) from Steele to his wife: "I write because I hear you give yourself up to lamentations. You have, indeed, no cause for it, and I beseech you to repose the confidence in me, which is deserved from you. . . ." No one but Steele would say that his wife's fears were entirely unjustified; nevertheless, he had broken all ties with the Tory Ministry.

Steele, a holder of patronage in army and government for more than fifteen years, was now no longer a soldier or courtier, but a politician running for office. His (or the Junto's) choice for the initial test was the borough of Stockbridge in Hampshire, according to Defoe "a sorry borough town, noted for its corruption in electing Members of Parliament." Defoe, one must remember, was Steele's bitter political foe and this judgment may contain a tincture of malice. Actually, from the point of view of the next century's electoral reformers, the Stockbridge seat was one of the more "democratic" since everyone who paid local taxes ("scot and lot") had the right to vote.[21] Paradoxically enough, cries of corruption in Steele's day generally rose from franchises like Stockbridge where there was at least the semblance of a contest; if a nobleman had a seat really in his pocket, the electors had little or no opportunity for protest. Steele's task was that of any candidate in a scot and lot borough of medium size: to secure the votes of several score electors by any means at his disposal, from promises of patronage or local improvements, to influence, threats (especially available to candidates who had large landholdings in the vicinity), and out-and-

[20] *The Importance of Dunkirk Consider'd* in *Tracts*, p. 113.
[21] Defoe, *A Tour through the whole Island of Great Britain* (6th ed.; London, 1762), I, 275; cf. Walcott, *English Politics* (note 15), p. 12, who declares that the franchise in Stockbridge "was at least as broad as that introduced by the first Reform Bill."

out bribery. Entertainment was an important and costly item: at a dinner given before the 1701 election, for example, forty-seven hearty electors of the Walpole borough, Castle Rising, in Norfolk consumed thirty gallons of port, great quantities of food and "beer and cider in plenty." [22] And this was considered a safe borough. Electoral politics was an expensive business, especially for a man whose income had recently diminished by the amount of his stipend and pension; Prue might well lament. Alexander Pope observed to a friend apropos of Steele's candidacy: "Some people say, that passage in Scripture may be applied to him, upon the resignation of his places: *I have left all and have followed you. But whether or no his Reward will therefore be great* is hard to determine." [23]

In July and early August Steele left the editorship of *The Guardian* to Addison and presumably threw himself into the contest. The Whig opposition needed seats in the new Parliament and must have given Steele important financial support; despite the expenses of the election, his finances were unusually healthy in 1713, only one action for debt being brought against him that year and that one for a mere £250. Unfortunately for the Whigs, the government had the safest of platforms: peace secured after a long war. The prospects of a reduction in the land tax, the principal means of financing Marlborough's war, would appeal to most rural electors. Opposition candidates could, of course, play on local concerns; an eighteenth-century legend tells of Steele offering an apple stuck full of guineas to be given to the elector voting for him whose wife was first brought to bed of a child nine months thereafter. According to a Hampshire chronicler writing eighty years later, "It is said that women here actually commemorate the knight to this

[22] J. H. Plumb, *Sir Robert Walpole: The Making of a Statesman* (London, 1956), p. 59.
[23] Pope, *Correspondence* (see note 8), I, 189.

day. . . ." [24] Though the story comes second hand, it is not inherently improbable (except, perhaps, with respect to the wives' reaction) and illustrates one possible way of securing electoral support in eighteenth-century England; there were others not much less bizarre.

Beyond purely local issues were those having to do with the peace, especially the eighth and ninth articles, the so-called "commercial articles" of the Treaty of Utrecht. These articles had been designed by Bolingbroke to lower the tariff barriers between France and England in the hope of reducing the commercial competition which had spread throughout the world during the previous half-century. English commercial interests, woolen makers, brandy distillers, and others, viewed the articles as a threat to their markets and flooded Parliament in the spring of 1713 with petitions opposing the enabling bill which would make the articles effective. Party lines wavered and broke; the Ministry was defeated on the bill's second reading, its first defeat in the House since the Tory landslide of 1710. Behind all the statistics and tables and economic theory which the commercial interests brought to bear like so many cannon on the problem were the genuine fears of hardheaded British merchants who knew well enough that France was England's greatest commercial rival the world over. Always available for association with economic arguments, of course, was the fact that France, a Roman Catholic country, harbored James, the Roman Catholic Pretender. All Englishmen knew that the Queen could not live many years longer. Would she be succeeded by the Pretender (whose claim to the throne, viewed from one legal aspect, was quite good; and who had the legacy of Stuart popularity

---

[24] Richard Warner, *Collections for the History of Hampshire and the Bishopric of Winchester.* . . . (London [1795]), I, Sect. 2, 190. Percival also tells this story of the election in 1722 (BM, Add. MSS. 47029, p. 219). There is, of course, no reason why Steele could not have repeated the stratagem.

with the masses) or the safely Protestant, but distinctly foreign, House of Hanover?

Symbolizing in a way Whig misgivings was the channel port of Dunkirk, which became for Steele an election issue. This great port, acquired by Cromwell in 1658, had been resold to the French in 1662 by Charles II when hard pressed for money. During the Anglo-French wars of the decades following it was a home port for privateers, who made English shippers pay for Charles' impecuniousness — goods worth millions of pounds were lost to the marauders.[25] The ninth article of the Treaty called for the razing of the fortifications and port facilities of Dunkirk within five months of the signing. English commercial interests came to look on the destruction as an indication of French good faith and were disturbed when in July, 1713, a representative of the Dunkirk magistrates came to London to seek revocation of the intended destruction.

Freed from all obligations to the government and with an election approaching in a few days, Richard Steele returned to *The Guardian* in early August with a fiery political paper on Dunkirk. The motto of the issue (No. 128) is *Delenda est Carthago:* Demolish Carthage, and the content matches the sentiment. Writing as an "English Tory," his opening sentence addressed to Ironside reads like a rebuke to Addison for his innocent *Guardians* of the preceding month. "You employ your important moments, methinks, a little too frivolously, when you consider so often little circumstances of dress and behaviour, and never make mention of matters wherein you and all your fellow-subjects in general are concerned." These matters prove to be Dunkirk, and "English Tory" affirms that "the British nation expect the immediate demolition" of the city. This phrase

---

[25] G. N. Clark, *The Later Stuarts, 1660–1714,* rev. ed. (Oxford, 1940), p. 57. Steele's uncle John was an English ship captain in these undeclared wars, it will be recalled.

was to be used by the Tories time and again as evidence of Steele's defiant attitude toward the Queen.

The essay is effective propaganda, in Steele's best hortatory, call-to-arms mood. He does not devote much attention to technical and commercial arguments but adheres to the question of the damage, past and future, to English properties and liberty that Dunkirk represents. And above all he reiterates the single, simple, inescapable fact that the destruction of Dunkirk provided for by the Treaty was not being carried out. The *Guardian* stirred up a hornet's nest in the government; Daniel Defoe, on Harley's payroll, had a twenty-three page anonymous reply on the streets within seven days, full of vigorous *ad hominem* arguments recalling Steele's lively past and reflecting on his treasonable demands, all with an eye to the election.

> Good Mr. Steele, be so just to your country, as to let the honest people of Stockbridge know who the gentleman who they are desired to choose to represent them in Parliament is, and how he has treated the Queen their Sovereign in Print; and tho' I know your election is necessary to you, to protect you from your just debts, which you are or might be able enough to pay; yet in generous justice to your country, which you have shown great inclination to serve in other cases, you can do no less than let them know how the case stands, and if they will choose you afterwards, none can be blamed but themselves.[26]

The Examiner also hastened to denigrate Steele in the eyes of the public and his electors, calling *The Guardian* a "scandalous libel" in the issue of 21 August and discussing the treasonable aspects of Steele's use of the verb "expect."

In spite of the government's opposition, Steele sailed safely into Parliament, returned by a vote of fifty to twenty-one.[27] It

[26] *The Honour and Prerogative of the Queen's Majesty Vindicated . . . in a Letter From a Country Whig to Mr. Steele,* p. 23. See also Goldgar, *The Curse of Party* (note 2), pp. 121–25.
[27] Steele's letter in *Guardian* No. 168.

was an election which held little cheer for the Whigs generally, but Steele was naturally elated. On 22 September he issued a pamphlet called *The Importance of Dunkirk Consider'd: in Defence of the Guardian of August the 7th. In a Letter to the Bailiff of Stockbridge*. The pamphlet, which rehearsed the arguments presented in the 7 August *Guardian,* printed also excerpts from Defoe's pamphlet and from the critical *Examiners,* the whole swelling to some sixty-three quarto pages and selling for a shilling. Assistance on technical matters, indeed whole passages of the text, were provided anonymously by Charles King, an English merchant who during the war had suffered considerable shipping losses from French privateers and who could thus bring to the controversy that personal knowledge which Steele, as a good editor, valued.[28] The issues the pamphlet deals with are dead these two centuries, Steele's ghostwriters ghosts indeed, but the opening sentences are pure Steele, full of zest and elation. The Irish orphan has become a Great Man, a Member of the British Parliament, and cynosure of London eyes. He addresses John Snow, Bailiff of Stockbridge:

> According to my promise when I took my leave of you, I send you all the pamphlets and papers which have been printed since the dissolution of the last Parliament; among these you will find your humble servant no small man, but spoken of more than once in print: you will find I take up whole pages in the *Examiner,* and that there is a little pamphlet written wholly upon me, and directed to me.[29]

Jonathan Swift was back in London at the urgent request of Oxford after his installation as Dean of St. Patrick's and some subsequent weeks in the Irish countryside recuperating from the strains of the previous three years. His head ached from the

---

[28] Cf. Rae Blanchard, "Steele, Charles King, and the Dunkirk Pamphlets," *Huntington Library Quarterly,* XIV (1951), 423–39.

[29] *Tracts,* pp. 83–124 and for publishing information, p. 640.

old ailment, and he was altogether in no mood to celebrate the political and journalistic triumphs of his sometime neighbor and friend. But there was, of course, more to his return than personal animosity; it is unthinkable that Swift would have bothered to make the wearing journey across the Irish Sea merely to reply to Steele. The Ministry was in difficulties. The Whigs had a good, concrete issue in the demolition of Dunkirk and a better one, as Queen Anne's health worsened, in the succession. Steele's *The Importance of Dunkirk* was selling, even at a shilling a copy; the third edition appeared just a week after the first, on 29 September, and by December Roberts, the bookseller, was offering versions in both quarto and octavo. There was trouble within the Ministry itself, too: the brilliant and ambitious Bolingbroke was maneuvering to get rid of Oxford and assume full control of the government. Oxford was drinking heavily, putting off business that urgently needed attention, but drunk and indolent was still a statesman and politician worthy of anyone's Steele, and he had the confidence of the Queen. The Queen held the balance of power.

All this the Whigs knew; secrets, personal or political, would not stay kept in the restricted society. The Whigs' course, too, had the virtue of simplicity; they were in opposition: continue to exploit the Dunkirk issue and press the Ministry on the succession. Meantime they could continue negotiations behind the scenes with representatives of the Hanoverian Court. Time, they must have reasoned, was on their side as the Queen's sands ran out, if they could dramatize the choice between James Stuart and Hanover, arouse public fears of James's Catholicism, and drive the wedge deeper between Oxford and Bolingbroke. All this required skillful journalism, for the Lord Treasurer had assembled a formidable group: two pamphleteers of talent in Mrs. Manley and William Oldisworth, and two of genius, Swift and Defoe. A party regular was needed, someone who knew printers and public, someone who could dramatize issues and who had the courage of his convictions, someone not to be intimidated by ministerial threats or swayed by promises. Richard Steele had written in *The Importance of Dunkirk:* "I say again and again, if once men are so intimidated as not to dare to offer their thoughts upon public affairs without incurring the imputation of offending against the prerogative of their Prince, that Prince, whatever advantage his ministers might make of his prerogative, would himself have no prerogative but that of being deceived." Steele was the choice.

The Guardian meanwhile came to an unannounced close with No. 175 of 1 October 1713. Addison's graceful pen had carried the paper through most of September and Pope had contributed a fine, half-humorous essay on a favorite subject, the advantages of naturalistic gardening, as No. 173. But Nestor Ironside's impartiality was out of place; great issues were being decided and Steele needed little persuasion, if any, from the Whig councils to end *The Guardian* and devote his full time to party journalism. "I have settled all things to great satisfaction," he wrote Mrs. Steele on 29 September, "and desire you would stay at home, but send the coach for me to come to you, to take the air and talk further."

CHAPTER VIII

The Englishman
and the Dying Queen

THE FRAY AHEAD was just the sort Richard Steele liked best and Joseph Addison detested: loud and public, with opportunity for swagger and riposte. Re-elected member for Malmesbury in August, Addison seems to have stood somewhat aloof from party machinations in the fall of 1713, certainly by choice. John Hughes, the librettist, wrote to him on 6 October 1713:

> I do not doubt but you know, by this time, that Mr. Steele has abruptly dropped the *Guardian.* He has published this day a paper called the *Englishman,* which begins with an answer to the *Examiner,* written with great boldness and spirit, and shows that his thoughts are at present entirely on politics. Some of his friends are in pain about him, and are concerned that a paper should be discontinued which might have been generally entertaining without engaging in party-matters.[1]

Hughes goes on to describe a sequel to *The Guardian* and asks Addison's help in the project. Addison's reply, often-quoted, is really more curious for what it implies about Addison's position than what it says about Steele. After putting Hughes off by pleading weariness, he writes: "I am in a thousand troubles for poor Dick, and wish that his zeal for the public may not be

---

[1] *The Letters of Joseph Addison,* ed. Walter Graham (Oxford, 1941), pp. 487–88.

ruinous to himself; but he has sent me word that he is determined to go on, and that any advice I can give him in this particular, will have no weight with him." [2] Addison was replying from his new estate, Bilton Hall, near Rugby, which he had purchased the previous February. There he remained until mid-December. The literary partnership was emphatically dissolved for the crucial months ahead.

The new journal, *The Englishman,* displayed Steele's "zeal for the public" in the first issue, from the motto (*Delenda est Carthago*) to Steele's assertion in the last sentence, over his signature, that "in the House, and as a Member of Parliament, I am accountable to no man, but the greatest man in England is accountable to me." The Englishman, the narrator or *persona,* reported that he had

> purchased the lion, desk, pen, ink, and paper, and all other goods of Nestor Ironside, Esq; who has thought fit to write no more himself, but has given me full liberty to report any sage expressions or maxims which may tend to the instruction of mankind, and the service of his country. It is not, said the good man, giving me the key of the lion's den, now a time to improve the taste of men by the reflections and railleries of poets and philosophers, but to awaken their understanding, by laying before them the present state of the world like a man of experience and a patriot. . . .

Nestor's parting words were "Be an Englishman."

An observer somehow able to see into Whig and Tory councils might have been amused to note that at the moment this Irish Englishman was asserting the true political faith, a fellow Irishman was preparing a devastating rejoinder to Steele's Dunkirk pamphlets. About this time, during the fall of 1713, the Ministry decided to move against Steele in two ways. One method was to be an indirect reply to his printed charges, through *The Examiner* and the efforts of Jonathan Swift. For

[2] *Letters,* p. 280.

the next several months Swift's talents were devoted to meeting and anticipating Whig propaganda, especially that of Richard Steele. The other method was more direct: expulsion from the House. Though Steele's pamphlet *The Crisis* and certain numbers of *The Englishman* provided the immediate pretext for his expulsion the following March, there can be no doubt that the decision to rid themselves of Steele was reached by the Ministry soon after his election in August, 1713, and that he knew of it. Peter Wentworth, a moderate Tory with an ear to the ground, had heard as early as 13 September that Steele was to be "turned out of the house." Defoe, who had Harley's counsel, spoke of the same fate in his *Reasons Concerning the Immediate Demolishing of Dunkirk,* published in September. Pope wrote Caryll only six days after the election: "Mr. Steele, you know, has carried his election, tho' 'tis said a petition will be lodged against him, and he is of that opinion himself." Most important of all, perhaps, considering its provenance, is a short paragraph in a news letter dated 10 September 1713 preserved among Robert Harley's private papers: "We hear there are informations taken upon oath of bribery and other corrupt practices at the late election in the west, and that two petitions are thereupon lodged against the author of the Guardian, who, it is said, is returned for Stockbridge, so that his sitting in the House may not be so long as some people expected." [3]

Now, bribery, threats, and promises were so ordinary in early eighteenth-century elections as to be the rule rather than the exception. As Walpole's biographer remarks, "[N]o candidate ever lacked grounds to petition Parliament against the return of his rival though he might . . . lack the money to do so." [4] The Ministry's move against Richard Steele was not in

---

[3] *The Wentworth Papers,* ed. James J. Cartwright (London, 1883), p. 354; Pope, *The Correspondence of Alexander Pope,* ed. George Sherburn (Oxford, 1956), I, 189; HMC, *Portland MSS.,* V, 335.

[4] J. H. Plumb, *Sir Robert Walpole: The Making of a Statesman* (London, 1956), p. 60.

the interest of better government. By February when the Parliament finally met, after deliberate delay, Steele had written and signed pamphlets which provided the Tories a better handle than the disputed election, but the basic decision to expel him, make a public example of him, had been reached months before.

He was a natural target. Sources like Mrs. Manley and Swift could provide a great deal of damaging personal information about him. He was well-known because of his writing, a much more prominent member than some Whig backbencher, yet he was not of the nobility or even of the English gentry; he was Irish. Above all, he had no family interest; no part in the great family connections which wound in and out of both parties in the eighteenth century and were sources of strength (and, frequently, embarrassment) to many political leaders of the time. He was fair game.

The obvious first step was somehow to neutralize Steele's effectiveness as a propagandist. To do this Swift prepared an anonymous answer to Steele's Dunkirk papers under the title, *The Importance of the Guardian Considered.* It appeared about the end of October. The tone is scornful, the argument *ad hominem,* the strategy to deflect attention from Steele's arguments on to the personal weaknesses of the writer himself: his vanity, his morals, his shallow learning, his lack of gratitude.

Mr. Steele is author of two tolerable plays, (or at least of the greatest part of them) which, added to the company he kept, and to the continual conversation and friendship of Mr. Addison, hath given him the character of a wit. To take the height of his learning, you are to suppose a lad just fit for the university, and sent early from thence into the wide world, where he followed every way of life that might least improve or preserve the rudiments he had got. He hath no invention, nor is master of a tolerable style; his chief talent is humor, which he sometimes discovers both in writing and discourse; for after the first bottle he is no disagreeable companion. I never knew him taxed with ill-nature, which hath made me wonder how ingratitude came to be his prevailing vice. . . .[5]

The author, a "Friend of Mr. Steele," demonstrates that Steele is a trifling bread-writer who has bitten the hand that supplied the bread. "As for the importance of Dunkirk . . . neither he, nor you [Snow, the Bailiff of Stockbridge], nor I, have anything to do in the matter."

A quality propaganda piece in the category of lampoons it was, but Steele had the issues. Who, after all, cared about Steele, and despite Swift's final disclaimer, who did *not* care about Dunkirk and the Pretender? Swift's answer apparently ran to only one edition. A more scurrilous and more popular tract appeared in early November, *The Character of Richard St——le, Esq.* . . . , probably written by Dr. William Wagstaffe of St. Bartholomew's Hospital. Scurrility outsells quality; four editions of the *Character* were in print by March.[6] Other writers lent their hands to discrediting Steele, alluding to his sister's insanity, his alchemy, his debts — always his debts. Tories who had hurried to the booksellers to buy Steele's plays, his *Tatlers, Spectators,* and *Guardians,* now hastened to retract their judgment, ascribing to Addison the merit of everything he had written, as Colley Cibber later wryly observed.[7]

Richard Steele was too busy to pay much attention. *The Englishman* appeared three times a week instead of six, but there was still much space to be filled. It was a party paper and every topic imaginable came under discussion: the commercial clauses of the Treaty of course, but also the election of Members for London, the plight of Protestant refugees from the Palatinate, the practice of the Tory clergy, the validity of lay-baptism.

---

[5] Swift, *Political Tracts, 1713–1719,* ed. Herbert Davis and Irvin Ehrenpreis (Princeton, 1953), pp. 5–6. Note that there is a contradiction in this text about the dating of the tract: p. xiii (2 November) and p. 201 (31 October).

[6] Swift, *Political Tracts, 1713–1719,* pp. xiv–xv and 201; Aitken, I, 410–11.

[7] Dedication to *Ximena.*

(Baptism was a lively topic; High Church Tories generally opposed baptism by laymen; Latitudinarian Whigs were for it.) Even wine drinking had humorous political overtones; good Englishmen presumably preferred Portuguese port, supplied by an ally, to French claret. And issue by issue Steele traded blows with *The Examiner,* from time to time signing his name, as in No. 13, for 3 November. Occasionally, as in No. 14 for Guy Fawkes Day, the Catholics were attacked, to remind the English people of what they could expect if James were introduced as the Queen's successor: I cannot "on this day omit to remind my countrymen, that the priests of that faith have equalled the utmost barbarities and cruelties committed by the ancient worshippers of the sun, or any other heathen idols." Adroitly quoting from a sermon by Swift's friend St. George Ashe, the Bishop of Clogher, Steele ends the paper with a call for unity.

Protestant unity: that was the sticking point. Although most Englishmen preferred an English Stuart to a German Hanoverian, that Stuart must be a Protestant. Bolingbroke knew this and was working frantically in secret negotiations aimed at persuading James to change his creed, if only for the nonce. To the deist Bolingbroke these religious questions were tiresome hairsplitting, but they were of the very highest importance to the mass of Englishmen; the Whigs had learned this once and for all at the Sacheverell trial. Steele's personal feelings went back to his Irish upbringing. The furor signified that if James refused to leave the Roman Catholic Church the English lower clergy, most of whom, like George Berkeley, were natural Tories, could not support his succession. After 1688 most Englishmen were not willing to accept a Catholic king.

The Englishman was almost but not quite immersed in politics. There was, for example, an early paper (No. 9) on one of Steele's favorite subjects, love and marriage. "Whatever fine gentlemen may think, or loose writers may suggest, there is not to be found in all the wild of pleasure through a whole year, half the satisfaction which the well-married man knows in one day." No man with five small children at home is likely to over-estimate the pleasures of the hearth; nevertheless, Steele appre-ciated the satisfactions of home, with the background of a bache-lor captain's life in Landguard Fort. Home was where he could direct a peremptory note for "clean linen" and find the linen there when he hurried to Bloomsbury Square between political meetings. Home was pre-eminently the place for plans and con-ferences; if other men kept their wives in separate spheres, ad-dressed them by their titles, Steele did not. Prue was always part of his public career.

In early winter 1713 Steele had a new project, the most am-bitious political project of his life. English politics were fluid, the Queen's health continued to decline, a crisis approached. *The Englishman* went well, but every attempt to bring the true state of affairs, as Steele saw it, to the attention of the public was countered by the Tory press. He had in mind publishing a pamphlet which would focus on the transcendent issue, the suc-cession. It would be called *The Crisis* and would, or should, have financial support from the Whigs to insure broad circulation. There would be an extended advertising campaign before pub-lication; he knew from experience as editor, from the success of Philips' play and of *Cato,* the power of advertising. The plan was good, but how to get it started? All the world knew, and the Tory press never tired of reminding the world, that Richard Steele would sound his own horn if no one rose to sound it for him. It was a condition of his continued existence in the society in which he quite literally lived by his wits, but there was a question of tact. He hesitated, discussed the matter with Mrs. Steele, then resolved to approach the Hanover Club for sub-scriptions in person. "[W]ith as gay an air as I can lay before them that I take it to be their Constitution to do it, as I am la-bouring in the common cause." And indeed, the name of the club itself should have encouraged an author writing on behalf of the Hanoverian succession.

The plan advanced. In *The Englishman* for 22 October the

publisher, Samuel Buckley, advertised a discourse by Richard
Steele, Esq., "now ready for the press . . . designed as an
antidote against the treasonable insinuations which are licen-
tiously handed about the town." The announced title rather
gives away the contents:

> THE CRISIS; *or a* Discourse plainly shewing, from the most
> authentick Records, the just Causes of the late happy Revolution:
> And the several Settlements of the Crowns of *England* and *Scot-
> land* on Her Majesty; and on the Demise of Her Majesty without
> Issue, upon the most illustrious Princess Sophia, Electress and
> Dutchess Dowager of Hanover and the Heirs of Her Body, being
> *Protestants;* by both Parliaments of the late Kingdoms of *Eng-
> land* and *Scotland;* and that no Power whatsoever can *barr,
> alter, or make void* the same: With some *Seasonable Remarks*
> on the Danger of a POPISH SUCCESSOR.[8]

The price, Buckley continued, would be one shilling and the
number printed according to the number of subscriptions. Thus
launched, the advertising campaign continued, with notices appearing in every issue but one of *The Englishman* for the week
following, and then intermittently until January.

Though Buckley's advertisement spoke of *The Crisis* as being
ready for the press, this was probably copy writer's license.
Steele's project was good on its face, however, and he soon had
help from various Whig sources. William Moore, a lawyer of
the Inner Temple, who had helped Steele on his lottery proposal
in 1712 and worked on the legal aspects of the Dunkirk *Guardian*
undertook legal research for *The Crisis*. Lord Halifax entertained the journalist-politician at dinner more than once and
prominent Whigs sold subscriptions like tickets to a lottery.[9] In
December the Hanoverian envoy, Baron Bothmer, wrote to his
superior at the Elector's court, proposing that the Elector finance

---

[8] From *The Englishman,* ed. Blanchard, p. 411. (Italics reversed.)

[9] Cf. *Corr.,* p. 293 (Steele to Prue): "I have left Mr. Craggs's subscription-
books at his house. . . ." Steele describes the circumstances of the pamphlet's
composition in the preface to his *Apology* (*Tracts,* pp. 285–86).

the printing of the tract and recompense Steele who was being assisted in the enterprise, he said, by Walpole and Stanhope.[10] This was powerful assistance indeed, for Walpole and Stanhope were Whigs of the younger generation just then rising to succeed the Junto. Stanhope was almost Steele's age and they had been at Oxford at the same time, both later entering the army, where Stanhope's ability, family, and money secured him frequent promotion, before his final defeat and capture, as Commander-in-Chief of the British forces in Spain, at Brihuega in 1711. Exchanged and back in London, he returned to politics; earlier he had been one of the Whig managers at the Sacheverell trial. He was Walpole's best friend — though a political foe in later years — and like that statesman aggressive, shrewd, tough-minded. These Whigs, men such as Halifax and Stanhope, were a formidable group and they had the immense advantage of being united on what was becoming the principal issue, the succession, as the Tories in office were not. Steele's project was, they saw, likely to prove fruitful and they backed it.

The Tory writers around Harley had a more difficult task. They could not, of course, support the Pretender; only an out-and-out Jacobite could do so, and men like Defoe and Swift would probably have left their employment rather than take such a step. On the other hand, they could not welcome the Hanoverian succession without seeming to echo the Whigs. One alternative was to attack individual Whigs and Whig publications, and this they continued to do, with Richard Steele and *The Englishman* as a preferred target. *The Examiner* sniped at Steele in almost every number, complaining of the allegedly libelous statements of the Whigs and alluding, from time to time, of the fate that awaited him. On 2 November the Tory paper hinted again at Steele's approaching expulsion, reminding him of Walpole's expulsion from Commons in January, 1712:

[10] James Macpherson, *Original Papers Containing the Secret History of Great Britain. . . .* (London, 1775), II, 521.

Mr. Steele can warp this hint to his own advantage: for after libelling the Queen and Ministry, he would now make his country amends by writing against the Pretender; by which he only means to lay in stock for future clamour, that if he should chance to suffer for the ill he has done, he may give his sentence a wrong turn, and say, as W[alpol]e suffered for his eloquence, he suffers for being in the interest of the House of Hanover.

Going ahead with *The Englishman* and *The Crisis* meant, then, certain expulsion. Steele chose to go ahead.

All was not politics that winter, though. His notoriety made him in a publisher's eye, valuable property. Jacob Tonson was not a notably sentimental man and he could overlook even some bastardy (especially since Steele had magnanimously taken the child into his legitimate family circle). Steele had been a good author and it was doubtless Tonson, publisher of *The Guardian,* who suggested that Steele put together a volume of poetry "by several hands." Tonson had published sporadically a series of similar miscellanies since 1684, with Dryden, while he was alive, as adviser and principal contributor. Joseph Addison had seen his first poem in English published in the *Third Part* (1693) of the miscellanies (along with a translation by a friend from Magdalen, later well-known, Henry Sacheverell). The *Sixth Part* (1709) had contained the famous pastorals by Philips and Pope. This was a distinguished series, in short. Steele's volume was not a direct continuation of the Dryden-Tonson miscellanies, but he felt the need to keep it clear of politics, or as clear as one could in those days. An advertisement in *The Guardian* of 4 May 1713 (No. 46) announced the proposed volume and called for contributions. In late December it appeared: *Poetical Miscellanies, Consisting of Original Poems and Translations. By the best Hands.*[11] Steele provided a graceful dedication to his old friend William Congreve who, though a Kit-Cat, had managed in his retirement to avoid identification

[11] *Verse,* pp. xviii–xx.

with either party and was respected by all. Steele praises Congreve's literary talents, especially his gift for lyric poetry. The poetical performances of Steele and his friends which follow are uneven — miscellanies cannot be otherwise — but the authors are, considering the temper of the times, a surprisingly assorted group. The Little Senate poets and poetasters, of course: Ambrose Philips, Thomas Tickell, Laurence Eusden (in later Whiggish days a poet laureate, and no good one), Eustace Budgell; but also John Gay, Swift's Irish protégé Thomas Parnell, Pope (who contributed his "translation" of the Wife of Bath's Prologue), and the eighteenth century's most distinguished female poet, Anne Finch, Countess of Winchilsea — a fair sampling of the day's poetic talent, except for Swift and Addison. Swift would not have answered Steele's advertisement in May; by then their final quarrel was beginning. Addison's absence is more puzzling.

In truth, Addison's actions in the winter of 1713–1714 savor somewhat of that disingenuousness which Pope was to immortalize in the Atticus portrait of the *Epistle to Dr. Arbuthnot.* There are his letters encouraging Pope in the proposed translation of Homer, followed a few months later by Addison's help and encouragement for Thomas Tickell's rival translation. This incident may perhaps be explained away, though with some difficulty; Addison may have felt he owed young Pope nothing. But he owed Steele something for years of friendship, and his withdrawal from town to manage his country estate, his disavowal of party at this juncture does not ring true. At every stage of his life, after all, since he left Magdalen, "party" had smoothed Addison's way: the grand tour, the under-secretaryship in Sunderland's office, the Irish post, the Parliament seat for Malmesbury — all these had been gifts of the Whigs. This was not quite the time, nor the tone in which it was said the proper one, to write John Hughes from the green acres of Bilton (in the letter quoted earlier) of being "in a thousand troubles for poor Dick." The hard-pressed Steele might have retorted, though he never would have done so, "Name one." In any case, Addison did not choose being in trouble to the extent of allowing one or two of his poems to be printed in the *Miscellanies*.

To the strains of political warfare was added for Steele that winter the exquisite torture of the gout. Steele hobbled about on crutches. As he had years before written *The Christian Hero* to fortify himself in his struggle with various sorts of temptation, so no doubt he now composed *Englishman* No. 22 to help quiet the pangs of gout, as well as to provide some of that religio-philosophical instruction which was always a popular ingredient of his periodicals. He relies mainly on the *Tusculan Disputations* of his favorite author, Cicero, but concludes that the Christian philosopher has the firmer support. As he often can, he freshens a trite subject with experience. We may imagine Steele, fighting the philosopher's battle with gout, scribbling the essay in bed, the Cicero volume at one hand and five wide-eyed children at the other. "With what shame, confusion, and repentance shall the man utter the least groan from the punction of the gout, who is furnished with so many precepts and examples of a contrary behaviour?" Yet he is forced to admit, " 'Tis true indeed that there is almost in every man naturally something wretched, weak, soft, and irresolute. . . ."

Perhaps the gout provided Steele time for reminiscence. In No. 26 he recalls his meeting Alexander Selkirk and describes Selkirk's adventures alone on Juan Fernandez Island. Selkirk had been placed ashore by the privateer Dampier after a quarrel and had been picked up nearly five years later, then had served at sea under Steele's friend, Captain Woodes Rogers. Other accounts of the adventure appeared, but Steele's has the detailed authenticity of what it was, the story from Selkirk's lips: the search for turtles, the reading of scriptures, making clothes from goatskins, and so on. Daniel Defoe was reading every issue of *The Englishman* with great care.

Sometime during the latter part of 1713 Steele had business in Oxford. Several friends were fellows there: Edward Young, Tickell, and his old companion of university days, Richard Parker, now Fellow of Merton. Though Oxford was thought of as a hotbed of Toryism, if not Jacobitism, the Whig persuasion had its Oxonian supporters too. Three of them, young students at Christ Church, had written academic exercises in Latin verse praising "Cato" and "the Censor of the British," which were read at the Sheldonian and subsequently printed. Steele strolled through the colleges like any alumnus, observed the new Clarendon Press, missed a favorite tree, toasted old times with an old friend, and regarded the University with great benevolence generally. The nation, he concluded, had nothing to fear from Oxford; "[T]hese noble foundations and monuments of the virtue of our ancestors are in their very nature directly opposite to tyranny and unlimited power, since as ignorance is a natural consequence of slavery, arts and sciences may be properly called the eldest daughters of Liberty." [12] Steele's instincts were optimistic and libertarian. Many of his sentiments ring familiar to an American ear because they derive from the classic liberal tradition in which the American revolutionary leaders were immersed: Polybius, Cicero, Locke. Besides, did not Richard Steele's experience prove these truths self-evident? Had he not first come to Oxford an impoverished Irish orphan of no family; was he not returning as a national celebrity, a Member of the House of Commons, a defender of the rights of people and Parliament? The one apparent exception to his liberalism, his hostility to Roman Catholicism, had roots in the same tradition, as well as in his Irish heritage. Steele and others of his views distrusted and attacked Catholicism because they felt it threatened men's civil liberties.

The Englishman on Oxford marked a turning point; henceforth the pages of the journal were closed to everything but

[12] No. 34 of 22 December 1713.

politics. Political debate generally begins with principles and ends in personalities; so it was with Steele. The next two months saw the intensification of the Whig-Tory struggle and the worsening of his relationship with Swift. In December matters were brought to a head by Whig attacks on Oxford and Tory attacks on Marlborough; Swift and Steele believed that the other was behind these attacks and both were to an extent right.

In an effort to minimize the Whigs' propaganda about the Pretender and Catholic tyranny, *The Examiner* breathed life into its attacks on Marlborough, hinting darkly of a "stratocracy," that is, a military dictatorship. *The Englishman* for 26 December (No. 36) struck back directly at Oxford, recalling his strategy of having a dozen peers created to secure a majority in the House of Lords. "I will shew him [the *Examiner*] an officer, who with only twelve men well posted, could introduce a greater innovation into this constitution than the Duke Marlborough . . . ever dared to attempt at the head of an hundred thousand." Two nights before Steele had dined with Lord Halifax; this paper, no doubt written at the party's call, represents the start of Steele's campaign against the Lord Treasurer. Oxford was Jonathan Swift's patron and personal friend; Swift could not fail to resent Steele's actions. There is no question that the attack on Oxford went against the grain with Steele; in fact a few years later, after the strife, or at least the Whig-Tory strife, had cooled, Steele apologized in public print to the Tory statesman, then out of public life, protesting that "I never writ any thing that ought to displease you, but with a reluctant heart, and in opposition to much good-will and esteem for your many great and uncommon talents. . . ." [13]

But the decision of the Whig leaders to single out Oxford for attack was from their point of view just and right. Despite the Lord Treasurer's fondness for the bottle — no very uncommon

[13] *A Letter to the Earl of O- -d, Concerning the Bill of Peerage* (1719) in *Tracts*, p. 525.

trait in those days — he was a resourceful politician, had the Queen's confidence, and was interested in and capable of forming a broad-gauge coalition which would include moderates of both sides. Bolingbroke was too closely identified with the extreme Tories, the High-Flyers; for all his brilliance, he probably could not realize his ambition of leading the nation unless he could secure the Pretender's succession. Quite correctly, then, the Whigs decided that Steele should attempt to split support away from the Lord Treasurer. Though neither could know this at the time, Swift had more to lose than Steele did; for the Whigs could easily do without Marlborough now that the peace was secured (as they proved when they came into office and turned the old general into his elaborate pasture, Blenheim), whereas the Tories could not at all do without Oxford.

He was no easy target. He was personally honest. He was not to be stampeded; cowardice did not run in the Harley family. And he was very fond of dealing by personal conversation rather than by writing, which made for that ambiguity convenient to politicians, especially those in office with preferment to dispense. Finally, he had vast connections in and out of Parliament, all going back to the family electoral influence in the Welsh border counties.[14]

That family background was Dissenting, and it was widely known that the Lord Treasurer himself had received part of his early education from a Dissenting minister. The incongruity of this background for the chief minister of a government relying upon High Church Anglican support, Steele or the Whig leaders decided, would be the main line of attack. The theory was that by emphasizing Oxford's "hypocrisy" in turning from Dissent to Anglicanism, the Whigs could split off his support from both Dissenters and High Church Tories. It was a good idea, such a good one that Bolingbroke himself adopted it for his own pur-

[14] Robert Walcott, *English Politics in the Early Eighteenth Century* (Oxford, 1956), pp. 66–68.

poses later in the year when he introduced the so-called Schism Bill, a measure designed to restrict the Dissenters' extensive (and excellent) educational system. Oxford, Bolingbroke realized, was bound to lose support from the Dissenters if he supported the bill and from High Church Tory elements if he opposed it. Both Whigs and High-Flyers, then, tried to portray Oxford as a religious hypocrite, a man who would change his religion with the seasons.[15]

Steele coined and put into circulation the epithet which expressed the Harleys' allegedly ambiguous position. In *The Englishman* No. 57 (15 February 1714) he prints a letter "to Mr. —— at Windsor." This Tory friend, presumably Swift, has told Steele that the "upper courtiers" are "for the Church. . . ." Steele asks ". . . what are your leaders, but what I used in private conversation to call them, the new converts?" After his expulsion from Commons in March, he continued the attack on the Harley family in his new periodicals, *The Lover* and *The Reader,* with new zest.

> The pleasantry of this excellent farce is, that all these fellows were bred Presbyterians, and are now set up for High Churchmen. They carry it admirably well, and the partisans do not distinguish that there is a difference between those who are of neither side from generous principles, and those who are disinterested only from having no principles at all.[16]

This was good propaganda but Steele did not relish the personal attack, especially since his relationship with Oxford had been for many years cordial. Still, a party writer must turn his hand from time to time to disagreeable tasks, as Swift knew from his own experience, but Steele's lampoons of Oxford constituted the irrevocable end of the friendship between Swift and Steele.

Much more congenial to Steele's talents and predilections was

---

[15] For a full discussion, see my "Steele and the Fall of Harley in 1714," *Philological Quarterly,* XXXVII (1958), 440–47.

[16] *The Lover,* No. 11 (20 March) in *Richard Steele's Periodical Journalism, 1714–16,* ed. Rae Blanchard (Oxford, 1959), p. 42.

the sort of propaganda *The Crisis* represented: the hortatory, the viewing-with-alarm, the call for a return to first principles. Whig drumbeating for this long-expected pamphlet palled early in Tory ears. "[W]hen I grow sceptical," *The Examiner* complained, "or too inquisitive and fond of novelties, I send and subscribe for the *Crisis*." On 26 December *The Englishman* announced that publication had been delayed "at the desire of several ladies of quality" in order to allow more members of the female world to exhibit their zeal for the public by subscribing. This bit of pomposity was too much for Swift; a few days later an anonymous poem appeared at the London booksellers entitled *The First Ode of the Second Book of Horace Paraphras'd: And Address'd to Richard St——le, Esq.:* It began

> DICK, thour't resolv'd, as I am told,
> Some strange *Arcana* to unfold,
> And with the help of *Buckley's* Pen
> To vamp the *good Old Cause* again,
> Which thou (such *Bur——t's* shrewd Advice is)
> Must furbish up and Nickname *CRISIS*.
> Thou pompously wilt let us know
> What all the World knew long ago,
>
> .   .   .   .
>
> That we a *German* Prince must own
> When *A——N* for Heav'n resigns Her Throne.

Swift, for these are his octosyllabics, goes on to advise Steele to leave politics ("For madmen, children, wits, and fools/Should never meddle with edged tools"), and repair with him to a cellar for a quiet drink.[17] The tone is good-natured. The strategy is, like that of *The Importance of the Guardian,* to turn attention off the issues and onto Steele, whose limitations as a statesman are made apparent. It is the strategy of *The Spectator's* treatment of Sir Roger the Tory squire, turned back on its author.

[17] *The Poems of Jonathan Swift,* ed. Harold Williams (2nd ed.; Oxford, 1958), I, 179–80.

One might note Swift's acceptance of the Hanoverian succession; there was apparently no question in his mind that this was the proper course. His political associate Bolingbroke, however, was still negotiating secretly with the Pretender.

Steele, undeterred, completed the promised pamphlet with unusual care. His assistant William Moore, the lawyer, would set down the points of law, what could legally be said, and Steele would revise the matter into paragraphs. After the draft was completed he sent copies to Addison, Hoadly (the pugnacious minister, friend of *Tatler* days), and two other Whig friends for comments and corrections.[18] These were incorporated, the copy sent to Buckley, and with a minimum of concealment the pamphlet was ready for the public.

When *The Crisis* appeared on 19 January, with its splendid subtitle and Richard Steele's name on the front page, it soon became apparent that a more serious answer would be required. Advertising and Whig zeal, together with the country's widespread uneasiness over the succession, produced a sensational sale. Whig agents set up a general subscription for the pamphlet all over England. There was a second edition almost immediately; within the week a pirated printing appeared to assuage the reader's thirst for politics. By the end of the year editions had been published in Dublin and Edinburgh, and translations in Amsterdam (in French) and Hamburg. A hostile writer estimated that 40,000 copies were sold by subscription.[19]

What was this pamphlet that generated so much interest, and had so much generated for it? Besides the title page, which is almost a tract in itself, *The Crisis* consists of a dedication signed by Steele "To the Clergy of the Church of England," a very long summary of the laws on which the Protestant succession rested, and a peroratory few pages bringing in, at considerable

[18] Edward Minshull and Nicholas Lechmere, the latter the manager of the Sacheverell trial, both Members.

[19] *Jack the Courtier's Answer to Dick the Englishman's Close of the Paper so Called,* as quoted in Aitken, II, 6n. Publishing information: *Tracts,* p. 641.

cost to the unity of the whole, remarks on the iniquities of the Treaty of Utrecht, the menaces of the Romish Pretender, and Marlborough's glorious victories. The dedication to the clergy was, of course, provocative in itself, since great numbers of the lower clergy leaned to the Tory side. Steele suggests that the Church is indeed in danger (the cry raised against the Whigs at Sacheverell's trial) — in danger from the Pretender. At least one clergyman, Jonathan Swift, was provoked, with good reason. Steele, it will be recalled, thought that Swift was behind most of *The Examiner's* attacks; he doubtless had the Dean in mind when he wrote, at the conclusion of the dedication:

> It cannot be expected but that there will be, in so great a body, light, superficial, vain, and ambitious men, who being untouched with the sublime force of the Gospel, will think it their interest to insinuate jealousies between the clergy and laity, in hopes to derive from their order a veneration which they know they cannot deserve from their virtue.

The body of the tract, a restatement of the laws of succession, stupefying to modern readers, employed a stock device of eighteenth-century controversialists: the extended summary. It has importance beyond the merely historical for a biography of Steele, however, because the summary and final comments illustrate a basic cast of the writer's thought already mentioned, his veneration for legalism, his high regard for the legislative power.

> As divided a people as we are, those who are for the House of Hanover are infinitely superior in number, wealth, courage, and all arts military and civil, to those in the contrary interest; besides which, we have the laws, I say the laws on our side. . . . Her Majesty's Parliamentary title and the succession in the illustrious House of Hanover is the Ark of God to Great Britain. . . .

Steele was fundamentally a "Parliament man" in spirit, as Swift had alleged in *The First Ode* ("To vamp the Good Old Cause

again"). Though no republican, he was comparatively insensi-
tive to the royal traditions of England. His grandfather's fidelity
to the Stuarts had become diluted; in the nineteenth century another Steele, probably one of grandfather Richard Steele's descendants, would be an Irish patriot, a fiery partisan of O'Con-
nell.[20] "[T]he greatest man in England is accountable to me"
as a Member, Steele had told his readers. *The Crisis'* mixture
of religion and legalism, however deplorable philosophically, is
familiar to Americans. "In the name of the Great Jehovah and
the Continental Congress," Ethan Allen cried when he stormed
Ticonderoga. An edition of *The Crisis* was published in Phila-
delphia as early as 1725.[21]

The propaganda impact of *The Crisis,* multiplied by its broad-
cast circulation, had to be countered. Parliament was convening,
at last, in mid-February and the Ministry could expect determined opposition over the succession question and the demolition of Dunkirk. As earlier noted, the main issue of *The Crisis,*
the Protestant succession, was one which the Tories could not
comfortably dispute. The obvious course, then, was to discredit
the author of the offending publication. Replies were not slow
in coming, some temperate, most abusive and threatening, like
that of the pseudonymous author of *A Letter to Richard Steele,
Esq.* who warns Steele darkly that "there is a time coming,
when you must account for this very *Crisis,* to a just and holy
God. . . ."[22] By far the most effective reply was the semi-

[20] Thomas Steele. See DNB.
[21] *Tracts,* p. 641. This curious edition (Evans 2703) by Franklin's employer,
Samuel Keimer, deserves attention. It was an exceptionally early example
of an American reprint of an English political tract. According to Caroline
Robbins, "Very few English political tracts or treatises came off the American presses before the reign of George III. . . ." (*The Eighteenth-Century
Commonwealthman* [Cambridge, Mass., 1959], p. 393.) Keimer, one of the
strangest men in an age of originals, was an extravagant admirer of Steele's
Christian Hero. See C. Lennart Carlson, "Samuel Keimer," *Pennsylvania
Magazine of History and Biography,* LXI (1937), 357–86.
[22] For a full list, cf. Aitken, II, 6n. *A Letter,* by "Philo Basilius," was not
published until 1715.

official one, Swift's *The Publick Spirit of the Whigs,* published, anonymously, on 23 February 1714.

Steele, meanwhile, had ended *The Englishman* with No. 57 on 15 February, the day before the opening of Parliament. In this paper he reviewed the issues raised in the columns of the paper, defended his right to "speak my sentiments with the freedom of an English gentleman," and complained that the opposition had "dwelt upon the author they writ against, in the articles of birth, education and fortune." The letter to his Tory friend, already mentioned, in which he alludes to the "New Converts," closes with a wish that the Elector of Hanover would signify the understanding he has with the Queen regarding the succession, Steele's implication being that the Ministry had created a misunderstanding between the monarchs. He closed the paper with his signature.

In the anonymous *Publick Spirit of the Whigs,* Swift met Steele's arguments by blandly denying that the Hanoverian succession was in danger at all, and proceeding against the Whig author himself. This was the method of the lesser Tories, but *The Publick Spirit* is charged with Swift's wit and power, and has some of the Gulliverian vigor: "A writer with a weak head, and a corrupted heart, is an over-match for any single pen; like a hireling jade, dull and vicious, hardly able to stir, yet offering at every turn to kick." Steele's wish that the Elector signify his understanding with the Queen Swift brands "seditious." It is a powerful tract, but the main interest for Steele's biography is Swift's use of the word "seditious." [23]

It was an age, of course, in which governments did not hesitate to charge authors critical of their policies with treason or with *scandalum magnatum,* defaming a nobleman; most writers hence published their political lucubrations anonymously. Steele's opponents had been muttering "sedition" for months; on 19 February Defoe, who had risked his ears in the pillory

[23] Swift, *Political Tracts, 1713–1719* (n. 5), pp. 43, 68.

in a matter like this, delivered the direct accusation in a letter
to Harley:

> The new champion of the party, Mr. Steele, is now to try an ex-
> periment upon the Ministry, and shall set up to make speeches in
> the House and print them, that the malice of the party may be
> gratified and the Ministry be bullied in as public a manner as pos-
> sible. If, my Lord, the virulent writings of this man may not be
> voted seditious none ever may, and if thereupon he may be ex-
> pelled it would suppress and discourage the party and break all
> their new measures.

Presumably Harley asked for detailed charges, for on the tenth
of March Defoe submitted a paper titled "Collection of Scandal,"
excerpts from Steele's writings, with comments on the seditious
nature of the remarks.[24] Most conveniently, Steele had published these over his signature; he could not evade responsibility
for them, as Swift was to do for *The Publick Spirit*.

Expulsion proceedings had a further attraction for the Ministry, of which Swift and Defoe were mercifully unaware: they
would consume time in which Oxford and Bolingbroke could
continue negotiations with the Pretender, looking to his con-
version to Protestantism. The decision to punish Steele, long
meditated, was implemented. On 2 March the Queen opened
Parliament, remarking in her speech prepared by the Ministry
how she resented the insinuations that the Protestant succession
was in danger under her government. Commons assured her two
days later that they would show their abhorrence of "scandalous
papers" which retailed such insinuations. The Tories pressed
rapidly on. On the eleventh John Hungerford, Tory member for
Scarborough, moved that the portion of the Queen's speech re-
lating to seditious libel be considered, with particular regard to
"several scandalous papers lately published under the name of
Richard Steele, esq." He was seconded, significantly, by Thomas
Foley, a cousin of the Harleys. Steele himself was not in the

[24] HMC, *Portland MSS.*, V, 384 and 392–95.

House, on Lord Halifax's advice. Both sides were maneuvering for advantage in the proceedings, hoping to make political capital at every stage. On 12 March Foley presented the formal charges to the House, citing *The Englishman* No. 46 (which Steele had signed) and No. 57, and *The Crisis* as "containing several paragraphs tending to sedition, highly reflecting upon her Majesty, and arraigning her Administration and Government. . . ." Steele was ordered to appear in person on the following day.

That Saturday, 13 March, Steele was confronted with the charges in a packed and noisy House. He asked a week's delay and, when the government objected, explained that he hoped the House would not oblige him "to break the sabbath of the Lord, by perusing such profane writings, as might serve for his justification." The Puritan phrasing was, of course, directed at the new converts; the delay was granted. On Monday the Whigs returned to the offensive. Steele himself moved that the demolition of Dunkirk be investigated by the House. The motion was defeated easily, 214 to 109, and Steele's case was in effect decided. It had never been in doubt.

Thursday, 18 March — After routine business, the Serjeant at Arms was ordered to clear the House of visitors. Steele was asked whether he acknowledged authorship of the writings under consideration. He rose and replied, "I writ them in behalf of the House of Hanover, and I own them with the same unreservedness with which I abjured the Pretender." At his side were James Stanhope and Robert Walpole, who were to act as his advocates. After considerable debate Steele was allowed to stay and make his own defense; Addison having assisted him in the preparation of his speech sat nearby to prompt. Steele prudently read most of it; this was no time for forgetfulness.[25]

The speech itself, which lasted for upward of three hours,

---

[25] *Apology* in *Tracts,* pp. 293ff; *Parliamentary History of England,* ed. Wm. Cobbett (London, 1809–1828), VI, 1267; *Journals of the House of Commons,* XVII, *passim.*

makes for dull reading today, consisting as it does of selections from his works, with appropriate comments. Steele acknowledges his fear of the Pretender and defends himself against the charge that he intended disrespect for the clergy in the dedication to *The Crisis* by citing passages at length from his works to demonstrate his respect for the cloth. He reaffirms his statements on the demolition of Dunkirk and takes a firm, and somewhat irrelevant, stand in praise of the Duke of Marlborough. "If it be a crime to speak honourably of the Duke of Marlborough, it is a crime that I must always be guilty of. . . ." At the very end he turns to what should have been a telling point: the doubtful legality of punitive action against a Member of Parliament for criticizing a Ministry. If he has broken the law, Steele asserts, he should be tried in a court of law. "Is not the executive power sufficiently armed to inflict a proper punishment on all kinds of criminals?" he asks. "[W]hy then should one part of the legislative power, take this executive power into its own hand?" By thus applying the doctrine of separation of powers Steele had scored a point, but most of his listeners were not to be swayed in their convictions one way or the other. Steele withdrew from the House and Robert Walpole rose in his behalf. This statesman never liked an apologetic or defensive stance; he proceeded to deliver a long, eloquent speech beginning with a justification of Steele, but moving to a criticism of the Ministry for attacking Steele at all. Seconding Steele's assertion, he held that charges of sedition should have been left to the due process of law. In fact, and here Walpole played what his biographer calls the Whig trump card, Steele was being punished for supporting the Protestant succession: whom then, Walpole asked by implication, did the Ministry support? It was a speech, reported the Prussian envoy to his government, "worthy of Augustan times." [26]

[26] J. H. Plumb (note 4), p. 190; Bonet, Prussian envoy, quoted in Wolfgang Michael, *Englische Geschichte im achtzehnten Jahrhundert* (Berlin and Leipzig, 1921–1937), I, 320.

Walpole's eloquence could not save Steele. The debate continued until far into the night, but on the question the division stood 245 to 152 in favor of the Ministry's resolution, that Steele's writings contained "many expressions, highly reflecting upon her Majesty, and upon the nobility, gentry, clergy, and universities of this kingdom. . . ." It was resolved therefore that Richard Steele be expelled from the House; little more than a month after the opening of his first session he was outside. Though he and his party had apparently suffered a crushing defeat, the defeat was only apparent. From the Whig's viewpoint, the debate, in fact, had not gone badly at all. Practiced observers noted the crucial fact that the Ministry's majority had declined; Berkeley's friend, Sir John Percival, who prided himself on his objectivity, wrote his cousin that "I know of several Tories who went away surprised at things which fell in the debate. . . . [V]ery many honest Tories left it in much discontent." [27] Outside the House Steele's expulsion was regarded from each individual's political point of view. With high satisfaction the Oxford antiquarian Thomas Hearne recorded the event in his diary, adding that "this Steele was formerly of Christ-Church in Oxford, and afterwards of Merton College. He was a rakish, wild, drunken spark. . . ." [28] On a different note Steele informed Prue: "I am in very good humour and in no concern but fear of your being uneasy."

But Steele was whistling in the dark. Though the Whigs had scored, the Ministry had after all won the expulsion skirmish decisively and, London heard, was determined to bring in the Pretender. Some Whigs were resolved to resist, by force if necessary. By the end of March Steele was convinced that civil war within the next few years was inevitable unless Divine Providence intervened; his friend and fellow-Irishman General William Cadogan was reported ready to lead a picked group

---

[27] BM, Add. MSS. 47087, letter to Daniel Dering, dated 23 March 1713 [/14]; *Journals of the House of Commons,* XVII, 514.

[28] *Remarks and Collections of Thomas Hearne,* ed. C. E. Doble et al. (Oxford, 1885–1921), IV, 325.

in an assault on the Tower should war come. Captain Steele
may have been one of the group.[29]

In a move of desperation Steele addressed Sir Thomas
Hanmer, whose nomination as Speaker he had supported, asking that Hanmer put two questions to the House: that Steele
should or should not be tried in a court of law and that Steele
was or was not eligible for re-election to the present Parliament.
This was ill-advised or unadvised impetuosity; Steele realized
the impropriety of his action immediately. Hanmer replied in a
temperate but firm letter that he could do nothing. Steele could
do nothing right. In the Easter term of court he was sued for
debt in two actions, one by his peruke maker. His enemies delayed not in commenting; Grub Street Tories exulted. Typical
was an anonymous imitation of Horace which appeared in April,
entitled *John Dennis the Sheltering Poet's Invitation to Richard Steele, the Secluded Party Writer, to come and live with
him in the Mint*. The Mint in Southwark was a sanctuary for
debtors. " 'Tis true," wrote the Horatian, "that Bloomsbury-
square's a noble place;/But what are lofty buildings in thy
case?" [30] Amid troubles with Parliament and perukier that
spring, Steele was addressed by his friend John Chamberlayne,
once with Steele a gentleman usher to Prince George and now
secretary of the Society for the Propagation of the Gospel in
Foreign Parts, the principal missionary society of the Church of
England. Chamberlayne congratulated Steele handsomely for
his service to the nation but reproved him for the "scandalous,
unaccountable, diabolical sin of profane swearing." Steele replied
with proper meekness, promised reform, but observed that "the
times are [the] worst that ever were for reforming that sin
above all others." [31]

---

[29] Basil Williams, *Stanhope* (Oxford, 1932), p. 144. Steele conferred with
Cadogan on the day before he expressed (to Prue) his belief that civil war
neared (*Corr.*, p. 299).

[30] Aitken, II, 27. Aitken believed, incorrectly, this to be by Swift. See
The Poems of Jonathan Swift (note 17), III, 1098.

[31] Assigned to Henry Newman in *Corr.*, pp. 87–88. I believe the writer
Chamberlayne because: 1) A copy of the original letter is not in Newman's

From this low point, when Tory, creditor, and pamphleteer seemed combined against him, Steele's fortunes began to improve. His case was still being debated in Grub Street but defenders were rising at his side.[32] This was heartening but much more heartening was money, three thousand pounds, which appeared for Steele's use via two intermediaries.[33] The ultimate source of the money has remained a mystery, but one may safely conjecture that it came from wealthy Whigs as a form of reward for Steele's service to the party. It was patently to the Whigs' advantage to keep their principal pamphleteer out of debtor's prison and cheat the expectations of the Tory press.

Steele's private life had been almost completely submerged in the deluge of public responsibilities since the publication of *The Crisis;* even the notes to Dear Prue are markedly shorter and less frequent. The loss of his domestic existence, on which his happiness depended, both annoyed and worried Steele. After his trial in the House he had written his wife, "Nothing can happen to [make] my condition in private the worse, and I have busied myself enough for the public. The next is for you and yours." But he was simply not able so to order his life and on Easter Sunday he told Mrs. Steele, "I am going this morning to a very solemn work and invoke Almighty God to bless you and your little ones, beseeching Him to spare me a little life to acquit myself to you and them whom of all the world I have hitherto least endeavoured to serve. But you and Betty and Dick and Eugene and Molly shall be henceforth my principal cares, next to the keeping a good conscience." Even with

letterbooks preserved at the Society for Promoting Christian Knowledge headquarters. 2) Steele heads his reply "Brother Ch.". 3) Newman always closed his letters "I am," etc. on the evidence of the letterbooks. The letter's presence in a volume (Bodleian, Rawlinson MSS., C 933) of papers collected by Newman can be accounted for by presuming that Chamberlayne sent it to his friend Newman — as the two often did, exchanging matters of common interest.

[32] See Aitken, II, 28.
[33] By one (William?) Ashurst and John Warner, a goldsmith. See *Corr.*, pp. 297–98.

the grant of £3,000, however, he was hard-pressed to meet his financial obligations and required to spend long hours and days at his many responsibilities away from home.

The resources of his pen had fortunately not deserted Steele; a writer of his energy could not be stilled. Hedging against his expulsion somewhat, Steele had begun a new periodical in late February, *The Lover,* "written in imitation of the *Tatler.* By Marmaduke Myrtle, Gent." This almost-forgotten periodical presents some of Richard Steele's best writing, and in his day *The Lover* was highly regarded: five collected editions appeared in his lifetime and four more before the end of the century. As the title indicates, the paper represents a return to the pleasanter days of *The Tatler;* here love, always a favorite theme with Steele, is made the organizing motif. The purpose of the paper according to the narrator Mr. Myrtle is "to trace the passion or affection of love through all its joys and inquietudes, through all the stages and circumstances of life, in both sexes, with strict respect to virtue and innocence. . . ." [34] Political writing was a duty for Steele, and an important one, but he yearned now for harmony, not conflict. Writing about love, "the source of our being" and "the support of it," was a pleasure. There is, of course, much for the ladies; readers got their twopence worth. To the surprise, no doubt, of his readers, perhaps to his own surprise, he could still write with the best of them when his subject was one of the old staples of *Tatler* and *Spectator* days. He had almost, but not quite, turned politician; the essayist of manners was still there. "It should," he opined in No. 24

> methinks, be a rule to suspect every one who insinuates anything against the reputation of another, of the vice with which they charge their neighbor; for it is very unlikely it should flow from the love of virtue: the resentment of the virtuous towards those who are fallen, is that of pity and that is best exerted in silence on the occasion. What then can be said to the numerous tales

[34] *The Lover* (note 16), p. 5.

that pass to and fro in this town, to the disparagement of those who have never offended their accusers? As for my part, I always wait with patience and never doubt of hearing in a little time for a truth, the same guilt of any woman which I find she reports of another. It is, as I said, unnatural it should be otherwise; the calumny usually flows from an impatience of living under severity, and they report the sallies of others against the time of their own escape. How many women would be speechless, if their acquaintance were without faults.

These spring months of 1714 were busy ones for Richard Steele and editing the paper, even on its thrice weekly schedule, demanded more time than he had to give. Correspondents were as always solicited and now and again Addison lent a hand, as on 18 March, the day of the expulsion trial. Eustace Budgell, Addison's faithful follower, helped some and so may have young Thomas Burnet, son of the Whig Bishop of Sarum. The paper, however, in writing, interests, and attitudes is very much Steele's. Politics was almost but not entirely excluded. The issue after his expulsion carried a satiric portrait of the Harley family relationship under the name of the Crabtrees. Four other numbers soon after this, continuing the Crabtree story, reflect Steele's brief bitterness; he continues to harry the Harleys as "new converts." This was not good policy, however, for even the Harleys were customers and they were naturally displeased. By early April he was ready to start a political paper, *The Reader,* to run concurrently. Politics disappeared from *The Lover* thereafter, and on 27 May the last issue, No. 40, appeared.

Alexander Pope disliked the violent character of Steele's political writings that winter; in fact, Pope was drifting into the group of Tory writers around Oxford: Swift, Parnell, Gay, the literary physician, Dr. Arbuthnot. But Pope maintained the air of political insouciance befitting a Catholic and he and Steele were on good terms. Marmaduke Myrtle used a quotation from the newly expanded *Rape of the Lock* which certainly did sales of the poem no harm. The *Rape,* of course, fitted the paper's motif. Steele was mending fences.[35]

But not political fences; not yet. Whigs were still in opposition, and Steele in or out of Parliament was the Whigs' principal spokesman. The political situation in April became suddenly better from the Whig standpoint; Oxford's and Bolingbroke's attempts to persuade James to abandon Catholicism had failed, though this of course was not generally known. Oxford began to put out lines to the Whigs; Bolingbroke pressed on in the hope that the Pretender's decision was not final. The Lord Treasurer thus came under attack from two sides: openly from the Whigs and covertly from his colleague St. John. In mid-April government ranks broke; during a debate on the succession Sir Thomas Hanmer and thirty Tories voted with the opposition.[36] The speeches of the Whig leaders, the propaganda of Steele and his fellows were having the intended disquieting effect.

The Examiner was still firing away at Whig high and low and on 22 April a new Tory paper, *The Monitor,* appeared to augment the cannonade. That same day Richard Steele issued the first number of his latest propaganda paper, to be called *The Reader.* For the three weeks in which this appeared (it ran to only nine numbers), Steele was publishing six papers a week and writing most of them. *The Reader* was a dull paper, totally engaged in wrangling, issue by issue, with the two Tory opponents; all the old subjects: the new converts, the succession, Dunkirk, are revived and thrashed once more. Surely defective circulation must have contributed to *The Reader's* early and unannounced end on 10 May.

Projects raced through Steele's mind. *The Reader* No. 6 revealed that Steele had in hand the materials for a history of Marlborough's war and that proposals for the work could be seen at Tonson's, an ordinary procedure in eighteenth-century

---

[35] No. 3, of 2 March 1714.
[36] Plumb (note 4), p. 194, citing the Brabourne MSS.

publishing. Steele's unflinching support of the Marlboroughs had won their confidence; the Duchess, who often quoted his works, spoke of his expulsion as being "far from a dishonour." [37] This would be, then, an authorized history, of the sort Swift intended with his *History of the Four Last Years of the Queen.* Like Swift's history, Steele's did not appear within the lifetime of the author; indeed, he apparently never got further than the plan. When the Duke and Duchess returned to England the following fall, however, the Duke interceded with the new King to secure Steele the governorship of the Drury Lane Theatre.[38]

May of 1714 was as busy as April had been; Steele apologized to Prue for this but apologies were all he could offer. His latest political tract, *The Romish Ecclesiastical History of Late Years,* was published on 25 May with a dedication to Daniel Lord Finch, son of Swift's "old Dismal," the Earl of Nottingham. The Finches were not Whigs but supported the Protestant succession; Lord Finch had backed Steele in the expulsion proceedings and Steele returned the compliment in his dedication, calling him "a true son of the Church of England and an exemplary patriot. . . ." The tract itself, a good-sized book of some 168 octavo pages, was ostensibly an account of the canonization of several saints by Pope Clement XI. Interspersed with the description of the ceremony are speeches by Cardinal Gualterio, Papal Nuncio at Paris, describing conditions in England to the Pope. These are, of course, fictitious; the Cardinal adopts in 1712 the term Steele coined two years later, the new converts, comparing the Harleys to Jesuits who "find their advantage by cajoling and managing of each side. . . ."

Steele's anti-Catholic propaganda needs to be seen in the perspective not only of his Irish youth but of the immediate situation. His targets are English Jacobites, whom he associates with the Tories. The analogy between the absolutism of the Pope and that of those Englishmen, especially English clergy,

---

[37] *Letters of Sarah Duchess of Marlborough* (London, 1875), p. 95.
[38] John Loftis, *Steele at Drury Lane* (Berkeley, 1952), pp. 37–38.

who profess to believe in unlimited royal sovereignty is conveniently easy. "[T]he clergy have nothing to say to us concerning government, but as other men have it, from the laws themselves . . . ," Steele writes in the preface, reflecting for the hundredth time his legalism. Thus the tract proceeds against not only the Pretender but also the High Church clergy and the Tory Ministry. The exposure of Popish practices is subordinate, used mainly to attract readers. As it had been in the days of the Sacheverell trial, religion was the effective issue in those last weeks of the Queen's life. In May Bolingbroke decided to rid himself of his colleague by the method the Whigs had used for months in their propaganda: by making the Lord Treasurer's religious position appear anomalous. A member of his High-Flying faction introduced a bill in Commons under the terms of which no one could teach, even in a private house, unless licensed by the diocesan bishop and certified as having taken the Sacrament according to the Anglican liturgy. The whole system of Dissenting education, which was very good and very extensive, would have been eliminated by the active enforcement of such a law. As earlier indicated, this put Oxford in a box; he was unable either to support or oppose the bill, which became known as the Schism Act.

Whigs were united in their opposition to the bill. Walpole and Stanhope fought its passage furiously in the House. As his part Steele wrote perhaps his finest political pamphlet, *A Letter to a Member of Parliament Concerning the Bill for Preventing the Growth of Schism*. Steele's libertarian disposition appears here in its best light; he was never skilled in the use of invective and he used none in this pamphlet. The debate concerns, he points out, a matter of the most fundamental rights. Talk of schism, he maintains, is inaccurate; since the bill applies to the United Kingdoms, logically the Church of England would be placed in the same disabling position in Scotland (where the established church is Presbyterian) as the Presbyterian in England. But the real purpose of the bill is to deprive the Dissenter of all rights, natural, religious, and civil; it is, in fact, an attack on the Act of Toleration passed in the reign of William and Mary, and a threat to every man's religious freedom. Remembering the religious persecution of the seventeenth century, Steele calls the bill a step backward. "Good will opens the way to men's hearts. . . . No man is persuaded by him who hates him, but all are easily prevailed upon by those who love them." [39]

It is a fine tract, full of Steele's best qualities: his compassion, his humor, his deep feeling for English liberties. He had managed to come through the spring's storms with his zest for life untempered, but apparently he was fighting for a lost cause. Bolingbroke, playing on the prejudices of the squires, carried the day; the bill became law after a close squeeze in the House of Lords. It was to take effect on the first of August.

The summer seemed Bolingbroke's; as the Whigs looked on in dismay he strengthened his hand with the dying Queen. Steele wrote one more tract on the demolition of Dunkirk, half-heartedly, as if seeking something better to do. Addison revived *The Spectator,* sharing the editorship with the dependable Budgell, but Steele did not contribute. Steele met with Wharton and Walpole, talked politics at the Kit-Cat Club, and waited, waited, waited, as did all the rest. He began to put together a summary of the expulsion proceedings and a defense of his conduct, to be called *Mr. Steele's Apology for Himself and His Writings;* this he planned to dedicate to Walpole, whose assistance had come when it was needed. Burleigh had completed the printing when someone, perhaps Walpole himself, suggested delay.[40] The times were simply too dangerous. No one knew what Bolingbroke would do, not even Swift, summering in the country, who professed ignorance of the Court and disillusionment with Party after three weeks' absence.

On 27 July Queen Anne dismissed Oxford. Final power seemed in Bolingbroke's grasp but Whigs and Hanoverian sym-

[39] *Tracts,* p. 250.
[40] *Tracts,* p. 283.

pathizers remained around the Queen, among them the Duchess of Somerset, Mistress of the Queen's Robes, and these exercised a partial veto by their presence. But some power, some choice still lay with Anne herself, and no person could know her mind. Bolingbroke or one of his group needed the approval of the Queen, the actual physical bestowal of the White Staff. Writing thereby one of the last chapters in the long story of the Royal Prerogative, the dying Queen from her bed handed the Treasurer's White Staff of office to the Duke of Shrewsbury, a Hanover Tory. Bolingbroke sought alliances everywhere but it was too late. On Sunday morning, the first of August, the last of the reigning Stuarts died. A Board of Regents safely Hanoverian in sentiment was formed to administer the government until the new King could come from Germany. The crisis was past; the Protestant succession was assured.

Richard Steele could afford some jubilation. He had come a way from the Liffey. He was forty-two, an essayist and dramatist of renown, a political journalist of national importance. His family was in good health and spirits; so was he except when a twinge of gout reminded him of his mortality. If the Peace of Utrecht represented the realization of Swift's goals as Tory pamphleteer, the succession of King George I vindicated Steele's decision to plunge into politics. The crisis had been real, the succession had been threatened. The Whigs had held good cards in the struggle for power and had played them well. Of all this Steele was, he could tell himself, no small part.

DEAR PRUE,

I have been loaded with compliments from the regents and assured of something immediately. . . . I desire you to send me a guinea. I shall have cash in the morning.

Captain Steele conferred with his old friend General Cadogan, two Irishmen with heads together about the future. Cash on hand was scarce but something fine would come out of all this. He knew it. He had always known it.

Epilogue

THE DEATH of Queen Anne was of course an event of momentous importance; although in the late summer of 1714 it was impossible to predict in detail what would follow from the queen's death, the general outline of the future was clear enough. All those who had not been publicly enthusiastic about the Hanoverian succession were in a distinctly awkward situation; this included Bolingbroke and Oxford, and to a lesser degree their propagandist Jonathan Swift, whose dreams of substantial preferment were at an end. The Whigs of the Junto, who had been in touch with the Hanoverian Court, would press their advantage on all fronts, with little reason as they saw it for magnanimous gestures toward those who had opposed them the previous winter and spring.

For Richard Steele new horizons were opened. He could expect to be and was, in fact, rewarded for his fidelity: within a few months he was knighted by the new king and was re-elected to Parliament from the safe seat of Boroughbridge. These were political rewards for political service; henceforth his activities and interests in public life were increasingly political, as indeed they had been since his election to the House in 1713, though as co-author of the great periodicals and author of two successful plays he remained a substantial man of letters. One of his rewards was the governorship of Drury Lane; as such he was also to be at the center of theatrical activity in England. He was no longer required to earn his living by his pen, however, and in fact was seldom able hereafter to find the time and incentive required for significant writing which the years in opposition had provided. If one conjectures that *The Conscious Lovers* was begun before 1714, it may be said that most of the literary work for which Steele is today remembered was done by the time of Queen Anne's death, though he was to undertake other periodicals and a large volume of political writing in the years ahead. The rewards Richard Steele received perhaps never quite measured up to his expectations but they were considerable nevertheless.

Steele could not know this, but his personal life was to be darkened by a series of misfortunes. The great partnership was over. Strained by the withdrawal of Addison during the parliamentary crisis, the friendship never recovered; indeed, a few years later the erstwhile collaborators, disagreeing over a political issue, engaged in an undignified pamphlet war which was dismaying to all but their enemies. Addison, like Steele, devoted most of his remaining energy to politics; in 1719, only a few weeks after their last and bitterest quarrel, he died. Prue had died, apparently in childbirth, the year before; his son and namesake in 1716. Richard Steele, then, only five years after the triumph of the Whigs, which had seemed to promise so much and which had provided him temporal rewards of various kinds, found himself bereft of his best friend, his son, and his wife. Sir Richard's is another, and sadder, story than that of Captain Steele.

Index

Addison, Gulston, 125

Addison, Joseph: at Charterhouse, 23–24; at Oxford, 27; ability recognized at Oxford, 35; gravity, 36; Macaulay's portrait, 50; criticized by Blackmore, 53; grand tour, 66, 71; admitted Kit-Cat Club, 71; Under-Secretary of State, 74; dedication of *Tender Husband,* 76; courtship of Countess of Warwick, 85, 96; and Gazetteer appointment, 92–93, 94; stands for Member of Parliament for Lostwithiel, 96; sale of RS's house to recover loan, 97n; Secretary to Wharton, 100, 106, 109, 122; contributes to *Tatler,* 110, 127, 128; and dramatic reform, 111–12; recommends Swift as prebendary of Westminster, 117; inherits estate of brother Gulston, 125; editor of *Spectator,* 131–53, *passim;* as Whig journalist, 140–42; his "Little Senate," 145–46, 163; interest in new science, 156–58; and RS-Swift controversy (1713), 165, 167; edits *Guardian,* 172, 174, 178; on RS's political activities, 179–80; contributes to Tonson's *Miscellanies* (1693), 188; possible disingenuousness, 189–90; assists on *Crisis,* 196; assists RS at expulsion, 201; contributes to *Lover,* 207; revives *Spectator,* 211; death, 214; mentioned, 41, 45, 108, 130, 183

Addison, Lancelot, Dean of Lichfield, 24

Advertising, 145–46, 150

Aitken, George A., 28

Albemarle, 1st Earl of (Arnold Joost van Keppel), 63–64, 66

Albemarle, Countess of (Geertruid Johanna Quirina van der Duyn), 63

Aldrich, Henry, Dean of Christ Church, 27, 31, 32, 33, 34, 35

Allen, Ethan, 198

American Mercury, 105

Amyntas, 163

Andromaque, 146

Anne, Queen: succeeds to throne, 66; orders dramatic reform, 69; distrusts Junto, 83–84, 92, 119; appoints Wharton Lord Lieutenant, 100; values High Churchmanship, 114; breaks with Marlborough, 121; replaces Godolphin, 124; creates "occasional" peers, 144, 160; declining health, 173, 177, 185; trusts Oxford, 193; opens Parliament, 1714, 200; dismisses Oxford, 211; death, 212; mentioned, 73, 138, 175, 188, 195, 199

Arbuthnot, Dr. John, 207

Arran, Earl of (Richard Butler), 18, 19

Arran, Countess of (Dorothy Ferrers Butler), 18, 19

Arsinoe, 135

Ashe, St. George, Bishop of Clogher, 184

CAPTAIN STEELE:
THE EARLY CAREER OF RICHARD STEELE
Calhoun Winton

designer: Edward D. King.
typesetter: Vail-Ballou Press, Inc.
typefaces: Text: Old Style No. 1. Display: Bodoni #375.
printer: Vail-Ballou Press, Inc.
paper: Warren's 1854 Medium Finish.
binder: Vail-Ballou Press, Inc.
cover material: Columbia Riverside Linen.